LEABHARLANNA CHONTAE NA GAILLIMHE
(GALWAY COUNTY LIBRARIES)

Acc. No. 135,800   Class No. 362.19

Date of Return	Date of Return	Date of Return

ORANMORE LIBRARY

Books are on loan for 21 days from date of issue.

Fines for overdue books: 10p for each week or portion of a week plus cost of postage incurred in recovery.

Published 2003
by Poolbeg Press Ltd.
123 Grange Hill, Baldoyle,
Dublin 13, Ireland
Email: poolbeg@poolbeg.com

© Rosemary Daly & Paul Cunningham 2003

The moral right of the author has been asserted.

Copyright for typesetting, layout, design
© Poolbeg Group Services Ltd.

1 3 5 7 9 10 8 6 4 2

A catalogue record for this book is available from the British Library.

ISBN 1-84223-160-X

Typeset by Patricia Hope in Sabon MT 10.8/14
Printed by
Cox & Wyman
Reading, Berkshire

www.poolbeg.com

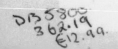

Co Author

Paul Cunningham is a correspondent with RTÉ News. He reported on the Lindsay Tribunal from its preliminary hearings in 1999 to the publication of the final report in 2001. He won the ESB National Radio Journalist of the Year Award 2000 for his coverage of the tribunal proceedings. He was the reporter on a television documentary, *Bad Blood*, concerning the practices of the US-based pharmaceutical companies making contaminated haemophilia blood products, which won the News and Current Affairs category in the Irish Film and Television Awards 2003.

Acknowledgements

Rosemary Daly

Shortly after deciding to attempt to write the story of how my life became inextricably interwoven with the tragedy which befell the haemophilia community in Ireland, I quickly realised that it would become almost incumbent on many people, friends, colleagues and family to give both their emotional and practical support. That support, without which this book could not have been written, was given sympathetically, unfalteringly and without pre-condition by all those concerned.

Thanks to Declan Kelly for the inspiration and motivation, and whose strident professionalism made the idea a reality. My co-author Paul Cunningham's dedication, understanding and compassion enabled us to portray this complex and often painful story. Your wry humour, Paul, often kept me from the edge. To colleagues, who couldn't but be friends, I owe a great debt; Margaret Dunne for her calm guidance; Nina, Marian, Ann and Fr Paddy for their encouragement and ever-available sympathetic ear. Michelle, whose nimble fingers danced over every draft, gave time and attention that only a true friend could give. Adrienne also provided invaluable assistance in research. To Gaye Shortland and all at Poolbeg for their support. To my clique of proofreaders, Brian O'Mahony, Ray Kelly, Michael Davenport, Paul McSharry,

Austin and Martin, whose criticisms were sensitively given and gratefully received. Thanks to my brother Billy for always being on hand. To my long-suffering and sometimes neglected family, Art, Aisling and John Joe, I need only say thanks for your love and thank you for caring.

Finally, to Margaret King, my mentor, my teacher and treasured friend, I am deeply indebted. Her kindness and humanity is appreciated by both myself and all those whose lives have been touched by this tragic story.

Paul Cunningham

I would like to thank my family for their unstinting support – Flor, Aisling and Isabelle; our editor, Gaye Shortland, for making an idea become a reality and all at Poolbeg; Brian O'Mahony for his shrewd analysis; Michelle Stenhouse, Nina Storey and Margaret Dunne at the Irish Haemophilia Society for unswerving assistance; my sisters Emer and Nuala who read and re-read drafts; Barrie Hanley, Joyce Jackson and Vincent Delaney for their advice; Ed Mulhall and all in the RTÉ Newsroom for allowing me the space to work on this project; and my parents, Connell and Mary. I wish to thank the haemophilia community for their support, bravery, resilience and good humour – without which this story could never be told.

For Shuala

Contents

Chapter

Foreword

In 1989, 105 members of the 400-strong Irish haemophilia community were known to be infected with HIV. This devastation hit the community at a time when the Irish Haemophilia Society (IHS) was a small, voluntary, totally under-resourced organisation with a tiny office, one staff member working only part-time, and dependent on a small number of committed volunteers. The IHS had to help many of our members deal with the fear, anger, uncertainty, guilt and sheer terror facing them in their now uncertain future. This was a time when public ignorance regarding AIDS was rife and the stigma associated with AIDS was enormous.

The assistance, services and help which were required could no longer be effectively carried out on a purely voluntary basis. The IHS felt it was time to employ an AIDS coordinator. This was the first time I met Rosemary Daly. Though other candidates were impressive, it was Rosemary's directness, enthusiasm and obvious desire to do the job that persuaded us to employ her. It was one of the best decisions we have made as an organisation.

One of Rosemary's strongest qualities is her ability to empathise. It was this that enabled her to form such close bonds with members who were living in a private hell and deeply reluctant to communicate with anyone from outside the community. Together with Margaret King, Rosemary initiated a unique scheme to help people in the terminal stages of AIDS-related illnesses to die with dignity, surrounded by their families. When the hepatitis-C disaster compounded the already horrendous situation in the early 1990s, Margaret and Rosemary expanded their critical-illness service.

Rosemary's role was not confined to the mammoth task of assisting individual members and their families, but also developed into a broader campaign. She was a key member of the IHS team which negotiated with five successive Ministers for Health and various departmental officials. The key issues included compensation for members infected with HIV and hepatitis C as well as some form of accountability for the catastrophic impact on them due to the manufacture and distribution of contaminated blood products. The work was multi-faceted, relentless and encompassed the establishment of two tribunals of inquiry and four State-sponsored compensation schemes.

Since the moment she joined the IHS, Rosemary has had a profound impact on the haemophilia community. It's a compelling story which needs to be told.

Brian O'Mahony
Chairman 1987-2003
Irish Haemophilia Society

Prologue

On Friday September 6, 2002, I found myself on a journey which I will never forget. I was driving home from the *Late Late Show* on the night after the publication of the Lindsay Tribunal report. The night was dark and so was the mood inside my car: I was giving a lift to Martin and his wife who had been in the audience of the TV show and were deeply upset by the findings of the tribunal run by Judge Alison Lindsay. Their son Stephen, a haemophiliac, had died at the age of twelve as a result of contracting HIV from a clotting-agent. They didn't feel that anyone had been made accountable for the disaster which ripped their family apart.

Martin is a big man with strong country values: there is very little grey in his world – black is black and white is white. I hadn't seen him for a time and so he started to fill me in about what life was like since young Stephen had died. Martin was always open with me, perhaps because I had in some small way helped his family to get through Stephen's death. The conversation turned back to the time when Stephen was in hospital in the terminal stages of an AIDS-related illness.

Martin pulled no punches: "Rose, I will never forgive myself for allowing him to stay in hospital for so long when I knew there was fuck all that anybody could do." I swallowed hard and kept driving as the frustration and pain welled up inside him. Angrily he continued: "There were so many times when Stephen was undergoing tests, like lumbar punctures or needles into veins, and his eyes would lock on to mine and beseech me to make it stop. And I did nothing, Rose, nothing."

It was now seven years since Stephen's death. I had thought that Martin and his family had gone a long way down the road to recovery. I was wrong. The emotion that erupted from him sent me reeling. He told me: "I don't feel a man anymore." I asked hesitantly: "What do you mean?" He said: "Jesus Christ, Rose, because if I was a man I would have gone out and killed the person who made my son suffer." I tried to calm him: "What about your other children? What use would you have been if you ended up in jail? They needed you at home." But my words didn't carry any weight. Martin said: "If I was in Mountjoy Prison they would have had more respect for me."

Martin clearly needed to talk so I kept quiet. He described himself as a man without a soul: "When I walk the dog, I don't hear the birds anymore or see the beauty of the sun. I've no soul. There's nothing left. My dignity has been stripped away. You know, I think I'd now make an excellent kamikaze pilot." Martin seemed to be oscillating between the pain of witnessing his son ravaged by an AIDS-related illness to the shame, as he saw it, of not seeking revenge.

I didn't know how to respond to such an outburst. I tried to be positive by saying he had done everything that was humanly possible for his son. I had sat with them in the hospital and in their home. I had witnessed their son's slow, painful death. I told Martin: "You couldn't have saved his life." But now, my words of comfort didn't reach far enough.

I was the one who had urged people like Martin, telling them that they might get some answers by participating in the proceedings of the Lindsay Tribunal. Martin had agreed to give evidence and had told his story. Now he said to me: "To be honest, Rose, I knew there would never be anybody held responsible. I just did it because you seemed to think it would be of use." He wasn't blaming me for the trauma of the Lindsay Tribunal. It was just his way of talking. But my heart sank as I realised that the pain of giving evidence would not have happened had I not persuaded him to testify. It was pain on top of pain.

Martin knew I was writing a book and he said: "Listen, you use anything you can to illustrate just how black things are." Fumbling for something to say, I told them both that I hoped the book might be able to explain a story that the public knew a bit about, but not enough. Martin said: "Well, don't hold back. Write anything you want to about Stephen and our family, but try to convey the level of despair we felt and still feel."

That's what I am trying to do. That is why this book is neither an autobiography nor a history of Irish haemophilia but a record of how I witnessed a small community brought to its knees and abandoned by the State.

Because of the stigma still attached to HIV and hepatitis C, I have to use pseudonyms to disguise people's identity. This secrecy means that this book can only recount part of what happened – the full magnitude of the pain and suffering can only be known by the community itself.

Rosemary Daly
February 2003

Introduction

On an April afternoon in 2002, I was sitting in the front row of the public gallery of Dáil Eireann. In the chamber below me, the Minister for Health and two opposition politicians were in the process of passing a compensation bill for members of the Irish Haemophilia Society who had been infected with HIV from blood products. The media had been heralding this legislation as a multi-million-euro settlement. It was a moment I should have been savouring – but instead it seemed so insignificant and so desperately late. Sitting beside me was a man with haemophilia who had full-blown AIDS, together with his mother, who had already lost two sons due to the virus, and a man whose thirteen-year-old son had died from an AIDS-related illness.

Haemophilia is a rare blood disorder in which a person with the condition does not have the normal capacity to stop bleeding. A person with haemophilia does not cut more easily or bleed more profusely – they simply bleed for longer as they have a limited capacity to make it stop. There can also be internal bleeding, the most common form of which is into the knee and elbow joints from friction caused by normal day-to-day activities. Haemophilia virtually only ever affects men. In the majority of cases, it is passed from one generation to the next through the mother. The large exception to the rule is that, in around one third of cases, there is no family history. In the 1950s, the life expectancy of a haemophiliac was around thirty-five years. However, blood products were developed which could stop a bleed and this transformed the lives of people with haemophilia. They now had a normal life expectancy. Tragically, these products are now known to have infected more than 100 haemophiliacs with HIV in the mid-1980s in Ireland. Considering that there are only around 400 people with haemophilia in the country, it is a devastating toll.

It had taken the Irish Haemophilia Society or IHS nearly two decades to secure a fair level of compensation for our members. Despite this, my mind began to wander as the issue was being debated in the Dáil. My attention instead focused on the Fianna Fáil TD, Dr Rory O'Hanlon. He was presiding over proceedings in his capacity as Leas Ceann Comhairle. Nearly thirteen years earlier, I had been sitting in the Dáil public gallery listening to Dr O'Hanlon who was then Minister for Health. The political response to the HIV crisis affecting the haemophilia community back then was very different.

In 1989, things seemed relatively straightforward to me: more than 100 people with haemophilia had contracted HIV by taking a clotting-agent which had been licensed by the Department of Health and distributed by the Blood Bank of the State. Accordingly, the IHS was seeking to establish a trust fund of £400,000 to help its members pay for special foods, additional heating and funeral expenses. I had only begun to work with the IHS a number of weeks previously and was visiting the Dáil for the first time. I was excited by being there, but also because it appeared the IHS demands were going to be met.

The Labour Party proposed a motion entitled: Policy In Relation To AIDS Sufferers And HIV-Positive Haemophiliacs. It called for the establishment of the trust fund and received support from Fine Gael, the Progressive Democrats, the Workers Party, Tony Gregory, Neil Blaney and Jim Kemmy. However, it was rejected by the Fianna Fáil minority Government. Dr O'Hanlon opposed the proposal on the basis that all persons with HIV should be treated equally and no special case should be made for people with haemophilia. He suggested that £250,000 be given to a fund which would help all people affected by HIV-AIDS. At this point, more than 800 people in the country were HIV positive and thirty-six had died from AIDS-related illnesses. In my opinion, his was a ridiculous argument as in this case a haemophilia blood product passed by the Government as safe, distributed by the State Blood Bank and often injected by doctors at Irish hospitals, had been infectious.

In the event, the Labour motion was passed by seventy-two votes to sixty-nine. I remember being so delighted that I jumped to my feet and clapped. In my innocence, I thought the IHS had secured a famous victory. The feeling of elation didn't last long. I sat down and looked at the woman beside me. I knew she had a young son infected with HIV who was already suffering badly. She also had several other children to look after and was not in a position to fully provide the extra protein diet or pay the heating bills required. The financial drain was compounded by hospital visits and special treats for her son who she feared might be dead in a year.

My sense of victory was also short-lived. Rather than

accept the Labour Party's motion, the Taoiseach Charles Haughey exercised his entitlement not to implement it. Fine Gael's Alan Dukes said: "The Government have lost the opportunity here to take a very compassionate action in a small sector that affects a number of people in a very very particular way." Brendan Howlin, who proposed the motion, said: "The issue is a moral one and the Government has a responsibility to respond to it."

Mr Haughey didn't refer to people with haemophilia but spoke in terms of the Government's fiscal policy being undermined. He said that the Government "would not tolerate any attempt to undermine their authority in financial matters". He also chastised the opposition: "The defeat of the Government was pursued with a determination which was not in any way relevant to the two proposals which were before the Dáil." He ruled out any possibility of implementing the measure. Yet the vote undermined the Government and Mr Haughey called a General Election shortly afterwards.

I remember feeling so depressed – seven people with haemophilia had already died as a result of AIDS-related illnesses by this time. Twenty other members of our society had developed full-blown AIDS. It was my first hard lesson in how the State could disregard its responsibilities to its citizens. I would come to understand that nothing the IHS ever achieved would come easy. Inevitably there would be lengthy prevarication from officials and their political masters. Our members were dying miserable deaths, but we had to waste time with politicians in an effort to get them to do what they should have done a long time ago. It was sickening.

Thirteen years on, in 2002, the same feeling of hurt and abandonment came back to me. My anger in 1989 had been directed at the Minister for Health and now here was Dr

O'Hanlon presiding over a Dáil debate which was finally going to lead to a settlement. I had witnessed dozens of people with haemophilia die between the two debates. Moving the debate along was the same person who I felt had let IHS members down all those years before when they were so vulnerable. I found myself staring down into the Dáil chamber. I couldn't take my eyes from him as I repeated over and over again: "Shame on you."

1

Nicholas And Alexandra

I was born in March 1957 into a family that had no connection with haemophilia. My father, Billy Marks, was a taxi-driver in Dundalk, County Louth, which claimed the status of largest town in Ireland. My mother, Rosaleen, worked in the home. My brother, Billy, was ten years older than me and left home when I was seven. It was always great to see him on his flying visits from Dublin as he was very protective of me and would always give me a few bob. As my brother was away, I became very close to my mother. She was a woman of great confidence and some of it rubbed off on me. She would often say: "The world is your oyster." It was something which seeped into my consciousness.

I went to Saint Louis Convent School in Dundalk and absolutely loved it. The ethos of the school was very advanced for the time and there were lots of extra-curricular activities. I was involved in debating and drama. My lack of interest in the academic side of things developed from being out of school through TB for five months when I was seven. I wasn't allowed any visitors for fear of passing on the infection. It was extremely boring. Afterwards, all I wanted to do was to talk to people. I was popular and a good organiser but paid little attention to my books.

The event which first evoked a sense of injustice in me was Bloody Sunday in Derry on January 30, 1972, when thirteen protestors were shot dead and another was fatally injured by British soldiers. Just shy of my fifteenth birthday, I remember going to Mass with my parents the following Sunday. When we came out of the church, I could see a line of buses parked ready to take people to a solidarity march across the border in Newry. I looked at my father and said: "I want to go." His response was emphatic: "You will do no such thing." However, he relented once he heard my cousin was going as well.

Once we came close to the border, the buses pulled in and we had to walk through the checkpoint. There were soldiers with guns everywhere. I had been across the border on numerous occasions, but the level of security this time was unprecedented and unnerving. Thousands of people marched peacefully in Newry that day and I was proud to be one of them. My cousin and I ended up walking the fourteen miles back home, but I didn't care. I felt my presence at the march might have contributed something. Looking back, I suppose I was a budding activist.

At the time, my mother and father took in boarders from the local Regional Technical College. I began to date a friend of one of the lodgers. His name was Arthur Daly. After the Leaving Cert, I followed Arthur to Dublin where he already had a job as a technician with the Post and Telegraphs company. I got a job there as a telephonist. However, I spent most of my time acting as a shop steward or organising basketball games. Relating to people one-to-one was far preferable to the salary job. At night Arthur and I spent most of our time either going to the cinema or to our favourite pub, *An Beal Bocht*, in Ranelagh where we listened to traditional musicians. However, we also liked going to see rock bands in other venues. Arthur and I married in 1976. We had a son, John Joe, in December 1979. After three months of maternity leave I returned to the telephone exchange on Exchequer Street but only lasted a day. I wanted to be with my son and so I resigned.

A few years later, my brother gave me a job as an administrator in his meat business. It was another example of taking a job just to pay the bills rather than out of any interest. By this stage, I was living in Coolock, north Dublin. When my daughter Aisling was born in 1984, I worked part-time. Yet as the job didn't really appeal to me, it wasn't all that surprising to my brother or my family when I left that too. A post had become available on a community employment scheme. The pay wasn't great, but the job of community youth activist was right up my street: it was outdoors and people-orientated. It was here that I first heard about Acquired Immune Deficiency Syndrome or AIDS. The topic would come to dominate my life.

In 1987 there was a lot of ignorance surrounding the Human Immunodeficiency Virus (HIV), the virus which causes AIDS. I was being repeatedly asked if it was possible to contract the virus by swimming in a pool with someone who was infected. Other urban myths included the belief that you could contract HIV by simply shaking hands with a person who was HIV positive. I didn't have the answers and realised that I needed to educate myself quickly.

I learned that a test for HIV had been introduced in Ireland towards the end of 1985. The virus was identified in three main groups: gay men who contracted the virus through sex; drug abusers who shared syringes; and people with haemophilia who became infected by using blood products which had been made from contaminated donations. People had already died. The pattern was always the same: a person's immune system would first be compromised by the virus and then they would die from a secondary illness like the rare cancer Kaposi's sarcoma or the form of pneumonia, Pneumocystis carinii. As there was no cure, the death toll was going to increase rapidly.

The thing which shocked me most about HIV was the stigma associated with it. Some young people would describe those infected as 'dirty'. Others argued that AIDS was a form of 'plague' being visited on the gay community. Such was the level of prejudice that people infected with the virus were terrified of their HIV-status becoming public. Many didn't even tell their own families. The more I read, the more angry I became. I felt if was unfair that people with HIV had to endure the sense of shame. The need for secrecy was unjust. I felt compelled to do something. The idea I hit upon was to arrange talks for young people with the aim of dispelling the myths. I had always been headstrong and didn't have any worries about seeking out the people who could make my idea become a reality.

With the assistance of Gay Health Action, the Bishops' Task Force, the Health Promotion Unit of the Department of Health and staff at Coláiste Dhulaigh, we put together a programme in 1988 to inform the students there both about the risks of HIV infection and the reality of AIDS. Critically, part of the programme included the participation of people who were infected with HIV. Three extremely brave people came forward: a gay man, Paul; a woman who had contracted the virus while working as a prostitute to pay for her heroin addiction; and Gerard Healy from Cork who had haemophilia.

At this time, I knew very little about haemophilia. There was no history of the disorder in my family and I didn't know anyone who had it. The only knowledge I had gleaned was through a film I once saw as a child, called *Nicholas and Alexandra*. It was about the Czar of Russia, Nicholas, whose young son, Alexis, had haemophilia. I was really taken by the story of the boy who was ill but who no-one really knew how to help. I remember swearing that I would name my first son after him. Maybe Alexis Daly wasn't such a good idea!

Gerard was the first real person with haemophilia I ever encountered. The first thing that struck me about him was that he looked the picture of health. Tall with black hair and sallow complexion, he was a good-looking man. Over the coming months we often went for a drink and ended up talking about what had happened to both him and his community. In a strong Cork accent and with passion in his voice, he explained how there were around 400 people with haemophilia in Ireland but, tragically, more than one hundred had become infected with HIV. Publicity in the national media about the situation led to haemophilia becoming synonymous with HIV. People fighting an incurable disease were also battling prejudice and fear.

Gerard explained that he didn't need to use very many blood products as his condition was relatively mild. He was therefore shocked when he was told he was HIV positive. My stomach turned as I imagined what it must have been like for him to go home and tell his wife of his diagnosis. Gerard was around the same age as I was and it began to dawn on me that here was a person who had to grapple with his own mortality. He was someone who was going to have to leave his children behind before they grew up.

One admirable thing about Gerard was that he took a decision which most people in the same position would recoil

5

from: he went public. In 1989, he was interviewed about his diagnosis in his home in Cork on RTÉ's *Today Tonight* and gave a very frank answer: "I was very frightened because I was a haemophiliac and was open [about that fact in the community]. Everybody was asking me was I [HIV] positive. And I denied it. I told everyone I wasn't positive – I was negative. I denied it to my mother, to my two sisters – I denied it to everybody . . . All my fears were that I could have passed it on to the kids as well. It was hell here in this house. We couldn't even talk about it."

I remember asking Gerard about how the devastation in the haemophilia community had occurred. He explained how he had 'haemophilia A' – the most common form of this blood disorder. It meant he was not able to produce the naturally occurring clotting-agent called Factor VIII. However, a blood product, which contained Factor VIII in concentrated form, was imported into Ireland from the United States by the Blood Bank. It was a cause for celebration in the haemophilia community when 'concentrates' arrived as they meant dramatically less time in hospital and fewer injuries due to bleeds. Yet by 1983, people with haemophilia were getting concerned about these concentrates. Stories were coming out of the United States about a mysterious killer illness which might be carried through blood. By 1984, the virus had been identified as HIV. By 1985, a test for the virus had been licensed. It revealed that more than a quarter of people with haemophilia in Ireland, all of them Factor VIII users, were HIV positive.

Things were slightly different for the minority of the haemophilia community who couldn't produce the naturally occurring clotting-agent called Factor IX. They had what was called 'haemophilia B'. Due to their low number, it was possible for their required blood product to be made from

Irish donations and manufactured by the Blood Bank in Dublin. However, Gerard said that six or seven Factor IX users had also become infected with HIV around 1986. It wasn't clear if Irish blood products were definitely responsible as some imported Factor IX had also been used by Irish doctors. Gerard said that the strange thing was that the Factor IX users who contracted the virus appeared to have been negative in 1985, the year when a means of eliminating HIV by heat-treating the concentrates was introduced. Therefore, how these infections occurred in 1986 was unclear. However, the main priority for HIV positive people with Factor VIII and Factor IX deficiencies in 1987 was fighting to stay alive rather than trying to figure out the cause of their infections.

Gerard wasn't the only person connected with haemophilia in the Coláiste Dhulaigh awareness programme. Another participant was Margaret King who had been the haemophilia nurse at Saint James's Hospital in Dublin. She was now a volunteer counsellor and executive committee member with the IHS. A small and slender woman, she was everything you would imagine a nursing sister to be: her facial expression was severe, she wore gold-rimmed glasses and dressed conservatively. On first glance, she stood in stark contrast to the other speakers. Some parents at the school thought she must be a nun when I introduced her as Sister King. One brave woman actually asked her. Margaret told the group she was the mother of eleven children who were not conceived by immaculate conception! She was quick-witted and had a tremendous sense of fun.

Meeting Margaret was a hugely significant moment in my life. What first impressed me was the way she could convey the devastating impact which HIV was having on the small haemophilia community. Though soft-spoken, she could grab people's attention by describing the fear, stigma and lack of resources the community faced. Her compassion and dedication were clear for all to see. The more I met Margaret, the more I respected her.

At the time there was nothing worse than having HIV. Most people didn't want to have any contact with people who were HIV positive or had full-blown AIDS. Very few knew what the difference was or cared. Yet, the HIV-infected people on the school awareness programme were going public in order to try to change things. To me, these were ordinary people battling extraordinary odds with courage and bravery. Because I had made a connection with these people, I felt compelled to support them and couldn't care less what anyone thought. I didn't have to consider the issue for any length of time – I knew what I wanted to do.

I was becoming deeply involved and believed that everyone needed to know about this disease, otherwise they were going to be at risk of contracting it. I began socialising with the speakers of the school programme and became as intolerant as they were of the obstacles being placed in their way. At its most basic, I believed that an injustice was being committed against people living with HIV. For the first time, I felt I was in a position to do something about it. While I got to know Gerard quite well, I was closer to Paul, the gay activist. The result was that I volunteered with Gay Health Action. They were determined to make a difference and had an energetic and aggressive approach which appealed to me. Within a matter of weeks I found myself going to gay nights in discos in Dublin. Some of the older members of GHA felt that younger men didn't believe HIV was an issue and so they had established an awareness programme. The approach was very direct: go to clubs, strike up a conversation with people and try to get them to practise safer sex.

While I had the courage of my convictions, it took quite an adjustment. I had never been to a gay night before and was now confronted by lots of men kissing each other. The first time, I remember standing on my own at the bar and not knowing where to look. While I felt that homosexual relationships were fine, it was a culture shock. I was scared that my facial expressions might give off the wrong impression.

Some of the other guys from Gay Health Action explained what to say and what to do. It was still difficult to walk up to total strangers locked in embrace and interrupt them with conversations about sexual health. Yet, within a short amount of time I got used to it and people began to know me, in part because I was usually the only woman there. I seemed to get along because I was non-threatening. It also helped that I could trade jokes and not react when they tried to shock me. I soon felt it was normal to ensure I was carrying dozens of condoms in my pockets before leaving home.

The volunteer job could mean that I was out two nights a week, but then there might not be another disco for a month. My husband, Arthur, didn't mind either the hours or the work. My children John Joe and Aisling, who were now nine and four, would usually be in bed before I went out. Part of the reason for Arthur's support was that he had met Paul who was by this time quite ill from full-blown AIDS. The personal connection had made an impact on my husband and he believed in what I was doing.

As well as going out at night, I was also working by day assisting another HIV support group, Body Positive, to plan a national conference on AIDS. The work was important and extremely rewarding, but it didn't pay the bills. I needed to get a job.

Possibly because I was moaning about this, one of the Body Positive volunteers, Christy, told me that he had seen an ad for the post of AIDS coordinator at the Irish Haemophila Society or IHS. While I had now an extremely good understanding of HIV/AIDS, I didn't have a third-level qualification or the medical training I felt would be required. So I dismissed the idea. It therefore came as more than a surprise when, about a month later, I received a letter from the IHS acknowledging receipt of my CV. For good measure, I was informed that I would be called for an interview. It was obviously Christy who had invented and sent in a CV for me. I didn't know whether to kill him or kiss him. I decided instead to ring him and thank him. I was overjoyed.

While the IHS letter of October 1988 said I would be called for interview "shortly", it didn't actually take place until the following February. It may seem strange but over those four months I didn't contact Margaret King or Gerard Healy. The idea just didn't cross my mind. It was a shock when I found Margaret sitting on the interview panel. The other person I recognised was Brian O'Mahony, the chairman of the IHS. Only the previous week I had read an article about him travelling to the European Commission to participate in discussions on HIV. I began to feel intimidated.

Their questions related to death, sexual relationships and my 'vision' of how best to provide care for the haemophilia community. My answers were reactive rather than illuminating. I felt uncomfortable in what was my first real interview. That sensation was accentuated by the fact that I had borrowed my interview suit from my mother-in-law as I didn't have one. My usual garb was jeans, runners and a sweatshirt. Afterwards, I went straight up to my mother-in-law's house and had a glass of brandy and a cigarette. I didn't even smoke at the time, but it seemed like a good idea. I sucked in the smoke more out of relief than satisfaction. I must have liked it though as it became a habit.

Less than two weeks later, I was called back for a second interview. This time I borrowed a suit from my sister-in-law only to find the interview panel decked out in jeans and T-shirts. The atmosphere was far more informal. They also told me that the advertised salary was above what the IHS could pay as they had forgotten to take into account the cost of PRSI. There was an air of embarrassment when this was disclosed, but I knew the IHS was an organisation run mostly by volunteers on a part-time basis. The interview board told me the job was now between myself and one other person. They said they would let me know as soon as possible. In fact, Brian O'Mahony telephoned me at ten o'clock that night to say I had got the job. I was elated. The next morning Arthur and I went out and bought my first car – a new Lada. After the repayments and childcare I would have a surplus of £10. It felt fantastic.

The position was described as mainly administrative. I would be coordinating the office, liaising with the executive and training volunteers. There was, however, a clear expectation that I would be getting involved with the members. What I could never have expected was just how deeply involved I would become.

2

My Boys

I had never anticipated being so intertwined in the lives of people with haemophilia. I found the job extremely difficult in the beginning. One incident burnt into my memory is that I inflicted extreme pain on a man with haemophilia who was in the final stages of full-blown AIDS.

Jim, who was married with children, was one of the few members to be infected with HIV from a Factor IX blood product. By the time I came to meet him, he was fighting the ravages of AIDS-related illnesses on the top floor of Saint James's Hospital Number 1 in Dublin. There were seven separate hospitals within the complex and a pub across the road, Kenny's, was nicknamed Hospital 8. Margaret King was giving more and more of her time as a volunteer counsellor to Jim. She asked me to help. This wasn't unusual as she was always introducing me to members in the office, hospitals and at their homes. My contact with them at this point was relatively superficial whereas Margaret knew them all intimately. What I picked up very quickly was that, if she indicated to the members that I was trustworthy, this was always accepted.

Jim had been having increasingly long stays at Saint James's. Margaret was spending more and more time with his immediate and extended family helping them cope. I was only getting to know Jim when his condition deteriorated very quickly. I found out when I received a phone call from Margaret. She said: "Jim is very low. Do you want to come up and say goodbye?" I wanted to, but was unsure about what he might feel. I asked Margaret: "Do you think it would be appropriate? I didn't know him that well – what would his family think if I suddenly arrived on the ward?" Margaret responded: "You're welcome, if you want to."

This was the first time I found myself in this circumstance. I was so naïve at the time about the reality of AIDS that I made an awful mistake. Walking onto the ward, the first thing I did was to greet Jim by covering his hand with mine. It seemed like the natural thing to do. What I didn't know was that Jim's nerve-endings were extremely sensitive due to his AIDS condition. Even the weight of a sheet on his limbs caused him pain. And there was I, in the hope of comforting him, as good as crushing his hand. I looked at his face and saw that he was gritting his teeth. I blurted out: "Jesus, I'm sorry!" Jim recognised my embarrassment and tried to play down the event. I felt terrible.

Jim died shortly afterwards. His funeral was the first such event I attended. It was just so sad. All around the church were other people with haemophilia and their relatives. I found myself wondering: "Who is going to be the next to die?" Margaret told me the biggest indicator of failing health was weight-loss. One key area of focus were the cheekbones. If this was protruding or more prominent, it usually suggested that a person was becoming seriously ill. It seemed everyone was assessing each other for any signs.

What made this awful situation even worse was the fact that nobody felt they could be candid about what had happened. The stigma of AIDS was so great that people were terrified about it becoming public. Families of those who died therefore covered it up. They knew the local community was probably wondering what had happened. More often than not, when people enquired, the answer they would be given was 'cancer' as that was socially acceptable. AIDS most certainly was not. I would often hear mourners at a funeral quietly talk about cancer being the cause of death and it struck me as being so unfair: a family already hurting was having to endure even more stress. Members would tell me about how they began to lie to their neighbours to cover up why a person went to the doctor or what prognosis had been given. The secrecy and fear of their anonymity being lost ate into them.

By this time, I was beginning to make friends with many of the other people regularly attending funerals. They usually stopped and spoke with Margaret King who always introduced me. Margaret had been forced to retire from Saint James's Hospital in 1988 after she accidentally became infected with hepatitis. She had been giving a person with haemophilia an infusion when the needle stuck into her by accident. As the man had hepatitis B, she contracted it. Margaret became very ill and spent many months in hospital. It took her nearly a year and a half to recover fully. She returned to work at Saint James's Hospital but decided to retire shortly afterwards because she became tired very easily. In 1989, Government funding became available and she was hired as full-time counsellor with the IHS.

At this time, the IHS's offices amounted to a portakabin situated on a site now occupied by Jury's Inn, Christchurch, in Dublin. The IHS now has a reputation for professionalism, but in 1989 the offices were makeshift. Essentially we had two rooms, the second of which was supposed to be mine, but which we turned into a counselling room. It was furnished with a second-hand suite. The 'main office' was one room containing two desks, a big long table, a few hard chairs, an armchair and a filing cabinet. The fact was that the IHS had very little funds. My position was paid for by the Eastern Health Board while the only other employee, Cepta, was a secretary working part-time on a FÁS scheme. The rent for the office came from donations and fundraising. It didn't feel like much, but it was certainly an advance on previous years where the IHS was run by parents and people with haemophilia on a voluntary basis from their homes.

One of the volunteers I became close to was Margaret Dunne. She had two children with haemophilia. Margaret was one of those people who never got ruffled. I, on the other hand, got very agitated. It made us a good team. Margaret had offered to help out with administration as Cepta was becoming overworked due to the HIV situation.

Members visiting from outside Dublin would usually drop in for a cup of tea before or after going for treatment at Saint James's Hospital. I came to meet Dermot through this casual system. On the first number of occasions it was rather strange: he would come in, sit down, have a cup of tea and say very little if anything at all. He wasn't being rude, but was simply very shy. After a few visits, Dermot began to open up and we became close. While Dermot was a quiet man, he loved to be in the middle of the fun. This became obvious when we held a weekend meeting in Dublin for male members. Dermot usually didn't have the opportunity to socialise with other haemophiliacs because he lived far away from the capital. He really enjoyed himself. The more ructions that occurred the more he enjoyed it. From this point on, Dermot took a keen interest in any meetings which he might be able to attend.

Margaret King continued to involve me in the lives of members. In part, she wanted me to meet those on whose behalf I was working. The other side of things was that Margaret had become completely stretched and needed help. By 1989, more and more people with haemophilia were getting ill due to AIDS-related illnesses. Due to an absence of State support, they were turning to the IHS for counselling and information. I was not a qualified counsellor but was happy to try. It was obvious that people were desperate for support and my reaction was to respond immediately and leave the thinking to later. I had by now formed an emotional bond with many members and felt duty-bound to do whatever I could. Margaret King and I became inseparable.

Margaret was originally from Limerick, but her family had moved to Dublin when she was in her early teens. Her ambition was to become a doctor, but, due to the untimely death of her father, this wasn't possible. She trained as a secretary, but gave up after two or three years and travelled to England to become a nurse. Margaret met her husband, Martin, over there. Eventually, she returned home when her mother became ill. She worked in the neo-natal units of Saint James's Hospital before moving to its National Haemophilia Treatment Centre or NHTC. With this experience, she was easily able to explain to me how haemophilia treatment had developed.

In the 1950s, if a person with haemophilia had a serious bleed, they were given transfusions of whole blood. The medical profession didn't have the capacity to separate the naturally occurring clotting-agent and so kept giving the patient blood transfusions until the bleed stopped. As this was a long process, it caused major problems. The main issue with not stopping a bleed quickly is that it leads to a build-up of blood internally. When this blood flows into a confined space, such as a joint, it causes stiffening. Eventually, it presses on the nerve, causing immense pain. Repeated bleeds lead to cartilage damage and early arthritis. Many people with haemophilia suffered horrendous pain as their ankles, knees and hips effectively seized.

A major development occurred in the late 1960s when scientists found that by freezing plasma and then slowly thawing it you could collect a white residue which was ten times richer in the required clotting-agent. This product was known as cryoprecipitate or 'cryo' for short and one treatment could be made from around five donations. As it was more concentrated, treatment was quicker and more effective which resulted in less trauma to joints. Cryo was a bulky product which had to be kept frozen. As there were not too many people with freezers at home in the 1960s, people continued to go to hospital for treatment.

However, the real breakthrough happened in the late 1960s when it was established that by treating cryo with chemicals and other procedures it was possible to manufacture a white powder of highly concentrated clotting-agent. These concentrated blood products or 'concentrates' amounted to a revolution in haemophilia care. Concentrates were liberating because people could treat themselves at home rather than having to go to hospital. At the first sign of a bleed, they could dissolve the white powder and inject themselves with the small solution which contained a massive quantity of clotting-agent. This meant they could stop a bleed more quickly and eliminate trauma. The bottles were the size of salt-cellars and could be easily taken abroad.

Concentrates were being imported by the Irish Blood Bank in the early 1970s and then distributed to hospitals. By the time Margaret King joined the NHTC at Saint James's Hospital, things were looking particularly good for people with haemophilia. Margaret herself, of course, was involved in administering the blood products.

However, within a few years, the HIV crisis hit. By 1985 it was known that the wonder-drug had turned out to be an apparent death sentence for a quarter of the haemophilia population. Margaret found herself working with a traumatised community as the realities and effects of HIV became known. She spoke to me constantly about this period. She would say: "If I had known what was in those drugs, I would never have administered them." She felt immense guilt as she had become effectively a mother-figure to many of the men who attended her centre. Now the 'mother' was having to nurse her 'children' to an early death. This was one of the reasons why Margaret felt so motivated to help people with HIV. It was a zeal which rubbed off on me. It didn't dawn on me to draw a line between myself and the members, because Margaret didn't. It was often commented that Margaret "didn't know what a clock was". She would always stay with a patient until they received attention – no matter how long that took.

People responded to her, particularly when she helped facilitate those who smoked but were confined to bed. Margaret would walk on to the ward pushing a wheelchair and say: "Come on, come on, it's time you were out of that bed for a while!" Though the other people on the ward wouldn't necessarily know, Margaret would wheel the person out to the smoking area of Top Floor 1. While Margaret had eleven children, most were able to fend for themselves by the time she came to work with people with haemophilia. She did have two children in their early teens, but somehow managed to work around it through the support of her husband

Martin. She had tremendous drive and fuelled her wiry frame by eating like a horse and had to have regular food-breaks of enormous proportions. However, her hepatitis B infection continued to have an impact and she would often be forced into taking a rest for an hour or two.

It was through Margaret King that I came to know Jerome Stephens. Jerome was unfortunate enough to have contracted HIV from a concentrate used when his appendix was being removed. The operation had taken place on Thursday November 4, 1982. Jerome was 27. It was his one and only treatment with this type of product. What made him different to most was that he went public in the late 1980s in order to press the Government for compensation so that his family would not be left impoverished after his death. When I first met him, he was in bed at his council home in Clondalkin. A sheet was pulled up to his neck; above that was a head with long hair, a bushy beard and dancing eyes. This first impression was something which the public also came to know: Jerome was interviewed on RTÉ's TV health programme, *Check Up*, in his bed speaking about the pain of AIDS and his financial fear for his wife, Liz, and three children Karen, David and Keith. The idea that a dying man had to be exposed in this way to get what he deserved was appalling.

The programme in March 1990 also happened to be the first occasion on which I was interviewed in a major way. I spoke about the pressures on mothers who were trying to manage when their partner became infected with HIV: "It affects the whole family. You have a mother trying to cope with young children and deal with a husband who is extremely ill. So the children in the end obviously suffer . . . She is trying to put a brave face on all the time for both her husband and her children, but inside she is torn apart, always having to be the strong one. And because of the nature of

19

haemophilia – that it is a hereditary disorder – we have families where there is more than one person infected. We have a mother who might have a son who has already died of AIDS and another son who is HIV positive."

Jerome was thirty-four when he gave the interview, but looked much older due to his grey hair and thin body. He explained how, when he was a child, no one really knew what haemophilia was: "They hadn't got haemophilia as a diagnosis. I was known in school as a 'bleeder' which didn't help at all." Jerome explained how he was beaten harder rather than treated with care due to his condition: "I went to Saint Joseph's school in Dorset Street. I got a rough time there. I got more broken ribs and more bleeds than anything else." He also explained about early treatment for his bleeds: "Before blood transfusions came in, haemophiliacs died if they got a bad bleed. Then when blood transfusions came in, they had to get twelve or thirteen pints. I had to get twelve pints in one night when I got my tonsils out."

When his doctor informed him he was HIV positive in 1986, Jerome said he didn't take it in. His father was with him at the consultation, but he didn't really comprehend what the diagnosis meant: "I hadn't a clue. I hadn't the foggiest. My father had about a hundred questions – I didn't have one. I was left speechless. If my father hadn't gone with me, I would have sat there and said 'OK, I'll see you' and walked out."

When it sank in, the impact was profound: "I . . . tried to commit suicide, at the earlier stage – maybe three or four months after I had full-blown AIDS. I looked at what I had up to then: it was nothing but pain and misery. Not just for me, but for Liz and the kids and everybody around. I was putting them through hell. My father had a heart attack because I wouldn't take the money off him for a coat in the winter and I felt very guilty about that."

Jerome recognised that his HIV status was having a major impact on his young children. One incident stuck in his mind – when news emerged of a drug being developed which could possibly slow down the rate of illness: "I heard the news on the radio and I got a bit excited. It was a compound which was supposed to halt the virus in its tracks. I told my sister and she came home and told Liz. And Karen [who was ten] was listening and she ran in and said: 'Oh, is there a cure for my daddy?' And she ran around the corner, all excited, and she told her friends: 'My daddy is going to be cured.' It was very hard to explain that there is no cure. [I told her] if it be God's will, he will cure me or take me. And either way it's OK. Because if he takes me, I'll be going to a better place than this. I'll have no more pain and no more suffering and I'll be able to run around with the deer and I'll be able to watch them and take care of them. And she was content with that."

While Jerome was most certainly a victim, the tag didn't catch one tenth of who he was as a person. He was a beautiful calm man who had a great love of art, sculpting and writing poetry. He drew a lot of imagery from going to the mountains where he formed a particular attachment to deer. Jerome had a great faith in the Catholic Church, but was by no means a 'Creeping Jesus' – even if he looked a bit like the Saviour! The Jerome I got to know was also a manipulative rogue who agitated for the IHS and was loved by its members, particularly for his sense of humour. He was extremely resilient. I must have sat on his bedside on three occasions when it was expected that he would die – only for him to pull through, yet again.

He was cute enough to recognise that I might be in a position to get him things that he wanted. Jerome had a great ability to get people to do things on his behalf and make them feel good about it. We got on extremely well as we both would lay into each other with jokes and jibes. He also had a

21

fantastic laugh. Once the cackle started, his bed would vibrate and his blue box of cigarettes, the ashtray and his books would fall off the edge. Jerome became one of 'My Boys'.

While Jerome was a father coping with illness and attempting to support and comfort his children, I also became very close at the time to a father whose eight-year-old son was HIV positive. Ray Kelly from Shankill in Dublin was witty and warm, but he was also extremely angry. His fury was in part due to his contention that he had not been informed about the chances of his son John contracting HIV before concentrates were used on him. Then, when John was identified as HIV positive, Ray had been assured that there was little chance of his developing full-blown AIDS – this was the conventional wisdom at the time. However, by 1989, even that little hope disappeared as people with haemophilia began to die. My connection with Ray came from his increasing distrust of the medical profession. He wanted to know what was happening and what was going to happen. He felt he could come only to Margaret and myself for advice and support. I was usually able to know when Ray was going to explode as he would become quiet and his face would be a giveaway. The joking would stop and you would be left with a man speechless at the fact that he could do nothing to save his son. My response was to offer him advice, information and access to experts. He would always follow up on this more quickly than seemed humanly possible in the vain hope that he might be able to reverse things. The IHS was a haven, especially as Ray didn't tell anyone else about what was happening at the time.

While John was in relatively good health, Ray and his wife Ann were living in a state of fear that he would find out about his condition. John's older brother wasn't told either. Their logic was that if John knew, then his friends might find out and they probably would not remain his friends for very much longer. The idea that their son could be both ostracised and severely ill was too much to bear. They wanted to protect him and his brother as much as possible. There was no easy formula or guidebook.

The first time I met John was in Harcourt Street Hospital in Dublin. He was in a room on his own because he was so ill. As I walked in, my mind was racing: "This boy will probably not want to see me at all. Why should he? Yet another stranger walking in to hassle him." I gave him a present from the IHS and, even though he was very weak, John put his arm around my neck and gave me a kiss. He was a beautiful child with blond hair, blue eyes and an angelic smile. John was around the same age as my son, John Joe, and both played tennis in the local Kit-Kat league. I wondered how Ray and Ann could bear the pain of what was happening to their young son.

With my background in youth work, I was also beginning to put some efforts into the youth group of the IHS. It was orientated around organising holidays and get-togethers so that the young could both have fun and talk. The first connections I made were with Paul and Kevin who were about seventeen years old. Both boys were HIV positive and finding it difficult to cope. My approach with them was different from the one I used with the adults. I never offered counselling or asked the dreaded questions: "How are you feeling? What are your fears for the future?" They would have run away and never returned. Instead, I asked them for a game of pool or inquired if they wanted to go for something to eat or drink as they would be more relaxed in that environment. Eventually, as we began to relax in each other's company, HIV was discussed. The conversation was on their terms – they decided when and for how long. Sadly, Paul and Kevin were often in hospital suffering from various infections. When I would visit there would be the usual initial banter and then, if we were alone, the conversation might move on to their concerns.

Both Paul and Kevin were old enough to know that their parents were terrified about what the future might hold for them. They always put on a show of coping well as they felt their parents had enough problems without them unloading their fears. The frequent illness also impacted on their schooling. Paul and Kevin had little hope of getting good employment even if they passed a medical.

Contact with Jerome, Ray, Paul and Kevin made me realise that the IHS had to provide a range of different types of support as each of their problems was unique. Jerome who had gone public about his illness had a different set of problems from Ray who was living in fear of his son being identified. Little John Kelly was in a totally different set of circumstances to Paul and Kevin. It took time to adjust.

My approach to people with haemophilia also had to be very different from that of my earlier dealings with the gay community. I realised, but didn't initially understand why, the haemophilia community had a heightened fear about being identified as being HIV positive. They were also more conservative in outlook. What was particularly sad was the fact that there wasn't all that much interaction between the two groups – even though it seemed they should be able to benefit from each other's resources and knowledge of HIV.

It became apparent that part of the problem was that some members of the haemophilia community secretly blamed the gay community for their illness. It was widely known that gay men had a tradition of altruism in being blood donors. Their plasma was used to make blood products for haemophilacs. A connection was therefore made between HIV in clotting-agents and gay men. It would be revealed much later that the pharmaceutical companies rather than the donors deserved the criticism – however, it wasn't known at this stage. The gay community was also upset about the manner in which the media portrayed people with haemophilia as 'innocent victims' on the basis that they contracted HIV from medicine. Gay men felt this was a misinterpretation as it seemed to suggest that they had gone out and deliberately infected themselves with AIDS. Their clear view was that they became infected with HIV through sexual contact at a time when it was not known what the virus was or how it was transmitted. They were innocent victims too.

I did manage to make some headway because the IHS and Gay Health Action had their offices in the same building. It was possible to get the younger members of the IHS to meet for coffee with volunteers from GHA. However, I also had to accept that it was not going to be possible to forge similar links between the older groups as the IHS members simply didn't want to know. Not everyone had a problem. One ally in this difficult position was Gerard Healy from Cork who'd come to talk to students about AIDS when I worked in Coolock. Gerard worked closely with gay men as he had identified at an early stage that the gay community had the most up-to-date information on HIV.

Gerard and other members with HIV began to call to my house. Initially, they were dropping in for a drink, but soon we were having people over for dinner and they would often stay. This wasn't all that strange as our house was a bit of a train station already with anyone and everyone dropping in. Arthur came from a family of nine and so was quite used to the house being turned upside down. He is a 'people person' and so loved to engage. He had a philosophy of welcoming people but never got hung up on formalities. I remember one man calling to the house when I had been unexpectedly called away to a member who was dying. He told me Arthur simply put some of his sausages and chips onto a plate with a slice of bread and handed it over. The man was so at ease that he didn't care if I never came back to the house.

Even at this early stage, some people used to ask me: "How do you manage to juggle your family and work life?" The answer was simple: on the one hand, Arthur was always around and, when John Joe and Aisling were younger, a friend, Peggo, was employed to live in the house for most of the week. Peggo had lived next door to me when I was in Coolock. We were always in each other's homes. The contact was so close that we ended up knocking down a piece of the wall separating our front gardens so that we could get to each other's front door more quickly. When Arthur, the kids and I moved to Swords, Peggo decided to effectively move with us. For the following year, she lived in our home from Sunday to Thursday and returned to Coolock for the weekend. Only when Peggo's daughter gave birth did our year-long arrangement came to an end. It had worked really well – I would bring Peggo breakfast in bed every morning and then head out to work. With her at home, it allowed me to do all of the things I wanted to do.

When Peggo left, I placed an ad seeking childcare in the local supermarket. A fantastic woman, Eilish, answered the ad and she is still with us eleven years later. There was, however, a big difference as Eilish worked part-time. John Joe and Aisling would be collected from school and looked after until six o'clock. After that, Arthur took over. Most of the time, I would be there as well in the evenings.

Even with these supports, I often felt at the end of the day there was someone I had not made contact with or work which I had not completed. This feeling really kicked in around the early 1990s when members infected with HIV began to die from AIDS-related illnesses with greater frequency. While Margaret King and I may have been very close to the family in the days preceding the death, we always stood back a respectable distance when the coffin was taken from the church for burial. We would be close enough to intervene if anyone became distressed, but far enough away so that the family could grieve over the loss of their loved one. Often, at this point, I would have loved to have Arthur standing beside me, but secrecy was such an issue surrounding those deaths that I wasn't able to tell him. This, however, would change as he got to know more and more of the members who called to our house.

One person with haemophilia who became a firm family favourite was Austin. It's deeply annoying that the stigma relating to being HIV positive was and is so strong that his condition remains unknown to many people and I am obliged to use a pseudonym now. The moment I realised how important he was to me was when I was standing at the graveside of yet another member who also happened to be Austin's friend. As he stood beside Margaret and me in the cemetery, I reached down and clutched his hand. In that moment, I knew that if Austin had died I wouldn't be able to cope or continue with my work.

Austin found out that he was HIV positive in June 1985 – just two days before his Leaving Cert began. He'd been taken into hospital to have his appendix removed. A young doctor came by and told him he had HIV. Asked if he had any questions, Austin said he didn't and the woman ran off the ward. Austin was put in an isolation area and people were putting on masks and gowns before entering the room. He simply thought he'd been given a room to himself. It wasn't until Margaret King kicked up a fuss that hospital policy changed: the gloves and gowns were no longer used.

The way Austin had been left alone and isolated at such a vulnerable age really rankled. That distance from the rest of the population was reinforced on leaving hospital. When he told his girlfriend about his HIV status, she freaked. Thankfully for both of them they'd not had unprotected sex. This bad reaction was the first, but not the last. One of his friends would not even sit beside him. He decided that he would not tell anybody else. He blacked it out. He got drunk instead, lost in the nightmare world that HIV meant AIDS meant death. He was eighteen and he was going to die.

By 1989 when I met Austin, he was already a person who'd bucked the convention. Most people thought he would be dead by 1988, but, a year later, he was still healthy and involved in the IHS. His outlook, however, was still extremely short-term. He agreed to accompany me to schools where I was talking to students about the disaster which had consumed the haemophilia community. Austin's view at the time was: "I might not be around for very long so why worry about a few school talks?" This was an amazing step considering the stigma associated with HIV.

One day we were travelling to a school in Arklow, County Wicklow, and stopped off for some lunch. Initially the conversation centred on what he was going to say at the talk. Then it led to him telling me his own personal story and he opened up for the first time. Austin was dressed in jeans and a jumper and I can still remember his big magnetic eyes recounting what had happened to him. At one point, he said that he was looking for love but had given up all hope of it ever happening. Looking at him – a young man who saw himself without a future – I felt I'd never met anyone more deserving of love. The way he was being so honest and open forged a unique bond between us.

Austin spoke to me about living in Ireland in the mid-1980s when the publicity surrounding HIV could only be described as horrific. He had decided to try one more time to open-up. Driving with two of his friends to Dublin, he began talking about haemophilia but went on to say that he was HIV positive. This was approximately two years after diagnosis and the first time he had discussed it since the initial bad reaction. Now he managed to disclose his status without being spurned. His approach to life was simply to work hard and enjoy each day. Everything was in the short term. It was an outlook reinforced by the fact that people with haemophilia were starting to die in increasing numbers.

The year I met Austin was the first time he realised that his life could end at any time. He badly damaged his leg and on being taken to Saint James's Hospital was informed that his platelet count was dangerously low. The doctor told him that if he had banged his head rather than his leg he could have died. While the accident reinforced his sense of mortality, it also motivated him to speak about what he was going through and this led to the school talks.

Our chat over lunch on the way to Arklow made me realise that this was a person who really needed to talk. I knew from my experience of working with younger members, like Paul and Kevin, that there was no point in trying to get Austin to come in for counselling. He simply was not going to talk about his fears across a table. My strategy therefore was to meet him in places he felt comfortable. As it happened, Austin also liked going to see bands and so I arranged to meet him at venues. One of the regular venues was the Wexford Inn in Dublin which was dark and packed but friendly. Outwardly no one would guess how troubled he was. Yet after these gigs, it became a pattern that Austin would come back to my home and talk. These conversations led to Austin finally beginning to confront his fears.

Austin effectively became a member of my family and

would regularly join us walking in the Dublin Mountains and on weekends in our favourite bolthole of Carlingford. He regularly attended our birthdays, confirmations and communions. John Joe and Aisling really warmed to him because Austin was always playing with them. He was always poking fun at Aisling and gave her the honorary title of 'Spill The Beans' because she seemed to continually dump them on John Joe. It went so far that Austin even met my family in Dundalk. My father and his mother became buddies too. Aisling became so close to him that Austin was her sponsor for her confirmation. She took his name.

Austin was relatively lucky. While he was tragically infected with HIV, he didn't come down with as many illnesses as others in his position. The longer he escaped the ravages of AIDS-related illness, the more calm he became. As months rolled into years, Austin began to plan for the future and the destructive side to his character fell away. This transition led to him stopping being public about his illness: he wasn't going to die just yet and so he wanted a degree of anonymity.

Austin was an example of how my job and personal life had begun to blur. When I left the office, I was often taking the work home with me in the shape of a frightened man looking for good conversation, safety and openness. The more the relationship developed with 'My Boys', the more I began to question how this tragedy had happened. I was now campaigning not for an ideal of justice or an amount of money, but for men and boys who had become my friends. They were people who had opened up and placed their trust in me. They were people who were beginning to die in increasing numbers, but no one on the outside seemed to know or care about their terrible secret. It was wrong. So bloody wrong.

3

A Cold Meeting

Over the past thirteen years, I've built up a lot of experience initiating campaigns and dealing with the media. But everyone has to start somewhere and my beginning with the IHS wasn't a glorious one. My big moment followed the 1989 decision by the Government not to accept the Labour Party proposal to establish a £400,000 fund for members infected with HIV. The executive committee of the IHS felt that if the State was not going to voluntarily provide financial assistance then it should be compelled to do so. A decision was taken to provide funds for members to sue. Financial support was going to be needed as no member was in a position to fund it themselves. The legal bill was estimated at £200,000. It was a significant decision considering the executive didn't have this money at their disposal and funds were going to have to be raised from the public and the members themselves. Minutes from an executive committee meeting on March 1, 1989 recorded how initial discussions with lawyers indicated that they were quite optimistic about our chances of success. A

A Cold Meeting

meeting was quickly convened the following month of all those infected, our solicitor Tom Barry from PJ O'Driscoll & Sons, and Nicholas Kearns SC.

The legal team told us that each member would be required to sign a form indicating their willingness to become involved. Despite being incapable of typing, my chore was to type these consent forms. After what must have seemed like an eternity to those at the meeting, I arrived back triumphant with a hundred copies. My hard work was certainly appreciated – the only problem was that I had misspelt haemophilia! They all broke their hearts laughing when they saw my distressed face. Dumb-blonde jokes were the order of the day. I was mortified, but, in retrospect, it broke the ice. Up to this point the meeting had been very serious. I was filled with admiration for those attending as they either had HIV or were relatives of those who had died. When the jokes started to fly, I got to see a completely different side. Friendships grew from this moment.

Within a matter of weeks, thirty-eight writs had been issued against the State. My less-than-sparkling form continued as the campaign gathered momentum. I was the officer charged with updating the media, but wasn't quite sure what I was supposed to do. Despite the amateur nature of our publicity efforts, there was substance to the case and it secured some coverage. RTÉ reporter George Devlin, who covered health stories, was very helpful because he always gave me time to find the right words and offered advice when he felt it was required.

Among those listed as defendants was the then Minister for Health. Legally it was usual to tie in the Attorney General. But the list didn't stop there. In the firing line also was the Blood Bank as this was the body that had imported and distributed the US concentrates that were mostly responsible for the infections. It had also manufactured the Factor IX blood product which was possibly responsible for infections. The irony wasn't lost on us that the IHS was suing the Blood Bank, even though its members continued to rely on it for their medicine. Another defendant was a body called the National Drugs Advisory Board which recommended what medicines should be licensed in the country. The board of Saint James's Hospital was also named as it was the home of the National Haemophilia Treatment Centre, or NHTC, where most people with haemophilia were treated.

The inclusion which caused most controversy among the members, however, was the medical director of the NHTC, Professor Ian Temperley. He was the foremost haemophilia-treating physician in the country. This decision to include him was difficult, not just because he had helped to establish the IHS itself, but because he was also rightly credited as having helped to significantly improve the lives of people with haemophilia. When few in the 1960s were interested, Professor Temperley stepped in and centralised haemophilia care. GPs and doctors at regional hospitals were not used to dealing with haemophilia and so a specialised centre was of major value. People with haemophilia no longer had to be met by ignorance but, instead, could go to the NHTC. He was medical director of the NHTC from 1971 to 1995. In essence, Professor Temperley became the champion of the haemophilia community. Many members revered him as he had worked hard to help a community which had been marginalised. He could have made a considerable amount of money by developing a private practice but chose not to. The work he carried out on behalf of people with haemophilia was only part of his brief. Professor Temperley was also responsible for setting up the first specialised haematology laboratory, the first leukaemia centre for adults and the first bone-marrow transplant programme. On top of this work, he also was Dean of the Faculty of Health Science from 1987 to 1993 in Trinity College and was a member of prestigious medical bodies abroad. He was also on the board of the Blood Bank from 1987.

Ian Temperley moved to Westport, County Mayo, from England when he was a toddler. He was later educated at Wesley College in Dublin and ultimately Trinity College which would bestow the title of professor upon him. His colleagues were in awe of his work-rate and many felt he was a visionary. However, his patients told me they felt he was detached: relaying bad news was not one of his strongest qualities. Tall and sporting a thick mane of dark hair, he spoke with a plummy accent and could have passed for an aristocrat.

Professor Temperley had supported the introduction and continued use of US-made concentrates. While these blood products were liberating for people with haemophilia, there was a flaw at the heart of the manufacturing process. The drug companies would collect plasma from thousands of donors and then pool the donations in order to make concentrates. This system was economical because to make clotting-agents from small pools would require more effort and therefore would be more expensive. The problem was that it took just one infectious donation to contaminate the entire pool. The probability of an infectious donation was also quite high as some pools contained as many as 100,000 donations. In Ireland, the Blood Bank used smaller pools when making the Factor IX concentrate – usually around 800 donations. A relatively small supply was needed and so the process was scaled down. However the logic remained the same: all it took was for one Irish donor to be infected with HIV for the pool to be contaminated.

At this stage, I knew who Professor Temperley was through meetings at the hospital and at the IHS. However, we didn't have much direct personal contact. One question I always wanted to ask him was why he had gone on sabbatical in the summer of 1985 when he knew that dozens of his patients had contracted HIV but hadn't yet been informed. Many of the members were extremely bitter about his absence for a crucial six-month period. They told me that they felt abandoned in their time of greatest need. Their 'champion' had deserted them. I remember looking at Professor Temperley and wondering what it must be like for him to be sued by his patients. One of my early tasks was to travel to the UK and speak to medical professionals dealing with haemophilia with a view to recruiting them as expert medical witnesses for the pending court case. When I met the professor I often felt he must have known what I was doing. We never spoke about it though.

Despite the apparent conflict of interest, the campaign continued. I remember one man expressing deep reluctance about suing the professor. He said: "I wouldn't be alive without Professor Temperley. Do we really have to do this?" My response was direct: "It's horrible, but when the law takes over, loyalties break down." To be fair to the professor, I don't recall any member telling me that he was any different in his dealings with them after the litigation commenced. A colleague who worked with him, Dr Fred Jackson, was also polite and helpful in his dealings with us.

While thirty-eight writs had been issued by early May 1989, it had increased to forty-five within a month. Money was also beginning to roll in. That said, most of it was raised through fundraising activities undertaken by the membership and staff rather than appeals to the public for donations. The person who was spearheading the campaign for the IHS was its chairman, Brian O'Mahony. He was a phenomenon, able to lead a huge law suit while retaining his lab job at Our Lady's Hospital for Sick Children in Crumlin. Brian had been involved in the IHS since 1982 because his uncle, an IHS stalwart, asked him to join the executive committee. Within a year, he'd been appointed honorary secretary. He was vice-chairman by 1985 and chairman by 1987. The titles sound rather grand but, in the late 1980s, the IHS was a tiny organisation with limited resources. It was fighting for a group of people who wanted to stay as far away from the media spotlight as possible.

I liked Brian for lots of reasons. On an immediate level he was easy to get on with and had a keen Kerry wit. He was in his early thirties, had sandy-brown hair and blue eyes, was always impeccably dressed and had an extremely charming manner. But beneath this affable front was a shrewd operator who knew how to punch above his weight. He had a huge drive and energy. Brian was part of a new leadership which was less in awe of the medical profession and more assertive in demanding a role in the decisions which affected the membership. Brian had haemophilia, although he was fortunate enough to have avoided HIV infection. His zeal in pursuing the compensation claim was due in part to the fact that many of his friends had been infected.

Brian was born in Killarney, County Kerry. He told me that due to his haemophilia he had spent more time reading than playing hurling and football. Physical contact could have resulted in hospitalisation and so he also developed an ability to steer well clear of fights in the schoolyard. He became a diplomat of sorts. This quality didn't always save him from injury: one day he was walking home from school and became so engrossed in his book that he managed to fall into a dustbin. Brian moved to Dublin after his Leaving Cert. He decided to become a lab technician and his first and only medical job was with Our Lady's Hospital. By the time I met him, he was married and would later have two children.

Brian's involvement in the IHS really expanded when the HIV crisis hit in 1985. It was a terrible time. One of the jobs Brian carried out was extraordinary. Doctors were telling patients that they had to protect their sexual partners as HIV could be transmitted through intimate contact. Yet condoms were actually illegal in Ireland at the time. Brian worked out a system with Dr Helena Daly who was working at Saint James's Hospital during Professor Temperley's absence in 1985. He later explained to the Lindsay Tribunal: "I used to go down to the clinic on Wednesday evening after finishing my work and Dr Daly would send people out to me and I would give them some condoms from the boot of my car. It was very demeaning for them because I was a young man in my twenties and many of these members were much older and didn't know me very well. Some of them knew me very well – which was perhaps even more embarrassing. You were in a situation where you were having to discuss their sexual relations with them, almost. There was . . . also a difficulty as many of them had very strong Roman Catholic views. Obviously, to them, this was a breach of their religious practice." Brian also set up HIV support groups so that people could talk to each other, as only those infected really knew what it felt like to be in such a cruel position.

By the beginning of 1985, a new means of eliminating HIV led to safer blood products. All of the drug companies making the Factor VIII concentrate introduced a system known as heat treatment. In essence, blood products were heated to a certain temperature for a defined length of time to eliminate the virus. Cryo was still being used by some doctors who had concerns about the number of donations contained in concentrates. Unfortunately, it wasn't possible to heat-treat this product as high temperatures killed off the clotting factor. The haemophilia community was informed by Professor Temperley that all concentrates were going to be heat-treated. This was a major relief to the people with haemophilia who were mostly using the Irish-made Factor IX. Only Factor VIII users had become infected with HIV and now, it appeared, those injecting Factor IX would escape the possibility of contracting the virus.

Yet in the middle of 1986, Brian got an awful shock while attending a seminar on HIV in University College Dublin in his professional capacity. Professor Temperley announced from the podium that there was a possibility that Irish-made Factor IX was infectious. This was alarming for Brian not just because no one using the Irish-made blood product had tested HIV positive up to this point but because he used Factor IX himself. He described it as "a terrible shock". While still reeling from the news, Brian looked up and found that Professor Temperley had put up a transparency which included the initials of the four people who he suspected had contracted HIV from Factor IX. Brian first scanned the list in alarm for his own initials. After the relief of finding he wasn't there, he looked at the list again. The horrible reality was that he could identify the people from their initials. He later said: "I was absolutely horrified by the fact that I could . . . look at these initials and these might have meant nothing to most of the people in the audience but these were not initials to me, these were people. I knew some of these people." Professor Temperley would later apologise for this at the Lindsay Tribunal.

The UCD conference wasn't interactive and so Brian didn't get the chance at the time to ask if heat-treated or non-heat-treated Factor IX caused the infections. Professor

Temperley had also said that it was possible that Factor IX imported into the country could be responsible. There was confusion. Brian went home worried. Just weeks later the Blood Bank withdrew its Factor IX and put all 'haemophilia b' patients on imported product. Brian felt the crisis was over, but would try to find out where the problem had been.

Brian was also good at explaining just how hysterical the public became over the issue of HIV/AIDS. He told me about an incident in 1987 when a young man with haemophilia who had cut himself went into hospital "down the country" and said he was HIV positive. He said: "Rather than treating him they burnt his clothes, burnt his crutches and sent him to Saint James's in a sealed ambulance. The headline in the local paper was along the lines that the local community had been saved from this dreadful disease which could have befallen them. You can imagine the effect that had on people with haemophilia in that locality."

One of Brian's key attributes is an ability to make things easy to understand. I discovered this on a flight to the Netherlands for a conference on blood products and EU directives. I was only two weeks in the job and didn't really know the first thing about the subject matter. Brian pulled out a piece of paper and explained haemophilia and the issues surrounding blood products brilliantly. He also explained in just a few sentences why haemophilia generally only occurs in men. The sex of a baby is determined by the type of chromosomes it receives from its parents. A boy inherits one of his mother's 'X' chromosomes and his father's 'Y' chromosome. A girl has two 'X' chromosomes – one from each parent. The defect that causes haemophilia rests in the 'X' chromosome. Accordingly, the son of a man with haemophilia will not have the disorder as he inherits his father's 'Y' chromosome. The daughter of a man with haemophilia, however, will inherit his faulty 'X' chromosome with its deficiency of clotting factors VIII or IX. However, the normal 'X' chromosome she inherits from her mother compensates for the defect. She will, however, be a carrier of the disease and she may have a lower than normal level of clotting factor which sometimes manifests itself as a problem. She has a 50 per cent chance that her son will have the disorder (if he inherits her faulty 'X' chromosome rather than her normal one) and her daughters will have a similar chance of being carriers.

The problem for me was that I had a fear of flying and nausea was overwhelming me. When we got to the conference, Brian was the life and soul of proceedings. At one point he came over and said: "You're very quiet, Rosemary." I told him: "I didn't really have anything to say as my knowledge is solely based on what you told me. And I'm sorry to say I didn't manage to take everything in as I was mostly scared that I was going to get sick on top of you!" He laughed first and then scolded me for not telling him to shut up. It may have been a short difficult lesson but the information stuck.

While the legal campaign continued apace in 1989, the new Government decided to make a move to specifically help haemophiliacs infected with HIV. At the beginning of the year, the preference of Taoiseach Charlie Haughey had been to call an election rather than agree to the Labour motion of handing over £400,000. However, by summer, the new Fianna Fáil-Progressive Democrat coalition wanted to resolve the issue. A lot of lobbying had taken place during the 1989 election and the Progressive Democrats had agreed to include a financial provision in their manifesto. This ended up being included in the Programme for Government. Mary Harney was particularly helpful. Very quickly after the Government came to office, negotiations on a trust fund were opened and a deal finalised. The result was the establishment of a £1 million HIV Haemophilia Trust Fund. The money came from a National Lottery grant.

I was relieved as members could now finally get some financial assistance. Up to this point, the IHS had been desperately attempting to help out by giving weekly payments to members in difficulty. It simply wasn't enough. The IHS also secured additional funds from the Government for the provision of services for those infected with HIV. We were now in a position to offer Margaret Dunne full-time employment as a secretary. It was a fantastic development as Margaret King and I were out of the office most of the time and we had the administrative and practical support we needed.

Yet despite the £1 million move, the legal cases continued. While the fund alleviated immediate financial strains due to HIV infection, it did not help or allow members to provide financial security for their families. The fact was that because people with haemophilia had a genetic condition, they often couldn't secure mortgages. The legal campaign had to keep going. One month after the establishment of the trust fund, fifty writs had been issued. With the number of writs increasing, our legal team had also been expanded to include the future Attorney General, Dermot Gleeson SC.

My ever-expanding job description now included liaising with the legal team. I would meet the lawyers but didn't see the documentation at the heart of the case. They would simply brief me in general terms about how things were progressing. On top of this I would also be doing the usual training, administration and media work as well as coordinating the youth group and assisting members who were unwell. While it sounds very involved, I was still effectively learning what it was like to live with haemophilia. Like most new posts, it was disconcerting to hold a title which gave an impression of in-depth knowledge when that wasn't really the case.

A Cold Meeting

A man to whom I will forever be indebted for helping me
out was Joe Dowling from Henrietta Street in central Dublin.
He was supposed to be carrying out research for the legal
proceedings, but probably spent as much time talking to me
about the hard times he encountered growing up. Joe was in
his early fifties and already disabled from constant bleeds into
the joints in his legs. He was a thin man who wore thick
glasses. He had a bright brain and an extremely caustic
Dublin wit. In an open and honest way, he explained what it
was like to be a man with haemophilia in the 1940s and 1950s
when the condition wasn't understood and there was little
treatment available. Joe's experience was pretty grim. Despite
his life possibly being endangered by internal bleeds, he was
beaten at school along with the rest of the pupils. He believed
some teachers hit him harder when he protested that he had
haemophilia. The story reminded me of Jerome Stephens.

Joe was also open about the fact that he was HIV positive.
I remember him explaining how his brother had already died
from an AIDS-related illness in the UK. He not only had to
deal with the loss of his brother, but also come to terms with
the fact that he would die the same way: before his time and
in pain. There were just six months between his diagnosis and
his brother becoming ill. He told later RTÉ: "I got a telephone
call from London saying my brother was critical. They wouldn't
tell me what it was – just a serious chest infection. We got
over there on the first flight the following morning and he was
put on a ventilator for a week and he [then] died of pneumonia."

Joe's motivation for getting involved in the legal case was
to ensure that he would not leave his wife and two children in
poor financial circumstances. Money was yet another strain
on someone with an already intolerable load. He needed
additional heating because of symptoms such as night sweats
and diarrhoea. He also needed a special high-protein diet to

42

help counteract weight and fluid losses. Joe said he got some of the items on the medical card but still needed more. He worked as radio controller in a taxi company but had to give it up shortly after I met him as the stairs there were too difficult to negotiate. Financially, this was a major problem.

Joe went on the *Kenny Live* TV show in 1989 to put a face on the hidden problem of HIV. He explained that he was constantly looking for any outward sign that he was moving from HIV positive to full-blown AIDS. He said the fear in the haemophilia community was terrible: "Lots of haemophiliacs I know won't get on buses because they are afraid of picking up people's infections. They are avoiding churches." In a later interview, he would explain what full-blown AIDS was like: "When a person dies in their sleep with something from AIDS, you can't really say they died a peaceful death. They will have suffered so many illnesses before the final big sleep . . . that's the frightening thing about AIDS."

As the year wore on, my job description expanded even further to include lobbying, which meant contact with the Department of Health. I had had some previous dealings with Dr James Walsh who headed up the department's response to the AIDS crisis. He had secured some funding so we could operate our AIDS awareness scheme at the school in Coolock. I liked Dr Walsh and trusted him enough to seek advice when going for the IHS job. However, my new work meant operating at a completely different level. Looking back, I was so naïve. The first problem with my approach to lobbying was that I was in awe of politicians and senior civil servants. I had never met a Government minister before and felt that we were making progress just by sitting around the table. If someone promised that they would do something, I took them at their word. Little did I realise how wrong I was.

Initial discussions centred on whether the Government

could devise a compensation scheme for those infected with HIV so that court proceedings could be avoided. My main point of contact was Gerry McCartney, a senior department official. A middle-aged man with dark hair, he exuded a sense of authority. We developed a good working relationship where contact was easy and the conversations were open. I remember calling down to the Department of Health one day to talk about statistical information on members infected with HIV. At one point he leaned over and said: "I know who you are." As it turned out, he was also from Dundalk and knew some of my relatives. It was common for us to hold informal meetings. Margaret King and I would often make coffee in his office while waiting for him to arrive. He was a smoker and distinguished himself by smoking his king-size cigarettes even during meetings when the Minister for Health was present. I wouldn't have dreamt of smoking in such illustrious company.

Gerry usually told me that he was trying to do his best, but there were limited resources available and politically there was a resistance to settling the cases. I believed him. My impression was that Gerry was all in favour of giving us the money but that the then Minister for Health, Dr Rory O'Hanlon, was refusing. It was not unusual for Gerry to ring me up late at night. I was more open than I should have been about our negotiating position. By this time, the IHS had moved on to a more professional footing, with a new office in Temple Bar. However, in relation to negotiations with the Department of Health, this was a case of a novice dealing with an expert. One evening in particular stands out in my mind, when I told Gerry over the phone that we couldn't take any less than £100,000 in compensation for a married man who was infected. He guffawed and maintained it was impossible but, in retrospect, he had acquired an important piece of information which should not have been divulged. In addition, despite the fact that I was giving all of this information to Gerry, he was not telling me everything about himself. I would learn just how much later on.

Another departmental official with whom I had regular contact was Michael Lyons. Much softer than Gerry, he often appeared to me to be upset by the members' stories. I remember on one occasion being driven home by him after a meeting and sitting outside the house for over an hour explaining our situation and mentioning the figure of £100,000. I was once again giving away our bottom line. The meetings dragged on for months and months. Brian O'Mahony was still leading our team, but now I was playing a more significant role in the decision-making process. Our focus was on the litigation as we felt the money was urgently needed and our pressure could well produce a positive outcome. Our cause, however, wasn't helped by difficulties with our legal team.

In November 1990, the IHS barrister, Nicky Kearns, advised the executive committee that our firm of solicitors P J O'Driscoll & Son viewed the HIV cases as untenable and his brief was being discontinued. This was the first the executive heard about the matter. We were all appalled, but could do nothing about it. Nicky felt we should try another company of solicitors that had the commitment, resources and time to push matters. We communicated this to all members involved in the litigation. Hoping that the cases would now progress quickly, we appointed the new firm, Taylor and Buchalter, on November 13, 1990. Our solicitors had changed, but our barrister, Nicky, continued working on the brief. By now, fifteen members had died from AIDS-related illnesses.

Initially, the litigation appeared to progress well. That was the feeling until a meeting of the full legal team in May 1991 at the solicitors' office, attended by Brian O'Mahony, Margaret King and I. Nicky indicated that he was intending to press one HIV test case as far as a court hearing. He said he felt the Factor IX cases would be the best ones to proceed with as they were infected at a time where it might have been expected that their blood products were being heat-treated to eliminate HIV. Nicky's feeling was that the State might fold in front of a robust legal approach and settle all claims. The IHS delegation felt it was a good strategy as there was always a question over Factor IX. They also agreed to his request that witnesses be identified, PR plans considered and preparation for counselling facilities put in place for our members.

The mood was optimistic. Then the legal firm's senior partner and future Labour Minister for Law Reform, Mervyn Taylor, joined the discussions. He quickly punctured the atmosphere by declaring his firm's intention to withdraw from the litigation. I wanted to overturn the small table in the room and smash it against the wall but somehow remained reasonably calm.

We walked out on to the street in disbelief. I was close to tears. This was one big disaster – we had no solicitors, very little money, our members were facing death and needing closure on the issue of compensation.

Things were not going very well politically either. We had a media campaign in place which was trying to put the coalition under pressure by pointing out that British haemophiliacs have been given compensation by their government. We held a meeting with the minister at his request. I had met Dr O'Hanlon once before and didn't have a particularly high opinion of him considering his opposition to the establishment of the HIV Trust Fund. At this second meeting, I found him to be distinctly cold towards our delegation. Maybe he felt this was appropriate considering the financial implications to the State of a settlement, but it struck me as odd and unnecessary.

Having been a community worker in Coolock just a few months previously, meeting the Minister for Health was quite unnerving. I wasn't expected by our delegation to say anything. Half the time I couldn't believe that I was actually there. The thought that went through my mind was: "If my mother could only see me now!" By the end of it, I was just disappointed. By the beginning of 1991, sixteen people had died as a result of AIDS-related illness. Yet the minister, who was also a GP, showed no human response. One member remarked to me – if sixteen people had died in a train crash there would have been a phenomenal response. The only difference, in his view, was that these people were dying one by one. And quietly.

Our response was to get four members to stand as candidates in the local elections scheduled for June 1991. Joe Dowling was one of those to run. I hit the campaign trail in the Artane electoral district with Joe and his family. It was a brave decision by Joe to stand considering the association between haemophilia and HIV. His gambit on the doorstep was: "Hello, my name is Joe Dowling and I'm HIV positive." An *Irish Independent* headline described him as 'The AIDS Candidate'. Asked why he was standing for election, Joe said: "What spurred me on to be a candidate is that the Government has suddenly found £142 million for potholes. Nobody is falling into potholes and dying. Our members our dying." Whether all this pressure had an impact or the Government decided to move, an offer was made. The manner in which it happened was very curious.

On June 10, 1991, Junior Minister, Chris Flood, was on RTÉ's TV programme *Questions and Answers*. He was asked why months had passed since the IHS submission had gone to Government, but no deal had been struck. Mr Flood responded by saying: "Very, very extensive discussions are presently taking place between senior officials at the Department of Health and the Haemophilia Society to try and bring this issue to a successful conclusion for the sufferers. It is a tragic situation. It should be brought to an end immediately." I wasn't watching the programme, but my phone started to ring after it went out. I couldn't quite believe it. There had been one meeting with officials in April after our concerns were submitted in January. This was hardly "extensive discussions" and so we sent out a press release outlining our case.

RTÉ's current affairs programme *Today Tonight* called Brian the following day and asked him if he would go on. Brian received another call later in the day to say that Chris Flood would debate the matter. A few hours later, Brian was told that the minister himself would be replacing Chris Flood. Then, out of the blue, Dr O'Hanlon called Brian at home and told him that a deal would be on the cards very soon. On the 9 o'clock news, the minister announced that the Government was to give £7 million to settle the litigation.

As soon as he heard, Brian rang me in Dundalk. He was talking extremely quickly as he was not only excited but also preparing for the TV interview. I attempted to listen to what he was saying above the din of my mother's swinging seventieth birthday. My first reaction was that this was a breakthrough. Then I thought about the amount: £7 million. The IHS had initially been seeking more than £20 million, but this had been reduced to £15 million. We were being offered less than half of our revised figure. While I was upset at the size of the offer, I also thought to myself: "We don't have a legal team. We don't have any money. People are dying. The offer is higher than what was given in the UK." I also knew that members infected with HIV were terrified about dying before a settlement. They desperately didn't want to leave their families in financial ruin. I might not have been equipped to lead discussions, but one thing I did know was the attitude of the members. I didn't see how we could walk away from the deal but believed some little advance could be gained if we held out.

The *Today Tonight* programme began with a short interview with Jerome Stephens which was conducted from his bed. It was a powerful picture – an emaciated face with a long beard and hollow eyes. In a voice choked with emotion, he explained why he wanted the issue settled: "I know I'm going to die, that's all right . . . but it's my family. How are they going to survive after I'm gone? I've been a burden up to now with this virus. And they deserve a lot more than they're asking." Jerome was very sick at this point, but he was still able to pile on the pressure. He went on: "I wish Rory O'Hanlon . . . could feel the way I am feeling now. Just a small piece of it." He was asked if he held the Government responsible. His response was direct: "Yes. Because it was their duty to protect us and we were not protected. They should pay the money out. If they had any decency or any morals they would have paid the money out without you having to come up here and film me in bed." Looking at the TV programme alone in a neighbour's house. I said to myself: "Jesus, Jerome, your body may well be failing but you still have the mental edge. You still know how to press the right buttons to get what you deserve."

After the recorded interview with Jerome, Brian was asked what his response was to the statement of Chris Flood the previous night. Brian said: "I was very surprised because to say there had been active negotiations all that time was in fact misleading. We had two letters from the Minister [for Health] and our staff had one meeting with some of his officials in

April and that was the last contact we had." Dr O'Hanlon was then brought into the discussion. He began by saying: "I can sympathise and understand what Jerome Stephens was saying and I can understand his anxiety and worry. And for that reason I was anxious to see a settlement." The words did not match my experience of meeting the Minister for Health. It seemed to me to be unfortunate that the first time he expressed sympathy publicly was on the State-owned national broadcaster. He certainly didn't express it to our delegation in any meetings. Dr O'Hanlon suggested that his department had been in negotiations with the other parties who were defendants in the litigation, such as the Blood Bank. When directed to Mr Flood's statement that the negotiations had been with the IHS, Dr O'Hanlon said that it was "a slip of the tongue".

By the following morning, the IHS had adopted the position that we would reduce our demand from £15 million to £12.5 million. A couple of days later we had another meeting with Dr O'Hanlon. I told him that £7 million wasn't enough. His response was to say that we should bring the offer to our members. In his answer, he also questioned me as to how I might know what our membership wanted when we hadn't discussed the matter with them. I was stung by the remark and shot back: "I know our members, you don't." It had not been expected by anyone in the room that I would make a contribution. I shocked myself by responding to his barb so aggressively. Yet afterwards, I felt justified: I might not know the detail of the compensation negotiations, but I most certainly knew what the membership's view of things was. A barrier of sorts had been broken: I was no longer in awe of powerful politicians.

We returned to the office and hit the phones to get the formal response from our membership. The executive of the

IHS was making no recommendation on the £7 million offer although our opinion was clear. As expected, 97 per cent opposed acceptance. A later meeting of members also ratified this position. The occasion was a nightmare as we were desperately attempting to avoid media attention so as to prevent identification. While I welcomed the members' support of our position, my overwhelming reaction was one of fury. I just couldn't believe that this compensation issue had not been sorted. I felt deep contempt for the officials and politicians who'd left us in the position of having to continue to battle.

Our next step was to contact Mary Harney of the Progressive Democrats who had been of assistance during the campaign to establish the £1 million HIV Trust Fund while in opposition. She was now in Government. Unfortunately, she was now very negative. We had a further meeting with Dr O'Hanlon who expressed disappointment at the rejection of the offer. He asserted that the Government's offer was the highest in Europe. He did however say that he would bring the matter back to Cabinet.

I left the meeting disconsolate. I realised that while we might get some increase, it was not going to be what we'd hoped for. One piece of light relief came a few days later when the local election count was held. I went down to the count centre, but Joe Dowling couldn't bear the suspense and spent most of the time at home. At one point it looked as if he could win a seat. Joe came down only to tell me: "I don't want to get elected!" Then he went back home. I did take some enjoyment from his discomfort. He came very close to becoming a local representative for the district of Artane. Yet, in the event, he was pipped at the post. In this instance, the candidate was indeed relieved.

A Cabinet meeting was held shortly afterwards but it

didn't increase the £7 million offer. Further meetings with officials were held which were also negative. I was beginning to get worried that I would have to face the membership with no progress. We were running out of options and I was running out of energy. The whole affair illustrated to me how weak the IHS was. We were a small group of people with massive pressures but limited time and financial resources. The State had many professionals at its disposal and unlimited funds. Their side could wait and sit the matter out while the IHS was desperate to get things resolved as quickly as possible.

This was underlined in the worst way possible: yet another of our members, Padraig, died from an AIDS-related illness. It was the first occasion where I was present at a person's death. The thing I remember clearly is the fact that the man endured a 'hard' death. It wasn't like the cinema-style passing where a person appears to fall into an easy sleep. This man died after spending hours gasping for air. It was deeply shocking. The terminal stages of Padraig's life had also been very difficult for him and his family as he suffered from AIDS-related dementia. Padraig knew he was losing his reason and often became very distressed. I remember him saying: "How am I going to stop this? I don't want to hurt anyone. I just hope I die before I do." Towards the end, his only outlet was going to a psychiatric clinic at Saint James's Hospital where he made baskets. He described the work to me as follows: "It's fuck all use to me." Yet it was the only outlet available.

Additional money was offered by the Government, but even then grudgingly. At yet another meeting, the IHS was told that a further £1 million might be made available, but the members would have to vote to accept it before a firm offer was made. I was just so angry at this constant war of attrition. We refused point blank and told the officials that we were going to hold a news conference the following day to go public on the way in which we were being treated. It was the only weapon we really had – shaming the department into doing something. Members were dying and they seemed to be playing games. It was both cruel and pathetic. Having been at Padraig's deathbed, I was in no mood to back down. We returned to our office. The conversation between us was ice cold: we were not going to be pushed around any longer. Suddenly a phone call came from departmental official Gerry McCartney to say that we could make an offer of £8 million to our members – the additional sum would also have to cover legal costs of both sides.

It stuck in my throat, but I felt the executive committee had to recommend acceptance. Even if they had recommended rejection, I am not sure it would have been supported this time by members, such was the desperation for some closure. I thought our members had been backed into a corner and, while deserving more, felt they had to put their families first. When the meeting was held, that desperate plight was underlined by the fact that there were a lot of obviously ill people in the room. They accepted. They didn't feel they had any other option.

I felt extremely uncomfortable about the decision. Shortly before the meeting I had a discussion with a friend, Norman. He had tested negative for HIV in October 1985, but was positive by May 1986. He had used the Factor IX blood product. Because the timing of his infection was late and Irish-made blood products might be responsible, Norman's case was considered to be strong. He could have decided to stay outside the settlement, but he chose not to. I remember asking him why. He told me he had full-blown AIDS and couldn't afford to wait. He also felt a loyalty to the other members who had been infected. If he withdrew from the group litigation it would reduce their chances of success and this was something he couldn't allow happen. Amazingly, he told me he had two bottles of the Factor IX which he believed had infected him with HIV. He said now that the settlement was agreed, he would throw them out and "let all bad luck go with them".

The horror for Norman was that his condition was beginning to deteriorate. I remember on one occasion he attended a holistic weekend for members infected with HIV and relatives of those who died. The aim was to provide the latest information on HIV, counselling and relaxation. It was traditional on the Saturday night to have a band playing. Norman always sang on these occasions, but by this time had begun to develop AIDS-related dementia. He began to sing the song *Sailing*, but then forgot the words. The room was willing him to finish it, but didn't want to be seen to be pressing him to a conclusion. It was awful. When Norman finally finished, the band said they were taking a break. There was a mass exodus from the room and Margaret King, Margaret Dunne and I ended up trying to comfort everyone. We were supposed to pause for ten minutes, but nobody was fit to regroup for more than an hour.

At the meeting which voted on the Government proposal, there was one dissenting voice – Gerard Healy from Cork. He argued that the offer simply wasn't enough and he was going to take the matter to court. The State had stipulated that all members must drop their writs but, in the event, the settlement was allowed to go through despite Gerard's stance. He continued to make his case but, in the end, he too had to bow under the might of the State. He was running out of time.

The High Court was later informed that the matter had been settled. Nicky Kearns, SC for the IHS, said he hoped this was the last act in a tragic drama which had played its way across the legal and political agenda for the past three years and which had troubled the conscience of the nation. He said twenty-two of the original seventy claimants had died, twenty more had full-blown AIDS and ten were seriously ill. Asked to comment on the steps of the court, I said: "No amount of money can compensate these people for what has happened to them, but at last they've been given some dignity to go and lead their lives. And for those who are not with us today, they're in our minds and our thoughts."

When the compensation situation had been sorted out, we held a European conference of haemophilia societies in Dublin, and the Department of Health official Gerry McCartney was one of our guests. Despite the negotiations, I still felt he was sympathetic to our cause. Following the formalities, we had a drink. I remember Gerry telling me cryptically that this whole HIV compensation story was incredible because it was defined by intense outside pressure. I didn't pick up on this comment immediately but asked him later what the inside story was. He said he couldn't tell me. I didn't think much about the comment until years later when we started our research for the Lindsay Tribunal.

4

The Bag

The haemophilia community is, in many ways, like one big extended family. Part of the reason for this is that, in a majority of cases, haemophilia is passed down from one generation to the next. However, many of the boys and men who are not related become close friends because they end up spending long periods in hospital together. Each death from contaminated blood products was therefore like a knife through the heart of the whole community. Now people with haemophilia were dying from AIDS-related illnesses in greater numbers. By the end of 1990, the death toll stood at eighteen and we knew it was only going to get worse.

Margaret King and I became deeply involved in trying to help not just the men who were ill or close to death, but also members of their extended families. As I have said, part of their families' struggle was that they were usually concealing the real reason for the death of their loved one. Death is hard enough, but having to cover up the cause of the death is extremely stressful. There was one protocol enforced by Irish hospitals which caused not just immense pain and anguish, but also threatened to reveal the cause of death. This was the practice of placing the body of a person who died as a result of AIDS-related illnesses in a body-bag.

Despite the pain this policy causes, hospitals have retained the practice to this day. Their logic is that many people will come into contact with the person's remains between the time they die and the time they are placed in the coffin. The only safe mechanism to prevent infection therefore is to put them in a body-bag. They argue that they can't take any chance that the infection might be passed on to a nurse or doctor on the ward, to the orderlies who remove the remains or to the staff at the hospital mortuary.

We accepted that HIV remains alive for several hours after a person dies. Consequently, a degree of caution is required. Yet the Department of Health's own literature was saying that it was safe to hug a person with HIV or an AIDS-related illness. It simply didn't make sense that immediately upon death the remains were in some way highly infectious. Just because body-bags were used in the UK did not mean we had to follow their lead.

The very term "body-bag" was also associated in our members' minds with a black rubbish sack. It conjured up the image of a person who was stigmatised in life and was, even at the end, going to be effectively dumped by society. While a body-bag is actually white, the image couldn't be diminished. Members were not just appalled that their loved ones were going to disappear into a bag, but the practice also denied them the right to grieve normally. If a man died, his body would only be retained on the ward for a short period of time. It meant that if all of his family were not close to the hospital at the time of death they would never be able to see their relative again.

A critical impact of the body-bag protocol was that it alerted the local community that this person's death was different from the norm. Why didn't they have a wake with an open coffin? In rural areas this was still a very strong tradition and it would be expected that friends and relations would be able to pray over the remains. If this was not being allowed it would raise the question: what have they got to hide? This caused immense strain on members as, even in their dying days, they worried that their death might result in their secret becoming known and their children and wives being stigmatised.

While hospitals retained their protocol, they did attempt to alleviate the pain by keeping bodies on wards for a longer period. In the beginning of the HIV/AIDS crisis, it was a much harsher regime. Without intentionally setting out to resolve this problem, I got involved in a very successful system of allowing people with haemophilia who died from AIDS-related illnesses to be buried with dignity.

The catalyst was the death of one of our members in 1991. Hugh was dying at home and Margaret King was involved in providing care and nursing. She knew that I had become friends with him and so, when he was coming close to death, I was told it was time to come and say goodbye. Hugh lived in a middle-class house and the wider community didn't know about the tragedy which was unfolding inside. Surrounded by his elderly parents, brothers and sisters, he was dying. I was actually a bit shell-shocked at this stage, having been at the death-bed of Padraig the previous week. That was the first time I had ever witnessed somebody dying and now it was happening again.

I watched in awe as Margaret busied herself talking the family through the process while also comforting Hugh and assisting him on his final journey. Immediately following

Hugh's death, I went outside with the family, made tea, and said things I thought were appropriate. In fact, I didn't have a clue about how to comfort them.

I felt awkward and out of place until Margaret came out of Hugh's room and said: "Rosemary, can you come in here for a moment?" I had no idea what I was getting into. Inside, it turned out that Margaret was dressing Hugh for a wake but was finding it difficult to get his suit on. True to form, she made it the most natural thing in the world for me to assist her in putting on his shirt and clothes. One of her methods was to speak to Hugh as if he was still alive. It was very strange to me when she said: "Hugh, Rosemary is now going to help put on your shirt." I didn't really think about what she was saying but carried out her request. As I helped put his arm in his shirt, the wasting process he had endured shocked me. His thin white arm, which was still warm, fitted into my palm. The whole situation was bizarre but felt totally normal because of Margaret's aura of caring. I just went with it. I did not see Hugh as a dead body: he was a friend and somebody's cherished son. The way Margaret casually involved me left no fear whatsoever. Instead of nightmares, I actually felt proud, privileged and got some comfort that I was able to do something to help the family. If I had been asked to help prior to walking into the house, I would have refused point blank.

Another four members died as a result of AIDS-related illness over the following nine-month period. Only one of those people died at home. Accordingly, body-bags were a huge issue with these other families. It was traumatic as Margaret and I were constantly trying to soften this blow, but it was an impossible task. It was as a result of this experience that we came up with the idea that if a person could die at home, then we would lay them out like we did with Hugh. The risk, if any, with this process was entirely ours as we never let any undertaker come in contact with a body. This would allow the family to have an open coffin and thereby eliminate any questions about the person's death being different from any other. Secrecy was still paramount.

What became known as the 'critical-illness service' came into its own in 1993, when thirteen members died. Having decided to undertake this duty, we had to buy the necessary equipment and have it close at hand at all times. We stored the material in a doctor's case which was kept in the office or taken home in case we were called out during the night. It became known as "The Bag" and could sometimes be found in my hallway. None of my family ever wanted to know what was inside and I didn't tell them.

Within a short space of time, we developed a relationship with an undertaker in Dublin who was aware of the problems facing the haemophilia community. We got to know him through a member. The system was that if a person died in Saint James's Hospital, then the undertaker would bring the remains back to his funeral home. Margaret and I would then remove the body-bag, lay the person out and 'coffin' them. This meant that neither the undertaker nor his staff would be at risk of infection. We would wear gloves and gowns just to be absolutely sure that we didn't endanger ourselves. I was, after all, a mother of two young children and had to take some precautions. Even while I believed the risk to be very small, the possibility of infection did play on my mind somewhat.

The undertaker was extremely compassionate and on many occasions would help us to transport the remains if someone died in Dublin and was from a rural area. This ensured that the local undertaker didn't see the sealed body-bag and realise that the person had some form of infectious disease. It probably seems difficult to understand now just how terrified families were of such identification. They were afraid that they would lose their jobs, their neighbours would shun them, and worse still their children would be ostracised. Even in Dublin, it didn't always work out perfectly as the undertaker came from the north side and members in the south of the city felt by using him they would be drawing unnecessary attention to the circumstances of death.

When Margaret and I felt that a person was going to die, we would arrange for them to be transported from hospital in a private ambulance to their home. The main problem was that our members were dying at an increased rate. Margaret and I would stay with the families where possible but, when two or three people were dying at the one time, it became very difficult. We had, thankfully, the assistance of the hospice nurses in Dublin who were absolutely tremendous. At other times we would employ agency nurses to step in for a while. At this time, it would not be unusual for us to go into the office expecting a normal day only to receive an emergency phone call from any part of Ireland. Margaret and I would head out in whatever clothes we stood in and might not return for a week.

At least money was not an issue. The £1 million trust fund established by the Government paid for all expenses for the critical-illness service and counselling. Members infected with HIV had decided that these support services were the priority. This meant that the cost of transport, whether it was securing a private ambulance or travelling by taxi anywhere in Ireland, was not an issue. The members wanted it guaranteed that if they needed assistance then they would get it immediately.

It was difficult for our families as it began to be common for Margaret and me to miss birthdays and other important occasions. I can't count the number of concert tickets that my husband had to give away. I was very conscious that this was something which I had undertaken but which he was also having to deal with. Yet Arthur understood what it meant to me and the members. Without his unwavering support, it would never have been possible. John Joe was eleven at this stage. While protecting him from the detail, I used to explain that I had to go to help a "daddy who was very sick" and was probably going to die. I tried to make a connection with John Joe by saying the man had a young son who wanted me to help because his family was very sad. When I would return, John Joe would ask me: "Did the daddy die?". When I inevitably replied "Yes", he would ask: "And how is the little boy?" I would respond by saying that the mother and son wanted to thank him for letting me go to their house.

While our arrangement with the undertaker in Dublin functioned well, he wasn't always able to help us when a death occurred outside the capital. It was difficult, therefore, to explain to the local undertakers why Margaret and I were there. In some cases, we would say we were friends of the family and the last wish of the person was that we would lay them out. This was respected by the undertakers, but they often became curious when we would appear in the same area on two or three occasions within a short period of time. They may well have suspected something, but they never asked any questions.

One of the key differences between cities and rural areas was that, on a small number of occasions, we told the local undertaker in a small place why we were involved. This was sometimes a matter of choice, but not always. In one case, a member of a family whose loved one had died told Margaret and me: "I have phoned the undertaker and he will be up in an hour to take him to the funeral home to embalm him." I responded: "Oh no, he will not!" I didn't say anything more as I wasn't sure if the relative knew about the cause of death. I had to go to the mother to ensure the relative was aware. Once I knew that he knew the situation, we discussed the dilemma: if the undertaker took the remains away, he could be at risk of infection and this simply couldn't happen. The family agreed. So Margaret and I travelled to the undertakers' office. He was emphatic that embalming would be nice for the family. He wasn't taking no for an answer so Margaret and I asked if we could speak to him in private. I told him: "The man has died from an AIDS-related illness. We have a service which the family wants to use and we will do all that is required. All we need is a coffin." The undertaker was shocked, but after a short while was very comforting and supportive.

Some families felt, for many complex reasons, that it wasn't possible to bring their loved ones home. A number felt the facilities at their home were not good enough while others were scared that their neighbours might find out. Another motivation was that many mothers felt their children couldn't cope with their fathers dying and it was best kept outside the home. On these occasions, Margaret and I would stay with them in the hospitals. Parents of children infected with HIV had a particularly difficult time. Many did not tell their other children what was going on. They rarely spoke about the situation to people outside their family circle. Instead they carried the burden of watching their child become ill without having any of the usual support. While some members died in hospital, a majority opted for home deaths. I felt this was beneficial to the families as the process was easier for everyone. When children were dying it was even more important. Fathers, in particular, were able to cope better with home deaths rather than having to spend long nights in hospital corridors. They could busy themselves with chores around the house and act as normal as possible. It was more intimate and less tense.

While offering support, we were also keenly aware that people needed space. I developed a sense of when to be available and when to disappear into the background. In Saint James's Hospital, we would go on to the flat roof of the intensive care unit. En route, Margaret would often get coffee. Smoking cigarettes, we would usually talk about the immediate situation, as we looked out over the Guinness plant and smelled the hops roasting. The big question was usually: "Will we go home and take a break or stay on for another while?" It was an important issue as after having completed a fourteen-hour day we needed rest. But there was also a danger that something dramatic might happen if we left. More often than not we stayed as we might only get home when the call would come through to return. Out on the roof, we would also counsel each other without knowing it. Another source of comfort to us and the members was a Dominican priest, Father Paddy McGrath, who volunteered his services as a counsellor. He possessed an inner calm and was always a source of comfort.

After someone died, I always felt heartbroken, traumatised and extremely lonely. We would have become extremely close to the families but then simply leave and return home. Despite my emotional state, my family was extremely supportive. It always struck me that all of my family were alive whereas the people we'd just left had lost a son, husband or a brother. It was a major source of comfort and helped me move on.

One death in particular stays with me – thirteen-year-old John Kelly. Throughout 1994 his father, Ray, was totally distracted as he desperately tried to save John. No words can describe how awful this was for Ray, his wife Ann and their family. Margaret had recently suffered a severe asthmatic attack so I was on my own. It was the first time I didn't have my friend and confidante. Ray and Ann did everything humanly possible to help their son, going so far as to ensure he had a water bed at home to avoid sores. My aim was to be as helpful as possible but also honest. This was hard when there were questions like: "Is John going to die soon?" I answered Ray and Ann truthfully at all stages.

On the night John died, I remember a beautiful little boy with his life ebbing away. Ray and Ann just wanted his pain and suffering to be at an end. It was something I had seen before with other parents – you want the dying process to be over but you don't want the person to be dead. I remember Ann asking me if John would live through the night. By this stage, I had enough experience to know that it was extremely unlikely. I looked back at her and said: "I promise you he won't." It's a moment I will never forget – one mother looking at another and promising that her son would be dead in the morning.

I felt immense anger. Some of it was directed at the disease but most of it was directed at the State. Like Jerome, I wanted to bring Dr Rory O'Hanlon out to this death-bed and show him at first hand the pain being inflicted on the haemophilia community. I wanted someone to be held responsible, be it the drug companies or whoever made the bad decisions over the contaminated clotting-agents. It all rolled through my head looking at Ann.

John died early in the morning. I had the privilege of dressing him. He was placed in a white coffin at his mother's request. It is difficult to place anybody in a coffin, but a child is simply the worst. I don't know how I got the strength to do it because I was cracking up inside. I kept waiting for someone to tap me on the shoulder and say: "Wake up, it's just a nightmare, you're all right!" I couldn't imagine what it was like for the family.

People with haemophilia have told me that it was very scary to see Margaret and me coming to visit. One or the other was okay. But when two of us approached it meant things were bad. Some people described us jokingly as the 'Angels of Death'. It certainly was a difficult job. It was very depressing but extremely rewarding at the same time. So many people let us into their homes and embraced us as part of the family. We were with them to share some of the most intimate parts of their lives. At times we were absolutely exhausted both emotionally and physically, especially if the person had been dying over a number of days. However, it wasn't all doom and gloom. Laughter was common. We encouraged the family to play their loved one's favourite music, to sit on the bed and have a drink. Many meals took place in bedrooms. It's also fair to say that some hilarity developed out of hysteria and the bizarre circumstances in which we found ourselves.

It can be very difficult to work out when a person is likely to die. I actually equate death with birth: if a woman is in labour you know that birth is imminent but you cannot tell the exact minute. Margaret and I were often asked: should I take tomorrow off work? Should I send the children to school? Will I go out now and will my husband/son/father be here when I come back? Unfortunately, one can never really tell. Often, a person looked very close to death and I would call the family to the bedside. As prayers were bring said, Margaret and I would move discreetly into the background. Then, within a few hours, the person would rally, become stronger. This was always a difficult moment: while you were happy that the person had made a recovery, you knew that, psychologically, the family was going to have to go through the whole process again.

A dramatic situation occurred at one house where a young man with haemophilia, Oisin, was in the final stages of an AIDS-related illness. Margaret and I were sitting beside him, after having told the family to go to bed and rest. We assumed he was in a coma and would not regain consciousness. Margaret was doing her crossword and looking very much alert. She always seemed to be able to keep awake, possibly due to her experience of working as a nurse late at night, whereas I found it very difficult. We were discussing the puzzle when Oisin suddenly woke up and spoke. I nearly jumped out of my skin. I could not believe that he had come back again. But there he was, awake, sitting up in the bed and asking for bread and jam.

Another bizarre moment Margaret and I shared with Oisin sticks in my mind. In the middle of the night, he asked me to give him a hug. The hospice care at this point ensured that it was possible to touch Oisin without causing pain. I lay down on the bed and embraced him. However, because of the workload, I fell asleep. Margaret also fell asleep in her chair. In the morning we were still in deep slumber when Oisin's mother arrived into the room. The sight she saw was me lying on the bed with my arms wrapped around her son. I then woke up to find her looking at me. All of us got a tremendous fright but, thankfully, she found the whole scene extremely amusing.

Just as much as being in people's homes, Margaret and I were as often to be found in hospitals. We usually received support from the staff working on the wards in places like Saint James's. They recognised that we could complement their services, particularly around the time of impending death. I believe that our presence and support alleviated the workload of the hardworking dedicated nurses on Top Floor 1. In some ways, we actually became part of the furniture.

Margaret and I were given access to the kitchens late at night. The usual menu consisted of those all-important items: tea and toast. I often wondered what medicinal qualities they had, but it couldn't be explained by science; tea and toast must have magical properties. We also took over hospital facilities, particularly when bad news was being communicated. On so many occasions, nursing staff would slip away from their offices so that the family could be brought in and told what was going to happen. The ever-present problem was that space was severely limited. On occasion, I would take a family into the dental room. It was embarrassing for the families, staff and us.

One of the worst feelings I had around this time was the realisation that I was assessing members as to whether an illness was minor or life-threatening. Within a short time it actually became regularised. Each January, Margaret and I would sit down with a list of our members and discuss how we thought they were faring. We would put a tick beside someone's name if it was likely that they would become seriously ill and need our home-care services. This was a necessary administrative job, but also a horrible task. It sometimes felt like we were playing God and this made us extremely sad. That feeling was compounded every time a prediction of failing health became a reality.

5

Money And Madness

At the beginning of 1992, the members infected with HIV and the families of those who had died began to come to terms with the fact that the difference between life and death was around £60,000. Money due under the HIV compensation settlement began to be released. It was a difficult period for all concerned. The hard fact was that there was a finite amount of money the State was prepared to give out and a system of dividing things had to be agreed on. The scale of payment was quite stark: parents of children who had died or those who left no dependents got £20,000 whereas a person who was alive received between £77,000 and £101,000. The categories were based on the British settlement which had been concluded more than a year earlier. The amounts given were worked out by the executive of the IHS, following advice from an actuary. It had been agreed by the members in advance. Coming to terms with the reality of that decision, however, was still hard.

The amount of the award wasn't the only part of the

settlement which was problematic. One provision enabled spouses of those infected with HIV who subsequently contracted the virus to also lodge a claim. It might appear strange now, but most partners had not been tested. Many were reluctant to do so in case they might be identified. Others were scared of finding out about their status at all. The fear of finding out you were a member of the world's most unenviable club was still extremely strong.

The settlement stipulated that any spouse who wanted to make a claim had to do so before August 31, 1991. For Margaret King and me this meant a lot of work as we offered counselling to members both before and after the HIV test. The counselling took place either over the phone or in their homes. Our first task was to convince the wives and partners that it was actually worthwhile to have a test. For many, they simply took the view that as there was no cure or treatment for HIV there was no point in knowing. The unknown was better than the burden of a diagnosis. The other factors were that many couples were using condoms following the HIV diagnosis and some women felt it was unnecessary to get tested. Some people took the decision to abstain from sexual relations. Others simply didn't want money and accordingly didn't see the point. The outcome was that after weighing up the pros and cons, some women chose not to be tested.

Professor Temperley ensured that the tests were undertaken in an expeditious manner. It was a major relief to establish that no spouse tested positive for HIV, although one would later be identified. The good news was conveyed to us in a phone call from the hospital. This clean bill of health was actually out of line with other countries. In the US, the rate of infection of partners through sex varied from between 10 per cent and 20 per cent depending on the circumstances. I firmly believe that this is due in a large part to Brian O'Mahony and his time spent on Wednesday nights in the hospital carpark giving out condoms. In attempting to save the lives of his members, Brian was actually breaking the law. It seems hilarious now, but it was a gutsy thing to do.

It was a strange time when the cheques were finally paid to our members. There was an air of relief that, at last, they could start making provision for their families. Yet there was also a tremendous sadness, particularly for the next of kin of the deceased. While the membership had fought for this settlement over many years it didn't make HIV disappear. A small number of members felt accepting a cheque from the State amounted to taking blood money. Quite a few had to be convinced to take the money, despite the fact they had voted for the settlement, but all did in the end.

A different range of problems quickly arose. The IHS helped by engaging financial advisors for each individual. Yet, once again, the stigma of HIV returned to complicate matters and unsettle people. I remember being in a house in a rural area when their washing machine broke down shortly after the couple had received their settlement. A new one later appeared in their kitchen but, incredibly, it was being paid for on an ESB hire-purchase scheme. When I asked why, the couple told me that they couldn't buy a new one because their parents or sisters and brothers would wonder where they got the money. The fact was that no-one knew the man was HIV positive and therefore didn't know about the award.

The choice which many opted for was to buy their own homes outright. This wouldn't raise any eyebrows, but the absence or reduction of a mortgage meant they had more disposable cash. Yet even this caused difficulty. It was hard for people to lodge their cheques in the local bank for fear of drawing attention to themselves. After a bit of work, I managed to reach agreement with some financial institutions in Dublin so that cheques could be lodged and questions would not be asked.

For those who did tell their relatives, the money sometimes caused a lot of strife as extended family members could feel it was a resource which everyone could avail of. I talked to one man who fell out with his family for a long period of time over the award. His brothers and sisters were experiencing financial difficulties and asked him to lend them money for cars and other home equipment. When he tried to explain that he was not in a position to use this money for that purpose it caused extreme stress and bad feeling. My advice to him was straight: "Your wife and children will need that money when you die. If your brother and sister do not understand, that's just hard luck. They might come to understand after a period of time, but if they don't, tough."

The reality was that while some didn't want the money, others felt guilty about taking it and most couldn't spend it for fear of drawing attention to themselves. The money eased immediate problems such as bills and fears for the future, but it came with strings attached. In essence, old headaches were replaced by new ones.

One detail which was annoying Margaret King was that the records of the IHS indicated that 103 people could apply for the compensation. However, she felt from her time at Saint James's Hospital that 104 people with haemophilia had contracted HIV. She went through the list of names, but couldn't identify who the missing person was. She tried to follow it up with the hospital, but got nowhere. The mystery would be solved only in the run-up to the Lindsay Tribunal nearly a decade later.

The IHS was given many donations from members in gratitude for the work which had been carried out on their behalf. Considering that most were facing the probability of death, the fact that they handed over some money to help sustain the IHS was deeply moving. It also reminded me of the fact that compensation was not going to cure anyone. Margaret and I felt spurred on to improve the services for people with haemophilia infected with HIV.

With this in mind, we set about redoubling our contacts with doctors, hospital administrators and their staff. The door was already open as Professor Temperley was amenable to greater participation by the IHS. During our initial meeting in 1989, I had garnered a very good first impression of him: he greeted each person with a handshake and poured everyone tea and coffee. In reality, at that time, I was very much in awe of him – he had a title and an air of gravitas. From my background, if you were having tea with a professor it meant you were someone very important. At the meeting, I made it clear that our objective was to be alerted to upcoming changes so as to be in a position to advise members and continue to complement the work being carried out by staff at Saint James's. This didn't mean consultation on every issue – just the major ones. The meeting led to further meetings. It was a major advance.

Professor Temperley was based at Saint James's Hospital, but I was also very involved in other parts of the country, in particular Cork. The IHS did not have a counsellor there and this caused problems as Munster members could not always travel to Dublin. After much searching to find the appropriate people, the haemophilia HIV trust funded counselling services in the region.

The year 1993 was the most difficult we had up to this point: thirteen people died, including two children. Margaret and I were constantly moving around the country as people became ill. The half past seven morning train to Cork became part of our weekly schedule. It was not unusual to get a phone call in the middle of the night looking for our assistance and support. It was in fact a nightmare – terrible things were happening and we seemed to be a ghostly presence slipping from one house to another. In effect, I was permanently on the road. I recall some nights being in Cork, flying back up to Dublin to be with somebody in Saint James's Hospital only to leave after a few hours to visit another home.

I felt guilty about the impact this was having on my family and felt torn between my job and Arthur and the children. Aisling was nine at this stage and it was clearly having a major impact. It became reasonably common for me to leave the house but then have to return a short time later. She would want me to explain to her one more time why I was going and repeat the goodbyes. Even though it was difficult to leave, she had Arthur with her. Aisling wouldn't come to any harm whereas in the place we were going to, people depended on us as they were going to die. I wasn't prepared to stop doing the work but did want to share the burden so that it would alleviate the pressure on family life.

It was a great relief therefore when Margaret Dunne and the IHS secretary, Teresa Mulvey, began to have more of an interaction with members who were becoming ill. They used to describe themselves as 'The B Team' because if Margaret King and I were helping somebody and another family got into difficulty, then they would go and assist them until we became available. The tag 'The B Team' was a misnomer as the comfort and support given by Margaret and Teresa was equal to anything we contributed. In the early 1990s, the community didn't realise the extent of the work we were doing. Margaret King and I never announced the service as something which you would ring and request. In part, we simply didn't want to highlight the body-bag issue which would cause unnecessary pain for those who were healthy.

Our beloved Jerome died on February 13, 1993. His death brought tremendous grief and sorrow to the haemophilia community. Margaret King was very close to him and would visit often. I usually tagged along, but soon ended up looking forward to the next time. He was a person you would drop in on maybe twice a week without really knowing why. Jerome was a magnetic character who always had a good story to tell, even though he was confined to his home. Some of the time he would paint a verbal picture of the place he loved most: the mountains. I can't now look at a picture of a deer without thinking of him. Everyone loved him because, on visiting, he always seemed delighted to see you.

As Jerome had gone public about his illness in dramatic terms on RTÉ, the news of his death got national media coverage. For many members his death came as a shock as they thought he would always survive. His death reinforced their own sense of vulnerability.

The last time Jerome had been seen by the public was on *The Late Late Show* in December 1990. He was wearing a green striped jumper and a pair of jeans, but had become so weak by that stage that he needed to wear a neck-brace to keep his head raised. He was also in a wheelchair. The programme had been devoted to people who were HIV positive and their families. Jerome clearly had full-blown AIDS. Gay Byrne said to him: "You're supposed to be gone by now, Jerome. You're supposed to be dead." It was the type of conversation which didn't faze Jerome. He responded: "They told me I died a few times. I outlived their expectations." Gay knelt beside him and asked: "How long do you think you have left?" Jerome answered: "As long as I can fight and as long as I can breathe and as long as God will let me live." Gay asked again: "How long do you reckon?" The answer was short and to the point: "I'd say about a year. I hope a year." It wasn't an insensitive conversation, just direct in a way that only Gay could have managed.

The tone of the subsequent conversation was not black but matter of fact. That was a quality which Jerome had in spades and something which endeared him to all who knew him. He went on to explain how he was experiencing constant pain in his back and the drugs designed to help him had harsh side-effects. As Jerome flicked through a book of his own poems entitled *Read My Mind*, Gay remarked that he had a lovely head of hair. Jerome quipped: "I believe in Samson. The longer it grows the longer I live!" The poem he read went as follows:

> A long fight
> A dream that perhaps
> will come to pass
> at last.
> It has come
> at last –
> but not the end.
> The beginning
> of beautiful things
> surround me –
> showing me the way
> to reality
> and acceptance
> of reality.
>
> As in where
> a child will laugh
> or newly born kittens
> will bounce
> and play.

For every winter
there is a Spring,
and even the Winter
is not without
many beauties.

Jerome finished the poem by apologising for the nervous delivery. He got a sustained round of applause from the audience. It was classic Jerome: open, honest, funny and heartbreaking.

When Jerome died, there was a clear plan as to what was to happen. He had accepted he was going to die and so had composed an invitation to his wake with the help of Margaret King and Margaret Dunne at the office. He also made it clear that he wanted to be buried wearing his biker leathers. The reason was that he saw himself being fit and healthy in heaven and wanted to be prepared to get on his bike when he got there. The funeral was very special. Around twenty bikers in black leather jackets drove ahead of the hearse from Jerome's house to the church. After parking their bikes, they carried the coffin inside. Among the mourners was U2 guitarist, The Edge, who came to know Jerome during a battle to save a wood in County Wicklow. So we said goodbye to a legend, but the misery continued.

Shortly after Jerome's death, I became involved with a family whose young son was dying. It's difficult to describe this type of situation – the only appropriate word is horrendous. However, once I arrived at the hospital, I switched on to automatic. My disconnection was reinforced by making myself think: "I don't feel I have a right to get upset as this is not my family." The philosophy worked but didn't take away all emotion. It just allowed me to function.

Stephen was twelve years old and in intensive care at

Harcourt Street Children's Hospital in Dublin. A bright, cheeky and intelligent child, I'd known him for a long time. The tragic thing was that he'd been on a family holiday which was only made possible by the compensation scheme when he became ill. Initially, it only seemed to be a bad cough. At the hospital, Stephen was prescribed medicine and would probably have been sent home, but his father, Martin, said the cough sounded like TB. What he didn't know, but the doctor did, was that TB is one of the first things which happens when a person starts to exhibit an AIDS-related symptom. To put it bluntly, it was sending a signal that Stephen was developing full-blown AIDS.

The doctor ordered an x-ray and the results indicated that Stephen's lungs were in such a bad state that he was much sicker than he appeared. He stayed a week in hospital, was discharged but returned within a couple of days. Things were going downhill rapidly. He was taken to intensive care.

Over the next sixteen weeks I was a regular visitor to Harcourt Street. It was a very difficult place to be. Stephen's parents slept on a makeshift bed on his floor at night and tried to offer entertainment and support for their son during the day. If that wasn't hard enough, all of this they did in secrecy. Neither Stephen's grandparents nor his siblings knew that he was infected with HIV. After a short time, I worked out their schedule. Martin's wife would stay in hospital with Stephen from Monday to Friday, with Martin visiting each evening at eight o'clock. On Friday night, Martin would take over and stay with Stephen while his wife returned home and attended to their other children. The hardest part for me was trying to help them as frustration mounted over the seemingly endless tests. As bad as that was, I knew that looming in the not-too-distant future was the appalling fact that I would soon have to talk to them about making a terrible decision: when was it time to stop the tests and bring their son home to die?

I remember driving to Harcourt Street knowing it was going to be necessary to have this discussion. There wasn't really a set time when this conversation took place. It was more something I sensed. That feeling was an amalgamation of things: the nurses would be coming to the view that not much more could be done; the parents would be getting frustrated at the battery of tests which were not going to help; the child would also be giving off signals that he had had enough and wanted to go home. Once I sensed the time was right, Margaret and I would have a meeting with the parents and suggest that they might talk to the doctors about bringing their son home if the hospital had no further treatment to offer. Beforehand, I tried to put myself in their position. But try as I might, it was impossible. Taking a twelve-year-old boy home to die is something that you can only know about if you have had the incredible misfortune to experience it. The only thing I did know as a near certainty was that they could provide more comfort and love for their son by taking him home and this would put less stress on everyone in the family.

In May 1993, Martin took his son home. He was in a pitiful state, requiring steroids to breathe. Martin later described Stephen's condition to the Lindsay Tribunal: "From the month of August on into September he was so thin you would be afraid to look at him. His teeth were so prominent, he was like a skeleton. His eyes were like golf-balls . . . He wasn't able to support his own body weight. It broke his heart to have to get into a wheelchair. Obviously an active little lad like that – it was a major blow to be seen out in a wheelchair when everyone else was able to run around."

Within a matter of weeks, Stephen was no longer able to

get out of bed. He also had two pumps attached to him – one for food and the other for morphine. Martin said: "I was able to carry him because I was big and strong . . . my wife wouldn't have been able to . . . it was handier for me just to pick him up and plonk him wherever he wanted to go." As his condition deteriorated, Stephen was finding even lying on a bed difficult: "Just the weight of the bedclothes was enough to hurt him." Martin never told Stephen that he had HIV, to protect him: "It was harrowing . . . he was a pathetic little sight. One day . . . he looked up at me with that little face. He said, 'Dad, what's wrong with me? Why am I getting these infections'? And I had no answer. It broke my heart."

Yet these are not the most vivid memories. What really stands out was the strength and love of his family. The house was constantly full of people and laughter. I could see that their hearts were breaking, but their son never knew it.

When Stephen died, Martin allowed me the privilege of being with him and dressing him. He was laid out in his favourite football kit. Forever ingrained on my memory is the image of Stephen inside a white coffin on his bed. All the walls were adorned with his football posters and memorabilia. I reflected on the fact Stephen's parents had not only watched him get ill and die a painful death, but had to do it all in silence so as not to alert the rest of the family to his condition.

I stood in the quiet room and felt devastated. What was getting under my skin was the fact that the politicians who were taking decisions never got to see the horror of HIV and AIDS. It was the same feeling which had coursed through my body when John Kelly died. Jerome had articulated it as well on *Today Tonight*. I was raging at the deaths and the fact that the public didn't find out due to the stigma and secrecy surrounding HIV. Our strongest weapon was the reality of how families were torn asunder and yet it was the story which could never be told. The public wouldn't know the reality until the Lindsay Tribunal. It was a violent feeling which, in some ways, was with me constantly, but only really bubbled up and got out of control at times like this. I wanted to grab politicians, thrust them into the room of the dying and ensure they saw the full reality. When the rage abated, I had to confront my reality which was that the politicians in power were people I was going to have to do business with to ensure the provision of future care for people with haemophilia. There was only one way of dealing with this: politically.

Nineteen people had died in the two years since Hugh passed away. That total included five fathers, two husbands, eleven sons and one child. Death no longer held either any fear or mystery for me. I had gained a level of knowledge about death which, to be frank, I really didn't want to have. However, I felt compelled to continue helping the members. Whereas in 1989 I knew statistics and theories, by 1993 I had come face-to-face with the pain, grief and suffering. I felt that no human being should have to witness this, let alone endure it. Rather than burn me out or slow me down, it spurred me on to do whatever I could.

6

The Long Fuse

The year 1993 was a difficult one because, while I had known for a long time that AIDS had the capacity to devastate the haemophilia community, the fear now became reality. It was also ghastly because something which seemed to be benign suddenly transformed into a nightmare. The nightmare had a name: hepatitis C. I was keenly aware that many people with haemophilia had contracted hepatitis over the years through contaminated blood products, but the virus had always been viewed as something which didn't really impact on their lives. In 1993, I realised that it was just a bomb with a long fuse.

Jaundice was a term which I was aware of in a general way before I came to work for the IHS in 1989. My knowledge was limited enough: a person became ill and yellow in appearance for a time before recovering and continuing with their life. It was something which could be dealt with.

Hepatitis C was first identified in 1974. Back then it was known only as 'post-transfusion hepatitis'. The number of people who contracted 'post-transfusion hepatitis' significantly increased when concentrated clotting-agents came on the market in the mid-1970s because of the fact that each treatment was made from the donations of thousands of people. Scientists called this unidentified virus 'Non-A Non-B hepatitis' for the reason, quite simply, that they knew it was a form of hepatitis but didn't have a test for it – unlike types A and B. The name seemed quite appropriate: people with haemophilia viewed it as essentially a 'non' virus.

Yet international blood policy stated that the transmission of any virus was undesirable and blood banks should seek to avoid collecting donations where there was a high probability of hepatitis being present. In 1975, the national director of the Blood Bank, Dr Jack O'Riordan, told RTÉ that the system of blood collection in the United States was not something he admired because in many instances donors were paid. He said: "There are dangers inherent in the type of person who comes forward as a donor. Unhappily, or too often, you find that people such as drug addicts come forward. And these people, in some cases, have passed certain diseases from one to the other – a disease such as hepatitis which is a form of jaundice. And obviously these would not be suited to a blood service's needs." Despite this, the Blood Bank imported and distributed these US-made blood products. Even though Dr O'Riordan described the US donors in the mid-1970s as "skid-row types", the Blood Bank declined an offer in 1979 from a company supplying blood products made from unpaid European donors. The US product was cheaper. The Blood Bank bought it.

In 1989, the Non-A Non-B virus was finally isolated and identified. As they already had hepatitis A and hepatitis B, the scientific community named it hepatitis C. We were taking more of an interest in it by this stage and seeking information where we could. In October 1989, we used our

AGM as an opportunity to invite a UK expert on hepatitis, Dr Charles Hay. He said, in his view, the hepatitis C virus was so closely associated with concentrated clotting-agents that most people with haemophilia had contracted it after their first injection. We brought in another expert, Professor Eric Preston, to discuss developments. He said the latest prediction was somewhat better than had previously been believed – 50 per cent of concentrate users would have the virus. The information caused some worry, but not alarm as it wasn't believed that hepatitis C was life-threatening.

The priority was to get our members tested as soon as possible so that we could quantify the scale of the problem. Unfortunately, this process was slow. Such was the lack of movement by June 1991 that I went to meet Professor Temperley. He said there were doubts about the accuracy of the 'enzyme-linked immunosorbent assay test' or ELISA. The concern was that there might be what they called 'false positives'. This meant that someone could show up as having the virus when in actual fact they didn't. Thankfully, an improved procedure became available shortly afterwards. The more specific 'polymerese chain reaction' or PCR test, however, didn't actually come on stream until 1993. While accuracy improved, there were issues over the speed of its introduction and how results were conveyed. Talking to the members, it appeared the manner in which the results were being delivered was somewhat piecemeal: some people were informed and some weren't. I believe this loose approach to the virus was due in part to the perception that hepatitis C wasn't the worst thing in the world.

This changed dramatically in 1993. The penny dropped when Margaret and I met Dr Ann Tobin who was based at Saint James's Hospital. It was usual for us to call in on consultants from time to time. However, on this occasion, I wanted to ask her about trials which were being conducted on people with haemophilia who had been exposed to hepatitis C. This appointment turned out to be no run-of-the-mill affair. Dr Tobin was the hepatology registrar. Tall, very slim and with short blonde hair, Dr Tobin had quite a studious appearance. I immediately liked her as she was very open. I remember she began to outline how people infected with hepatitis C were progressing to serious liver disease. This wasn't one or two people but a substantial number. I began to get very worried. The moment things really hit home was when Dr Tobin said that a person who contracted the hepatitis C virus might not begin to feel any major adverse effects for twenty years. Initially, I thought: "That isn't too bad." Then I remembered that most of our members began to use concentrated clotting-agents from the mid-1970s and so would be reaching that point now. This was a major problem which was going to engulf us very quickly.

When I tuned back in to what Dr Tobin was saying, she was explaining how the virus impacted on the liver. First it becomes scarred and then it begins to harden. This process, known as cirrhosis, can in some cases lead to cancer. The medical community was of the view that once this progression commenced, there was very little they could do about it. My response was to blurt out a quick invitation to Dr Tobin to address the executive of the IHS. Margaret and I walked out of the room and began to make our way along a very long corridor on the bottom floor of Hospital 1. My mind was racing: "It couldn't be that bad. Maybe it isn't." I needed to confirm what I had heard so I asked Margaret: "What do you think?" She responded: "It does not sound good." This was not the answer I wanted to hear. I had hoped that she would say that everything was going to be OK. As I wandered down the corridor in a bit of a daze, my mind began to flick through images of those I felt might have the virus. I began to panic.

The executive meeting was held on July 15, 1993, in the IHS's office in Eustace Street, Temple Bar. In a broad outline, Dr Tobin detailed what the statistics from hepatitis C tests were indicating and the medical prognosis for those who had the virus. We now had to consider that this was something which was facing at least 50 per cent of our members. After Dr Tobin left, there was a discussion on what policy to adopt. In reality, everyone was still coming to terms with what they'd heard. The meeting was crowded which added to the uncomfortable atmosphere. As the conversation shifted towards the future, I realised that my policy of truthfulness with the membership was going to mean imparting a lot more doom and gloom. If someone asked me what hepatitis C meant, I was going to have to detail the progression of an illness which seemed impossible to reverse. It was clearly going to be a difficult job as so many men were carrying this virus. For those who had HIV, it was going to be yet another problem to deal with. For those who escaped HIV, the wonderful sense of freedom was going to be cruelly stripped from them. And Margaret and I were the people who were going to have to pick up the pieces. Even more illness, death and misery was about to engulf an already traumatised community.

The only light at the end of this dark tunnel was a drug called interferon. It had been developed to treat forms of cancer, but was now employed to treat hepatitis C. The hope was that interferon would reduce or possibly even eliminate the virus from a person's body. However, it was only in trial stages. One problem with the drug was that it was known to be difficult to take. Side-effects included fatigue, weight-loss, depression and hair loss. A person taking interferon also wasn't allowed to drink alcohol. The trials in Saint James's were not limited in numbers so things looked good from that perspective. However, interferon wasn't available free of charge. Members were being asked to pay £15 per month for the drug. A lot of people were on disability pensions and this was another financial burden. For those who lived outside Dublin, there were transportation costs as well.

Members were seeking information and so the IHS set up special meetings around the country featuring experts on the subject. It was hard to believe that people who'd gone through so much were once again being told that they had been infected by a potentially lethal virus. One of the most upsetting aspects of the emerging knowledge was that hepatitis C was particularly dangerous for those who were already infected with HIV. Here were people who were just emerging from the horror of the mid-1980s only to be catapulted back into the darkness. Tests would show that most people infected with HIV were also infected with hepatitis C. Professor Preston's prediction proved to be the more accurate. Just over 50 per cent of people with haemophilia contracted the virus. The other prediction which proved prescient was death: in 1993, two people died as a result of having been infected with the hepatitis C virus.

Yet another shock was in store for us when one of our members who died from liver failure as a result of hepatitis C infection was placed in a body-bag. The same procedure for AIDS-related illnesses was going to apply to hepatitis C. As the scale of the disaster became clear to the members, they began to actively seek interferon treatment. Even though the chances of it having an impact were slim, the desire to neuter the virus was overwhelming. The affair also brought in new members and, unfortunately, we were meeting them at a particularly low ebb. I remember a stranger coming in off the street and telling me that his brother had haemophilia, but never required much treatment and so had never joined the IHS. However, he'd just found out that he had hepatitis C and was already on interferon treatment. The man was very agitated and it was clear to me that it had taken a lot for him to tell the story. The thing driving him was concern for his brother who was suffering greatly as a result of the treatment. Just to complicate matters further, he was also facing problems with his employer after disclosing his status. We made contact with the brother and he called into the office. It was his first contact with the IHS. He was clearly independent, a man who would usually never view himself as being a person requiring assistance from a support group. None the less, he had reached such a level of desperation that he had to do something.

This difficulty with interferon began to be replicated around the country. The drug was a self-administered injection which was taken three times a week. Having hepatitis C means a person is already lethargic, but interferon wiped them out. The depressive nature of the new drug extended the impact of the illness to the rest of the family. I was getting calls for assistance from partners who were at the end of their tether because their husband had had a personality change in which they withdrew from their role as parent.

With the scale of the problem now emerging, Brian O'Mahony and I went back to the Department of Health to ensure treatment, services and support were available for our members. As these discussions looked as if they could continue for some time, the IHS decided to pay for the interferon treatment for members. In our overall budget, the amount wasn't that much, but it was likely to increase as more members sought treatment. We never raised the issue of compensation with the department at this point as our priority was to secure treatment for our members. It was, however, always in the background. I remember, at one meeting, Gerry McCartney asking me about the 'C' word. [Gerry was the senior official with whom I had lengthy discussions over the HIV infections.] I thought he meant hepatitis and went off on a long ramble before he interjected and said: "No, I meant compensation." We secured a financial commitment on treatment from Health Minister Brendan Howlin. Yet it took quite some time for that to turn into action.

Hepatitis C was a depressing re-run of the HIV disaster in so many ways. One particular thing which annoyed me was that so few lessons appeared to have been learned by the medical profession. It does not take a rocket scientist to know that conveying information, about a life-threatening illness must be done with sensitivity. Other important factors include ensuring privacy is maintained, that speed of imparting the information is crucial, and that a person does not necessarily take in what they are told immediately after a diagnosis is given. The haemophilia community had, to say the least, a bad experience when receiving the results of their HIV tests in 1985. People were told in hospital corridors rather than offices that they or their children were infected with HIV. They would often leave in a bewildered state, armed only with the knowledge that they should make contact with their doctor once symptoms of an AIDS-related illness began to show. In 1993, we began to learn that things hadn't moved on all that much. Members were coming into the office and informing me that they had been diagnosed with hepatitis C but didn't know what it meant.

Margaret and I quickly assembled information packs which would bring people up to date. The information was stark: "In most countries the sero-conversion rate [ie the percentage of people who were negative and then test positive] is 60-80 per cent." The key point which most people were interested in was what happened next. The booklet gave the statistics: 15 per cent completely recover and do not progress to liver disease. 85 per cent of people develop either chronic persistent hepatitis or chronic active hepatitis. Of this group, 50 per cent to 70 per cent would develop severe liver disease and of these, 20 per cent would develop cirrhosis or hardening of the liver. The statistics on treatment with interferon were not too uplifting: only 50 per cent responded to treatment and of that number, half relapsed once the course of medication was over.

One case which stands out in my mind is that of John, who had haemophilia. His case showed that a new disease meant referral to new hospitals and a new learning curve for everyone. Like many men of his age, John had always shouldered his illness without complaining. He chose to live his life to the full. He enjoyed his family, job, hobbies, and dealt with the effects of his medical condition as they arose. He knew from the 1980s that he had signs of Non-A Non-B hepatitis and at one point even had a liver biopsy.

By the time I was becoming aware of the true impact hepatitis C was going to have on our members, John was already getting into major difficulty. The virus had damaged his liver so seriously that it was felt the only solution was to secure a liver transplant. He was referred from the National Haemophilia Treatment Centre at Saint James's Hospital to the National Liver Transplant Centre at Saint Vincent's Hospital. The transfer created a number of difficult situations for John and his wife Isobel and these were compounded by a feeling of isolation. Thus began a very stressful period for them. An early indication of the difficulties ahead was an anxiety about how John's haemophilia treatment could be managed by the staff at Saint Vincent's Hospital. Isobel told me that the consultants who were responsible for John's care were very specialised and excellent in showing a willingness to receive information. She attended all of John's medical appointments where they got information from the doctors on what tests were required and what procedures had to be undertaken to obtain approval for the transplant.

A good example of how unsettling things were, however, was when they attended a progress meeting. When John and Isobel arrived at the hospital and entered the designated room, approximately fifteen people were present. As they tried to work out who these people were, the news was conveyed that the transplant had been sanctioned. A formal atmosphere was maintained during the meeting which lasted less than ten minutes. Then the meeting was concluded and everyone left.

John knew he needed the transplant to save his life. The information he received that day was hugely significant. Yet they left without asking the questions in their mind: Who were those people? Who called the meeting? Who was being informed of what? Was the consultant telling the transplant team about John or was he being informed by the meeting at large about what was going to happen? In essence, this was unnecessary stress and confusion being imposed on someone seriously ill. Isobel has since then realised that they could have spoken to the designated coordinator of the transplant team, but at the time, because the referral to Saint Vincent's Hospital had happened so quickly, they were in a state of shock. Difficult circumstances were compounded by John having to radically change his diet and lifestyle while continuing his job as was his wish. No-one from Saint James's Hospital got in touch with John or the family to see how they were coping. In the changed circumstances, no new systems had been put in place. No one took responsibility. There was no one to walk the road with them.

John received a bleeper, as a transplant liver could materialise at any time. One person on the transplant team was dedicated to liaise with the family and answer as many questions as possible once John was admitted. It was a difficult time for John, Isobel and their children. He was armed with a pager which was going to herald his own survival, but only at the cost of someone else's life. About fourteen days before John was due for a check-up the bleeper went off at eleven o'clock on a Sunday night. His life was thrown into disorder as he considered the real possibility of a liver transplant and what that could mean for him and his family. Within an hour, his bleeper sounded again. The news was that the liver was unsuitable. The information on the bleeper was all he received, despite the dramatic nature of both messages.

A fortnight later John's health deteriorated and he was admitted to Saint Vincent's Hospital. It was decided that a scan was needed. Isobel told the hospital authorities in absolute terms that she wanted to be with her husband when the results of the scan were being conveyed the next day. She confirmed when she would be in. She and John had been through everything together. Isobel arrived as normal but knew that something had happened when she saw John's face. Despite her clear instructions, John had been informed about the scan results while on his own: he was no longer a suitable candidate for a liver transplant due to his deteriorating condition. This meant that he was dying. John asked Isobel to go down to the liver clinic in the hospital to learn more. It was outrageous.

John died thirty-six hours later. Isobel told me of the kindness and help of the hospital staff during those hours, but John's death was a devastating blow. He had been in hospital for only a week.

John's story was deeply disturbing. Not just because a founding member of the IHS had died as a result of a virus which we'd seriously underestimated, but the sad fact was that it was the beginning of another chapter of hospitals, illnesses and deaths for the haemophilia community. Worse still, it was going to be a journey with some of the same frustrations encountered in the 1980s. This time the disaster was one a larger scale: by 1994 we knew that more than 150 members had tested positive for hepatitis C.

7

Two's Company

One night in 1994 I returned home to find a brief message waiting for me: *Jane O'Brien rang and wants you to call her back*. I didn't recognise the name at all. In a few months the whole country would know it as she would be splashed across the newspapers as well as the radio and TV bulletins: Jane O'Brien was from the group Positive Action, formed to support mothers who'd become infected with hepatitis C. They had contracted the virus after receiving a blood product called anti-D which was made from Irish donations. Anti-D was given to a mother when her blood was found to be rhesus negative but her child was rhesus positive. Without the blood product, her body could develop antibodies which would attack the red cells of a foetus from any subsequent pregnancy. Prior to anti-D, it was estimated that 100 newborn infants died every year from what was colloquially called 'blue-baby syndrome'.

I arranged that Jane and some of her group would meet

Brian O'Mahony and myself at the IHS offices. Jane was a quiet-spoken person but clearly driven and very assertive. She was focussed and took control of the meeting to ensure that all of the information she required was secured. She also had some like-minded members of Positive Action with her – one of them being the late Brigid McCole who appeared older than the rest of the group and also somewhat physically weaker. A mother of twelve from Donegal, she would become a household name for her bravery in the face of appalling State cruelty.

Positive Action's agenda was to get details on how the IHS had dealt with the issue of compensation in relation to HIV. In particular, they were seeking advice on how to deal with the State. Brian and I related our experiences and offered any support we thought might be worthwhile. I think Jane felt we were the only group which had already successfully achieved what Positive Action were hoping to do. She certainly hoovered up any information which was going to help them in their task.

It was a strange feeling: I was being considered something of an expert. Jane later asked me to address a meeting of her members at Liberty Hall. I vividly recall walking into that meeting which was extremely well attended. Looking out over the room full of women, my overwhelming feeling was one of immense sadness. The haemophilia community had a long experience of dealing with the medical profession and so could adapt more easily to the new situation. However, unlike our members, these women didn't know each other and had few dealings with the medical system. By the end of the meeting, there was a silver lining: it was clear that the officers of Positive Action had both the courage and organisational skills to cope.

One thing which was common to both groups – apart from the virus – was the fact that confidentiality was a major issue. It therefore came as something of a shock when, looking out from the platform at Liberty Hall, I recognised one woman. I didn't think she'd caught my eye so for the rest of the afternoon I made strenuous efforts to look anywhere but in her direction. A couple of months later in my local shopping centre the same woman came up to me and introduced herself saying: "I saw you in Liberty Hall." Standing in the aisle, we spoke about how she was coping. I was surprised at her openness and, in particular, that she would speak frankly in a public place. We maintained regular contact afterwards.

The anti-D scandal was beneficial to the IHS in so far as it brought public awareness of hepatitis C to a new level. People had latched on to the idea that a virus could be transmitted through a blood product and this made it easier for the haemophilia community to communicate its message. However, there was no question of our organisations amalgamating because the experiences were just so different.

As the shock of the anti-D scandal began to abate, the IHS renewed its campaign of seeking help for its members infected with hepatitis C. The following month we arranged a meeting with the Minister for Health, Brendan Howlin. Having only previously dealt with Dr O'Hanlon, this was much easier. Brendan was the person who in 1989, in the Dáil, proposed giving £400,000 to those affected by HIV. He was also supportive of the IHS in 1991 when we were seeking compensation from the State. The meeting was warm and we seemed to strike up a good working relationship. I was, however, conscious of the fact that concern expressed in opposition didn't always produce results when in Government.

On the medical front, I was not convinced that everyone who had hepatitis C had been told of their diagnosis. This was prompted by meeting members who had not been tested or had not been informed of their results. It led to a policy whereby anyone phoning our office was asked about their situation regarding hepatitis C. During the HIV crisis, people who were infected with the virus often experienced unacceptable delays in receiving test results. To avoid a repetition, in August 1994, we arranged a meeting with Professor Temperley. He told us he was aware of the need to communicate the information about a diagnosis effectively. He argued, however, that it took time to tell people individually. He reminded us that there were only a limited number of employees at his centre and a large number of patients to be seen. He also stated that he didn't want such information to be conveyed by letters, something with which I agreed. A further complication was the fact that newer, more accurate PCR tests were coming on stream. However, the number of different tests led to some confusion in the IHS over who had been checked and by which test. By September 1994 things still had not been resolved, although Professor Temperley said he was making every effort to inform people. At the time, it sounded like a reasonable position. I didn't like it, but I felt I had to accept what he was saying. Yet, we did offer assistance to speed up the process.

The year 1994 proved to be a difficult time as preliminary results from the interferon treatment were very discouraging: only two out of forty people had responded. The statistic didn't surprise me as the drug didn't seem to be helping the patients I was seeing on a regular basis. Yet on viewing the statistics it began to dawn on me that maybe interferon was no use at all. This posed a dilemma as many members used to seek my advice before going on the trial drug. While I was now very concerned about its effectiveness, I didn't want to take away the hope that it just might work for the person who was asking me. My solution was to deliver the information and make sure they understood: the drug isn't proving effective, it has serious side-effects, but the only way to know for sure if it will work for you is to take it. While Margaret and I continued to provide the critical illness service to ten members who died from AIDS-related illnesses in 1994, hepatitis C was the major focus.

There was a change of Government the previous month, although no election had been called. Brendan Howlin remained in cabinet as Minister for the Environment because Labour pulled out of coalition with Fianna Fáil but went straight back into Government with Fine Gael and Democratic Left. I was sorry to see Brendan Howlin go as Minister for Health as I felt he was very approachable and it was possible to discuss a problem with a hope of getting something done. He had resolved the issue of interferon payments and also funded the publication of a booklet on haemophilia. However, I did discuss the issue of body-bags with him and this wasn't resolved. He referred the problem back to Saint James's Hospital and, despite meetings with administrators, pathologists, doctors, nurses, social workers and funeral directors, the practice continued.

The new Minister for Health was Michael Noonan. At the beginning of 1995, he moved to assist the women represented by Positive Action. Of course, any provision for women infected with hepatitis C was going to lead the IHS to claim similar treatment for people with haemophilia. The first step was to make contact with the Department of Health and request a meeting. I felt that it was in the IHS's interest to liaise with groups like Positive Action but not to come under one campaigning umbrella. While both organisations represented people infected through blood products, the needs of the individual memberships were different and so it was best we remain separate. Positive Action were of the same view.

A meeting was scheduled. Prior to it, we had many internal meetings to ascertain the personal circumstances of our membership. I never really had much time for or interest in statistics, but my experience with the fight to secure HIV compensation led me to understand that this was the only language which the Department of Health and the State understood. The method we employed was to anticipate the questions which the officials would ask. Then this information would be included in a submission. The idea was to avoid the possibility of wasting time: if you didn't have the data, then the department would have an opportunity to offer platitudes and delay things. Brian O'Mahony cut short a working visit to the United States to attend the meeting but, at the last minute, it was postponed due to an abortion debate in the Dáil.

A rescheduled meeting took place in April 1995. I found Mr Noonan to be friendly and unassuming. I didn't know very much about him, but my first impression was that he was interested and would be accessible. That said, we still felt that the IHS was second in ranking on the issue of hepatitis C. It wasn't surprising considering Positive Action had four times as many members infected. There was also a lot of public support for their cause. Walking out of the Department of Health I felt progress had been made on the issue of compensation. Discussions had centred on whether any agreed sum from the State would be paid following an individual assessment or if the money would come as a lump sum to be divided by members.

Brian O'Mahony was leading the delegation, but this was about to change. He had been elected President of the World Federation of Haemophilia and so now wasn't always going to be as available for domestic meetings. I remember him saying that he felt I'd now acquired the skills to be able to head such meetings without his presence. This was after a meeting where I'd really done my homework and made good interventions. He said he expected to be able to attend many meetings, but that we were now in a position to alternate the leadership role between us.

I was terrified. On the one hand I felt that I was now able to do the work, but then again, he was always around. The idea of going into a meeting without him was scary. I was just going to have to get used to it. Meetings were going to happen at short notice and we were not going to be able to reschedule until Brian was back in the country. But in my favour, I was totally on top of my brief. The other saving grace was that Brian was so approachable that it was always possible to ask him any questions – even at four o'clock in the morning when on the far side of the world. He gave me the confidence to go forward.

Talks continued over the following months without the Department of Health indicating their preference for either a tribunal which would assess each claim and order a payment, or a group scheme running along the same lines as the HIV settlement in 1991. We reiterated that the IHS wanted action as soon as possible. Years of negotiation would not be tolerated.

I wasn't convinced myself as to what would be the best way forward. A compensation tribunal appeared to offer the fairest opportunity for members to secure the money they deserved. However, I was deeply concerned that it might take a long time to get up and running. There were other considerations: people with haemophilia had already died as a result of hepatitis C. For dozens of others, the fact that they were co-infected with HIV heightened fear of serious illness setting in. A compensation tribunal would also make awards on medical criteria and we were not confident that all of the material would be easily accessible. One final consideration was the emotional stress of having to take part in a compensation tribunal hearing. My gut feeling was that it was better to get some money while people were alive and reasonably healthy than a lot of money when they were dead or seriously ill.

The worry was that the State pay-out could be conservative. The other issue was the fact that the payment was on an ex-gratia basis – meaning the State would not admit liability. This was the same approach the State was taking with the anti-D women and so it wasn't unexpected. The main issue for our members was to quickly obtain fair compensation; the question of an apology was never considered or discussed. It just wasn't expected.

Meetings scheduled for the summer fell through. By the time of the next meeting, the Government had already announced it would expand the tribunal to all groups affected by hepatitis C. The only thing we could agree on was to have another meeting. While progress was minimal, I felt far more confident at these discussions. Whereas I used to feel intimidated, now there was a feeling of normality about them. I had become a better negotiator. The main difference between these discussions and the previous encounter in 1991 was that I pressed for results and, as much as possible, tied decisions down to dates. Things didn't always work out the way you wanted them to, but it avoided a lot of stalling.

The skills I had learned included saying a little rather than a lot. I would prepare my two or three points and know them back to front. This would then allow me to concentrate on what was being said by the officials. I was also able to pick up on what wasn't being said. I could analyse questions and see what was coming around the corner. The meetings were usually quite formal, with our delegation on one side and the Department of Health's officials on the other. Nobody ever expressed anger: it was a bit like a poker game with no emotion being shown.

Aside from negotiations, the normal job was continuing. Duties included checking the electrical capacity of UCD where the IHS were hosting an international meeting on haemophilia scheduled for June 1996. I was also organising special weekends for members infected with HIV so they could support each other and avail of counselling. The hotel where the event was being held wasn't told the meeting related to HIV. On the Saturday night, we had the usual sing-song. I looked at the staff on duty and thought how oblivious they were to the grief and pain inside this seemingly happy room.

While preparing for further meetings with the department, we recognised we were not going to get our preferred option of ex-gratia payments. Accordingly, we decided to examine the possibility of employing a legal team to help members process their claims. The big trouble with this idea was that the IHS had had a bad experience with two previous firms of solicitors. Our main criterion was that the successful company would have an employee working in the same building as the IHS. Access to legal opinion was essential in our view. I wasn't prepared to be treated as a second-class citizen any longer. At times solicitors made clients feel as if they were doing them an honour by simply turning up. Usually the timing of the meeting was convenient only to them.

The initial search wasn't very good with many pompous lawyers hawking for business. As we ran out of options, a member of the IHS executive committee, Frank Bird, suggested that a better strategy might be to engage a company from outside Dublin. The hope was that it might see the case as an opportunity and therefore be more agreeable to our demands. The first we contacted was a firm Frank had had dealings with in the past: Carlow-based Lanigan-Malcomson Law. It seemed like a reasonable idea to me. Frank Lanigan had previously helped organise a fundraising cycle event from Malin Head to Mizen Head. The solicitors who participated raised £11,000 for the IHS.

So, in December 1995, a meeting was arranged with Raymond Bradley – a solicitor and partner at Lanigan-Malcomson Law. However, at the appointed time, it was Mr Lanigan who arrived at our offices in Temple Bar. The rather embarrassed visitor blurted out that his colleague had been delayed at a court hearing. Not the best start to a first meeting. When Raymond eventually turned up, the first thing which struck me was that he appeared to be so young. Tall, in his early thirties and wearing steel-rimmed glasses, he was sporting a sharp suit. Raymond was very soft-spoken and focussed intently on what he was saying. For some reason, I happened to be sitting a little behind him during the interview. I could pick up that he wasn't particularly enjoying being assessed by a person who was out of view, saying virtually nothing and taking notes.

When we eventually got down to business, I quickly formed the impression that this, as Margaret Thatcher once famously said, was a man I could do business with. For a start, Raymond had no airs or graces but told things as they were. Another major plus was the fact that he had some experience of working on a hepatitis C case in the High Court for a client who had been infected by the anti-D blood product. The deciding factor, however, was that he declared he would be willing to move from Carlow and work exclusively for our members in preparing claims. This was the dedication which we felt was necessary. In the end, Raymond actually ended up working above the IHS offices in Eustace Street.

Our new solicitor was originally from Ardee in County Louth, which helped, as it was just up the road from my home-town of Dundalk. My experience of the legal profession had led me to usually dislike these Trinity College types, but Raymond was far removed from that. I liked the fact that he'd been an apprentice with his firm and was now working his way up to the title of managing partner. As Raymond began to work very closely with our members, one of our secretaries began to work in his office to ensure there was a familiar face there.

When the meeting finally happened with the Department of Health at the beginning of December, as expected, the compensation tribunal was the one and only choice on the table. I knew this was going to happen, but it still terrified me as I fretted that the administrative side of things would be immense. With no other real options, the proposal was put to a meeting of the members, who endorsed it.

While 1995 ended with progress made on the hepatitis C issue, a further six members died as a result of AIDS-related illness. One of them was a young boy, Mark, whose mother had been sitting with me in the Dáil back in 1989 during the bid to secure £400,000 for people infected with HIV. I received a phone-call at two o'clock in the morning to say that Mark was seriously ill. Within a matter of hours he had died. Mark was laid out in his favorite football strip. After he was buried, the talking continued.

8

A Hellish Year

The first time I kicked a barrister was during a meeting with Professor Eric Preston, one of the world's leading experts on liver disease. I had travelled to London with Brian O'Mahony in preparation for the newly established Hepatitis C Compensation Tribunal.

The aim of the trip was to get a number of lawyers up to speed on what hepatitis C meant for a patient and the probable course of the illness. Things began to go wrong when one barrister asked the professor not about cirrhosis, the hardening of the liver, but psoriasis – the skin complaint. It might sound similar, but has nothing to do with having a virus. I let it go the first time, but acted after he repeated how the development of psoriasis as a result of hepatitis C was something which was afflicting many Irish members. A good kick under the table to the man's shin worked wonders for his powers of recall of medical terminology. But it wasn't just one-way traffic – I was also learning a lot about the legal approach to such situations.

While 1996 began somewhat optimistically with the focus on the compensation tribunal, the year quickly descended into the worst I ever had to endure. It was hellish both professionally and personally.

My mother had been ill since the previous summer but became bed-ridden in the spring of 1995. I employed a nurse to help my father cope during the week, but it wasn't financially possible to sustain this level of care over the weekend. The result was that each weekend I had to go to Dundalk. This was difficult for Arthur as we had very little time together. My work schedule during the week was intense. We considered moving the family to Dundalk each weekend, but it really wasn't an option. For a start, our son John Joe had sports and other commitments lined up and afterwards wanted to be with his friends. However, my daughter Aisling, who was younger than John Joe, was happy to tag along with me. The compromise reached therefore was that Aisling came to Dundalk with me each weekend while Arthur remained in Dublin with John Joe. We would always try to meet up at some point over the weekend. What got us through the time was simply that there wasn't another option. We didn't dwell on separation but simply got on with matters.

Though I had hoped to divide my time between work and my family, I was forced to abandon my plans when one of our members, Sheila, became seriously ill due to her hepatitis C condition. As haemophilia affects men and boys, it might seem strange that a woman was a member of the IHS. But Sheila had a clotting disorder which was very similar to haemophilia and was treated accordingly at Saint James's Hospital. Unfortunately, she had a long history of difficulties and was quite a familiar face on Top Floor 1.

The possibility that Sheila could die caused significant

problems. Not only was it a tragedy for her and her family, but there was also a financial aspect: the amount of money awarded by the compensation tribunal is significantly reduced if a person dies before their claim is heard. The legal thinking behind this is that "pain and suffering" is a category for which a person can claim compensation. Yet once a claimant dies, they can't feel pain or suffering any more and so can't get financially rewarded for it. So, if you die the award is lower – possibly by as much as 50 per cent. I realised this was the time for action.

Six days into 1996, Sheila suffered a brain haemorrhage. I heard of the development relatively quickly and resolved to speak to her family. It wasn't an easy thing to do, but I approached her mother and her sister about the possibility of pursuing a claim. It was an awful conversation as the only thing they cared about was Sheila's wellbeing. Compensation came nowhere in their list of priorities. I still persisted. I explained that the tribunal would pay out a lower amount if Sheila died and said that she would want her mother to have the comfort of financial security. Sheila's mother was not wealthy and had spared no expense in taking care of her daughter for over thirty years. Eventually they agreed to meet Raymond.

I was in the job seven years by this stage and the members used to put great stay on what I said. If Margaret was backing me up, it was almost unheard of that they would oppose us. They simply didn't believe we would be acting against their interests. It's also fair to say that some of the newer members were probably intimidated by my aggressive style and were not inclined to go head to head with me.

Feeling extremely nervous and looking highly uncomfortable, I dragged a reluctant Raymond to meet the family. It was a baptism of fire but he coped well. The family agreed that

Raymond should make arrangements with the tribunal to hear an emergency application. This was quite a task as the tribunal at this stage didn't even have a venue for hearings. The date of our first ever hearing was set for Monday, January 15, 1996. The fact that we had secured a hearing was absolutely fantastic. That is, until we began to think about the amount of work involved in preparing a case in just days. The sense of foreboding was accentuated by the fear that a mistake could set a precedent from which we might never recover.

The first step in the process was to gain access to Sheila's medical records. To do this, we needed permission from Dr Owen Smith – the man who had succeeded Professor Temperley as the medical director of the National Haemophilia Centre. Dr Smith was totally different in style from the professor. For a start, he was quite happy to be direct. He told it the way he saw it and if you had a problem with that, then tough luck. My first impression was that it was a breath of fresh air. Dr Smith was also younger than me and I certainly wasn't going to be in awe of him or deferential in my approach.

Dr Smith agreed to hand over the records. The problem was that we would only get access to them on Sunday, January 14 – the day before the hearing. With no other option open to us, we arranged to meet at seven o'clock in the morning at Saint James's Hospital – it was not possible to remove the records from the ward because if a patient required treatment, then the physician needed to have access to the records. So while Sheila was on Top Floor 1 fighting for her life, we were on the ground floor studying the progression of her illness.

I managed to make it to the hospital fifteen minutes early. Margaret King was already there – once again displaying her ability to go without sleep. The clock ticked closer to seven. No sign of Raymond. The appointed time arrived and still our solicitor hadn't come. By four minutes past seven I was dialling his mobile. He answered very quickly. I barked down the line: "Where are you?" He responded: "Thankfully, at the other end of the corridor." I put down the phone and smiled – it was good to hear him lighten up.

Our job was to read the medical records and identify what could be relevant at the compensation tribunal. There were lots of records, but thankfully Margaret could interpret the medical language and, even more fortunately, knew the patient intimately. Margaret took the lead and I was the official photocopier – running back and forward from the machine with pieces of paper.

Raymond was clearly uncomfortable about the whole situation. He had to run a very important case, but also knew that he would be interacting with a family as their loved one neared death. I remember looking across the room and wondering: "Does he have it in him?" He proved to be perfect on both counts. The family had to sign certain documents and it became clear very quickly that they trusted him. His quiet and gentle way won through.

While we worked away piecing together Sheila's case, the unexpressed fear of all of us was that she would die before the hearing. Margaret and I visited her on several occasions that day. We knew from previous situations that things were not looking good. Her family's support knew no limits. Thankfully, Sheila was still alive on Monday morning. The international expert, Professor Preston, had arrived in Dublin the night before. Yet there was a major hole in our case: our Irish medical expert, Dr Owen Smith, wasn't able to attend. He informed us on the morning of the hearing that he had another engagement.

It's difficult to find the words to express my emotions as Raymond and I drove down to Ballsbridge in Dublin for our first ever hearing with the Hepatitis C Compensation Tribunal – minus our chief witness. The best way of phrasing it is: *total panic*. The hearing was taking place in a hotel as they didn't yet have a permanent venue.

We felt it was essential to Sheila's case that we have a medical expert on bleeding disorders attend the hearing. I could think of only one person who knew Shelia and might be able to prevent total disaster – the retired Professor Templerley.

Sitting in Raymond's car, I dialled the professor from my mobile. He luckily was at home. No doubt my voice betrayed my anxiety. After outlining the circumstances, I asked him to assist us. Professor Temperley dropped whatever he was doing and immediately drove over to Jury's Hotel in Ballsbridge where the hearing was to take place. I didn't hear the professor's testimony as it was our policy to absent ourselves during expert evidence so the doctor could speak openly about the patient. I was outside with Sheila's sister. I met him before and after, however, and thanked him for his help. He didn't have to help but obviously felt loyal to his former patient.

The last-minute bid to secure Professor Temperley's assistance was in keeping with a very surreal day. For a start, Jury's in Ballsbridge had been the venue to several IHS AGMs. Now on a Monday morning we were in the boardroom facing Mr Justice Seamus Egan and talking about the life and suffering of a person who was in a coma in Saint James's Hospital. Somehow, we managed to get through.

The policy of tribunal hearings is that the judgement is announced immediately afterwards. Thankfully, our first case was successful. The amount of money didn't really count – what mattered was that the case had been heard and won. I was pleased. It still galled me though to think that the State would save money if one person happened to die quicker than another.

Armed with a successful result, we returned to Saint James's with Sheila's sister to tell her mother what had happened. She was amazed that the case had been heard, but saddened that Sheila hadn't been able to participate herself. Despite our success, I began to feel empty. Sheila had suffered so much and was now not even aware of what was going on around her. On the one hand the absence of pain was welcome, but it was also the end of her life. I knew that she would never live to enjoy in any way the money which had been secured for her. Looking down at her, I was reminded that one of her great passions in life was clothes. For a moment I imagined her going on the spending spree she had never been in a position to enjoy; I thought of the style, cut and colour of what she might buy. Images of how she might look flickered through my mind. I smiled. I then looked again at her face on the hospital bed and knew it was an unrealisable dream. Sheila died soon afterwards.

Just two days after the tribunal made its first award, another of our members became seriously ill from a hepatitis-C-related illness. This time it was a person I knew well: Dermot. A single man in his late thirties and from a rural area, I got to know him as he visited our office on a regular basis. Our friendship had taken a bit of time to cement as he was the person who used to come into the office for a cup of tea and didn't say very much, but who, it turned out, loved to be in the middle of fun. He was always keen to participate in meetings – mostly to enjoy the social side of matters! On one occasion he travelled to Athens for a conference of the World Federation of Haemophilia. These meetings were open to anyone with haemophilia who wanted to attend. The Irish delegates decided to go to see the ancient site of the Acropolis overlooking Athens. Dermot preferred to stay in the city and have something to eat. He bumped into Brian O'Mahony returning from the ruins and memorably asked him: "Brian, would you ever go back up there and take a photo of it for me?" The chairman demurred. Then Dermot indicated his clear preference for people over history: "Sure, what is it only a heap of stones."

It came as quite a shock when Dermot was admitted to Saint James's Hospital suffering from acute liver disease in 1996. I had heard that he was in the hospital, but was not aware of how bad the situation had become. A series of tests was being conducted to ascertain the full extent of his problems. His father had requested that he should be with his son when the results were conveyed to him. This request wasn't adhered to. I happened to be in the hospital around ten minutes after Dermot was informed he was going to die. I noticed there were curtains around his bed and, unaware that anything was happening, pushed my way through. He looked distraught. I sat on his bed and asked him: "What's wrong?" His response was short and direct: "I am going to die." My head was spinning. Automatically rather than consciously, I switched into supportive mode: "It doesn't have to be now. Maybe you can go home. Maybe you can have a good quality of life for a while . . ." But as I spoke I could see that the spark of life had disappeared from his eyes. He just held my hand and cried. I had no words which could comfort him.

I was crazy about Dermot. I had thought that I would fall apart when this moment came, but I didn't. It is like a mother, who worries about how she would cope if her child was in an accident. More often than not, what happens is you act rationally until the crisis is over and then you collapse. I became an expert at crying once I knew there was no-one else around. I would just let it all come out before pulling myself together and moving on. My rock was Margaret King. We sustained each other in times of crisis. Another mainstay was Margaret Dunne from the IHS. In the case of Dermot, he was so close that all of my family were upset.

It became clear that Dermot's position was similar to that of Sheila's – we would need to apply for an emergency hearing of the Hepatitis C Compensation Tribunal. On this occasion, I was allowed to listen to proceedings. The reason for that was that I had been asked to explain to the tribunal what Dermot's life had been like as I was very close to him. Giving evidence was horrific. At the time, I wasn't able to put any distance between the job I was there to do and my personal feelings.

Dermot retreated into himself after the diagnosis, disengaging from the outside world. He never read the newspapers again. It spoke volumes as one of his greatest pleasures had been reading them cover to cover. After a short space of time, we arranged for him to leave hospital so he could die at home with his family. I sat with him on the ward as his parents went to prepare the car. We helped him into the vehicle and then I waved as they departed. It really cut me up as I could see the sadness in his face as they drove off. I also knew that part of the angst was the fear inside him that he was bringing more pain and suffering on parents who'd done so much for him. He had tried to protect them by not discussing the fact that he'd contracted both HIV and hepatitis C.

I made many journeys up and down to his home. Austin often accompanied me as they were also pals. Dermot kept stating his desire to go to top Dublin tailor Louis Copeland and buy a top-of-the-range suit with his award from the tribunal. As his condition deteriorated, he changed his story slightly and asked if I would buy the expensive suit and use it to lay him out in after his death.

His deterioration at the end was so fast that I didn't have the chance to get Louis Copeland to make a suit, despite this being Dermot's last request. Instead, I went into the local town with his mum and sister. We bought a suit there and Louis Copeland graciously organised a suit-bag to be sent down with labels. Dermot's sister sewed the labels onto the inside of the suit and we presented it to him. He was very impressed.

A short time later he died. I had lost another friend. Dermot was quiet, unassuming and a joy to be with. I still miss him. As was his nature, he slipped away quietly in the early hours of the morning. I just remember sitting in the room with him on my own. I was listening to the birds singing as it started to become light. I wondered how life could go on as normal outside when this disaster of AIDS and liver disease was being played out in all the various families throughout the country.

At this time in 1996, my professional and personal lives were merging in an alarming fashion. The weekend Dermot died stands out in particular. As he was ill, I didn't travel to New York with Arthur to see Aisling perform with the Aer Lingus Pipe Band. I was without my husband's support. On Friday morning, I realised how much of a problem that was going to be. Margaret Dunne told me my father had rung the office. He told her his brother had been found dead at home in Waterford. I was immediately on the phone to make arrangements with the undertaker. The gardai were also involved as my uncle had died alone and so I had to liaise with them as well. With Daddy leaving Dundalk, I also had to ensure that my mother could stay in a home over the weekend. My father, John Joe and I then travelled down to

Waterford and made arrangements with the help of our relatives. The burial was on Saturday morning. Any time I could get the chance, I was on the phone to Dermot's family to find out how he was doing. A tug of war developed in my mind about where I should be. The debate ended at half eleven that night when I got a call to say Dermot was dying and I should go immediately. Shortly after midnight, a taxi collected me for a two-hour dash across the country. I sat in the back of the car with my mind reeling. As it was the middle of the night I couldn't even try to distract myself with the view. My mind bounced from my mother to my father to Dermot. I even had to leave my son John Joe in Waterford. I felt I was doing the right thing, but it was still an extremely lonely place to be.

When I got to Dermot several hours later he was thankfully still alive. I was able to spend some time with him. He wasn't conscious, but it was wonderful to be able to sit and hold his hand. He died later that morning. I assisted Dermot's sister in laying him out in his new suit. My father then travelled from Waterford with my son to collect me. It was difficult for him as I couldn't say where I was, to protect the family's confidentiality. I had to make an arrangement to meet him in the town centre. By the time we made it to Dublin, I was absolutely traumatised. Despite this, there was no time to recover. After a change of clothes and a short sleep, I was back on the road heading to Dermot's home-town for his funeral. Thankfully Arthur and Aisling were now back from New York. Arthur knew Dermot and wanted to accompany me to the funeral. Austin was also on hand to give emotional support. To cap it all, I spoke with Raymond who told me he had not been able to attend as he was involved in a serious crash in which his car had flipped over several times and ended up in a field. It was so badly damaged that it had to be hauled out by crane. In typical Raymond style, he went to work the next morning.

The year continued in the same vein. Mostly I was working with Raymond and the legal team, preparing the cases for the tribunal which was now located in Dublin's Smithfield. The rest of my time was spent travelling up to Dundalk to be with my mother whose health was deteriorating rapidly. By April I was travelling to see my mother on evenings during the week and then returning to Dublin each morning. All of this was taking place against the background of the IHS preparing to host a major international conference.

My mother died on May 25, 1996. Margaret King was there with me because, despite all the experience of death I had, I found I was unable to cope without her. I rang Margaret and told her: "Get down here." When I saw her getting out of the car it seemed like a weight lifted off my shoulders. I had been supporting my father and now I had some support myself. In one sense, my job gave me the knowledge of how to get through things as I was able to understand the phases. I knew what was happening. At the same time, I wasn't in control either. I remember attending to my mother at one point and hearing visitors whispering in another room. For some reason it got to me and so I marched in and told them all to "speak up" as death was "perfectly normal". Clearly, I wasn't 'with it'. I realised then just how hard it was to say goodbye to someone you love. One source of comfort was my mother's gold necklace. After she died, I put it on and never took it off again as it made me feel she was close.

Less than a month later, the IHS hosted the World Congress of Haemophilia. It was widely heralded as one of the most successful ever, but I was, in reality, totally detached despite having been involved in its preparation for several years. And still it didn't stop: on the last night the IHS held a celebration, but a phone call came through in the middle of the festivities. Another member was dying from a hepatitis C-related illness in Saint James's Hospital and Margaret and I were needed. We left the revellers and went off to comfort yet another shattered family.

The tribunal worked speedily through cases. By the middle of the year, twenty-three had been dealt with. My function was to attend the consultation between our member and the legal team before the hearing. During the proceedings, I would sit with them and explain the process as best I could. Often I would simply be on hand to talk, make tea and provide a distraction. Many found coming before the tribunal a challenge. They had coped with infection by keeping it boxed away. Even the preparation was difficult as not only did they have to face the reality of their infection but also visit many experts. By the time they reached the day of the hearing, they were usually emotionally drained. Their biggest fear was having to go before the tribunal and talk about intimate details they might not even have imparted to their own family. The person infected would talk first and their partner second. We often found that each had been hiding information from the other. To protect them, we got them to testify individually.

It's extremely difficult to talk about your personal life in front of people you don't know. While the three-member compensation tribunal panel did their best to make it easy on witnesses, it was still hard. We were of course briefing our membership about what was going to happen, but nothing could prepare them for the actual hearing. I was allowed to bring witnesses up to the room before a hearing so that they could acclimatise. There were nice waiting-rooms for our members and refreshments available. At Raymond's request, the tribunal sat for two weeks in Cork to hear claims from our members from the southern part of the country. One advantage was that members could eliminate some of the suspicion that might have developed had they been forced to travel to Dublin.

Secrecy remained a major issue. One case which stands out featured, Clement, a member who had sworn his children to secrecy. Not only did Clement want to protect his family by ensuring no one else knew about the illness, but he also became extremely fearful that his children might become infected while taking care of him. Clement demanded that everyone use rubber gloves when touching him. His son, William, would later say: "Even up to the end, he wanted to protect us . . . It was hard because my mother died quite suddenly and we didn't get a chance to talk . . . [My father] was upset about Mam and, you know, we were talking . . . we both got upset. I was crying and he started to cry and I just saw a tear roll down a cheek and I reached out and wiped it away and he shouted at me. He just shouted – you can't do that, you can't touch me without wearing the glove. I don't know. It hurt."

Clement's family made contact when he slipped into a coma. We tried to take an emergency case with the tribunal, but unfortunately he died on the morning of the hearing. Maybe it was the fact that I had been with Clement when he died, but I went on to have a major row with Raymond. What sparked it was the fact that I couldn't contact him at seven in the morning to inform him of Clement's death and the collapse of the case. I eventually reached him and let fly, saying that he had to keep his mobile phone on permanently. I was incredulous that he could have ever turned it off. He responded quietly that he turned it off at half past ten at night and felt this was a reasonable position. This explanation failed to placate me. I verbally abused him for a time and then hung up. On returning to Dublin I had to go and apologise. Raymond was big enough to understand what prompted my outburst and never mentioned the row again.

Looking back now, I used to go into a 'sub-world' as a person neared death. Within this bubble, dying was the only thing which mattered. It was therefore quite difficult to comprehend that people in 'the real world' didn't understand it or have the same values. At this point, I was living in this sub-world for a lot of the time. Sometimes for weeks. As a result, my reasoning of what was going on in other people's lives began to become impaired, particularly when I was tired. So while it was entirely reasonable for Raymond to turn off his phone when his working day was over, it was an incomprehensible act viewed from the place where I was living.

Just two days later there was yet another crisis. The plan was for me to travel to Cork where the tribunal was sitting for two weeks. However, on the morning I was due to leave I received a call from the wife of Joe Dowling. (Joe had been the person who helped me get to grips with the IHS in the very early days and also provided so much enjoyment when he nearly got elected as a councillor in Artane.) His wife told me Joe hadn't got out of bed. While she could hear snoring she wasn't able to get into the room as the door was locked. I immediately told her to call an ambulance and then try to break down the door. While I didn't mention it, my experience of people with haemophilia and AIDS-related illness was that they tended to have brain haemorrhages and often made a snore-type sound. I knew that sound.

An ambulance arrived but, despite my loud protestations on the phone, Joe was taken to Beaumont Hospital rather than Saint James's. While Beaumont was closer to where Joe lived, the staff didn't have experience with haemophilia. I rang Margaret

King and we went to Beaumont immediately. Joe was in the emergency room by the time I arrived. I was already highly charged and suspected the medical staff were considering inserting tubes. My concern was clear: if they tried such a procedure it could lead to a serious bleed. I felt I knew more than the doctors and wanted to force my way into the emergency room. I considered it. Then I tried to talk myself out of it: "I am a representative of the IHS and it might reflect badly on the organisation." The logic was sound, but I was just so angry that no-one was listening to me. I burst into the room leaving two doctors and a nurse quite startled. I said: "Don't touch him. He needs Factor VIII." I was gently led out of the room.

My initial concerns about bringing Joe to Beaumont were confirmed when we learned that they didn't have the clotting-agent required to stop his bleeding. Joe's relatives engaged in a mad dash to his home to pick it up as delivery from another hospital would take longer. At this stage, I knew that he was not going to live. Margaret and I spent the night with him and his family. We had some lovely time with our friend on our own when the family needed rest. Yet it didn't take away from the awful fact that he was leaving us. It hurt me as Joe had such a strong presence, quick wit and a great mind. At the same time, I was grateful to be there with him. In the early hours of Monday morning Joe slipped away, surrounded by his family. The fact that he died in hospital meant we faced the possibility of a row over a body-bag. Thankfully, we were able to find a compromise.

The insanity of the life I was leading was exemplified by the fact that later that day I flew to Cork to attend a hearing of the compensation tribunal. The member due to attend was particularly anxious and would definitely not have gone had I not been there. Once the hearing was over the following morning, I flew back to Dublin.

I went directly out to Beaumont and met Margaret. It was particularly difficult to go into the mortuary and find a body-bag waiting for us. It was compounded by the fact that when we opened it there was the body of someone I admired, loved and respected. The comforting thing was the feeling that we were able to give Joe his dignity before his family said their goodbyes. I attended Joe's funeral the following morning before returning to Cork for more sittings of the tribunal.

This was a very difficult year for me at all levels. On the one hand, I was still grieving for my mother. My father was devastated and needed a lot of support. Work was also extremely intense. I felt like everyone wanted a piece of me and the stress was beginning to tell. Yet, if I am honest, I liked being integral to so many people's lives. When confronted by serious illness or death, most people offer their support but are not in a position to contribute meaningfully. I was. It was impossible to stop the process of death, but I felt I could help soften the blow. I was contributing, but also getting something out of it.

Five people with haemophilia died in 1996. Of the more than 260 people with haemophilia infected with HIV and hepatitis C due to contaminated blood products, sixty-three had died. I had been involved in some capacity in nearly all of their lives at the terminal stage. The IHS had achieved a lot in the previous seven years, from compensation to HIV settlement to the critical-illness service. However, I was a very different person from who I had been in 1989. One consequence of the job was that I probably became more reckless in the way I lived my life. After seeing so much death, my philosophy was very close to the old line: 'Seize The Day'. I was also harder. It was a quality I needed to make tough decisions.

9

Walking Out Of The Tribunal

October 8, 1996, began relatively quietly. I was working in the office on proposals about how the Government could provide additional support for our members. Then Raymond walked in.

He had a sense of urgency about him and, unusually, discarded the niceties in favour of immediately talking about the main news story of the day: the Minister for Health, Michael Noonan, had given a commitment to set up a tribunal to examine how so many women became infected with hepatitis C through the anti-D blood product. In his announcement, the minister had said: "We are doing so because of the serious public concern about the circumstances surrounding the contamination of blood and blood products and the consequences for the health of a significant number of people." I had heard the story and was happy for Positive Action, but it didn't really mean anything to me.

Raymond was clearly perplexed. My reaction to his furrowed brow was to ask: "What are you on about?" In a more animated voice than usual, he said he felt that if the anti-D situation was being investigated then it surely followed that haemophilia blood products should also be examined. Now I was the one who was confused. I looked back at him and said: "Sure, we already know how our members were infected." He responded: "Yes, we know how they were infected – through blood products. What we don't know is why contaminated blood products were being used. What are you going to say to your members when they come seeking an answer to that?" I was stumped. We already had evidence to suggest that serious questions needed to be asked about how some people were infected with hepatitis C at a time when all products should have been free of the virus. In particular, a number of children who were using Blood Bank-made Factor IX had become infected in the late 1980s. After a bit of reflection, I realised I obviously hadn't grasped the full significance of what a tribunal could do for our members.

This was a key moment in my relationship with Raymond. The way he presented the argument was interesting because he kept repeating the same phrases until the force of what he was saying hit home. He now understood how to make an impact. He used words like "your members" and "they had rights" which always struck a chord with me. Raymond obviously had worked it out. I still remember the moment – Raymond standing rather than sitting and his hand accentuating his points. When I realised his analysis was correct it was like a slap in the face: "Why didn't I think of that?" Raymond had his finger on the pulse and so I gave him the green light to get the IHS involved, subject to the executive committee's approval. Had it not been for Raymond, the IHS might well have delayed taking action until a later stage. By then, however, the impact would have been significantly lessened.

Two days after the Michael Noonan's announcement, we

made a preliminary submission to the Department of Health asking to be included in the terms of the inquiry. It was a brief document of five pages but encapsulated what we needed. It stated: "It is with some trepidation that it is noted by the IHS that the proposed terms of reference may be limited to . . . anti-D." Drafting the document was important for me as it helped clarify why a tribunal was important.

We knew that the terms of reference were going to be finalised very quickly. Accordingly, I was on the phone constantly to officials from the Department of Health, in particular Donal Davitt. There were numerous meetings which Brian and I attended. We became convinced that the concerns of the IHS would be taken on board and that the terms of reference would include an investigation of haemophilia blood products. The focus was solely on hepatitis C. We didn't raise the issue of HIV as it was clear the tribunal was not going to investigate that matter. This, at least, offered the opportunity of finding out about the other virus.

Through these discussions my own view of the hepatitis C infections completely changed. I had always perceived that the virus was an inevitable consequence of taking concentrates. But I learned that it wasn't as black and white as that. Perhaps some of the infections could have been avoided. My realisation came when the negotiations on the format of the tribunal were being concluded. I moved from a position of thinking "What's the point?" to "This has to happen!".

On the evening of October 15, 1996, just a week since the decision had been taken to try to get involved with the tribunal, we knew that the terms were going to be published and were pressing the Department of Health to fax a copy to us before it was released to the media. We wanted be prepared for the inevitable questions. I remember that night very clearly. Raymond and I were sitting in the office waiting for the fax to hum into action. We waited. And waited. Eventually there was a ring-tone followed by a number of loud noises as our old fax machine got into gear. The pages of the terms of reference began to be pumped into the Eustace Street office. Raymond and I gathered them up and laid them down on the table. I looked up and down a couple of times and could see references to anti-D in the nine points which were going to be investigated. There was reference to "other blood products", but our clotting-agents were not mentioned specifically. I waited on Raymond. He simply said: "We're not there." I was confused: "But I was sure we would be included!" Raymond repeated slowly: "We're not there."

This was a turning point. My last discussions with departmental officials had led me to believe that our concerns would be taken on board. I was wrong. I also realised that the executive committee of the IHS might now think, along with the public at large, that I had been taken for a fool. Trusting Rosemary. I felt humiliated and betrayed – the anger came a short time later. I got back on to Donal Davitt and roasted him. I said: "You knew what we wanted and it's not there!" He suggested that our concerns were in the terms of reference, if only we looked harder. He'd done his best. My tone was cutting. I terminated the call with a curt: "Thanks for nothing!"

The immediate task was to work out what we were going to say to the media. It wasn't just that journalists would be ringing us, but most of our members were going to find out what happened through them. It was doubly difficult as the IHS executive committee were not around and I had to phone them individually and explain.

We worked late into the night preparing a press release. It was a rather strange operation as Raymond was appointed to type it up. He wasn't very skilled in this department, but I happen to be even worse. I dictated and he typed and edited. Slowly.

Our criticism was in print the next day. We stated there was ". . . a failure by the Government authorities to recognise that the present hepatitis C outbreak occurred and affected amongst others blood transfusion recipients, anti-D recipients and concentrate recipients equally. Each hepatitis C sufferer is entitled to know what went wrong." Just over twenty-four hours later, the Dáil passed the terms of reference which effectively excluded us from the tribunal. It didn't cross my mind to contact the Minister for Health. It just seemed pointless.

The other problem was that Positive Action were reasonably happy with the terms. As this was viewed by the public as 'their' tribunal, I realised that the IHS could be damaged by delaying proceedings. Even though the haemophilia disaster had been connected to the collapse of a Government, there still wasn't a deep understanding by the public of what we were trying to achieve. There was also a significant scepticism about tribunals anyway in the wake of the investigation into the beef industry here. As our members were not going public on the pain they were enduring, people simply didn't connect with our cause. It meant our negotiating position was not strong. The secrecy surrounding the viruses was hurting our case: people were dying, but the public didn't know about the tragedy.

A short time later we got the chance to rake over the coals of the debacle at the Department of Health. My feeling prior to the meeting was that I wanted to smack the first official who walked into the room. I felt we'd been strung along. Donal Davitt told us that they also had difficulties. The first problem was that there was pressure to draw up the terms of reference for the tribunal as quickly as possible as Brigid McCole had tragically died earlier in the month. I recognised that Michael Noonan was in a difficult position as he had faced huge criticism over the case.

Mrs McCole had initiated legal action in 1995 over her infection, along with hundreds of other women. All who issued writs received a letter from the Chief State Solicitor which characterised the approach of the State to the claims. They were all warned that if they chose to ignore "the privacy, informality and speed" provided by the Government's scheme of compensation in favour of "the uncertainty, delays, stresses, confrontation and costs involved in the High Court action" then "any resulting litigation would be fully defended by the State, if necessary to the Supreme Court". Despite this threat, Brigid continued with her case. She would fight them all the way. When she tried to take her case under an assumed name it was contested and she was denied anonymity. She tried for an early trial in April 1996 due to her deteriorating condition but this was rejected. Instead of June the case was listed for October. In May 1996, the Blood Bank made a lodgement to the court which meant that if she refused to settle and failed in her legal bid to secure a higher amount than what was lodged then she would face paying not just her own legal costs but also those of the other side from that date on. In late September, the Blood Bank finally admitted liability and apologised but the pressure continued: Mrs McCole was told that if she proceeded to try to secure aggravated damages then it would be contested all the way. Mrs McCole by this stage was on her death-bed. She ended up accepting the offer. The High Court case had been due to take place on the October 8, 1996. She died just a few days before it.

Whatever about the State's legal policy, Mr Noonan drew particular condemnation on himself when he made remarks in the Dáil about the McCole case. He criticised her lawyers, who included the former Attorney General John Rogers, for taking her case to the High Court rather than the Hepatitis C Compensation Tribunal. He said: "Is it not accepted in the legal profession that the tribunal is working very well and that Mrs McCole could have received a significantly higher award by going before it? She would not have had to face the enormous stress of court proceedings. Could her solicitors not, in selecting a test case from the hundreds of hepatitis C cases on their books, select a plaintiff in a better condition to sustain the stress of a High Court case?"

His comments resulted in a walk-out by the Positive Action delegation, from the Dáil public gallery. Jane O'Brien told the waiting media: "In commenting on Mrs McCole's case and her right to take it to court in this way, we feel he has shown an insensitivity that means we cannot trust him to continue to deal with this issue. And if the minister can't apologise to Mrs McCole's family and to the other anti-D mothers – we feel he should resign." Mr Noonan was back in the Dáil chamber a short time later to say: "I would like to avail of this opportunity to apologise unreservedly for any offence. It was not intended whatsoever." Unfortunately for him, the damage was done.

Donal Davitt did say that our preliminary submission to the minister was viewed as being "most helpful". However, he went on to say that many things we wanted investigated, such as how blood products were made and how the Blood Bank operated, had already been dealt with in an earlier report and the recommendations were being implemented. We were not impressed. I argued that the proposed inquiry would be incomplete if it only focused on one blood product. Regardless of what reports had been published, all issues would have to be addressed at the tribunal if public confidence was to be restored in the Blood Bank. I left the meeting feeling despondent and without any expectation that something was going to be done. The meeting had been held at our request and, probably, they were simply allowing us to let off steam. Raymond was invited to attend this meeting with Brian and me.

Brian and I had opted to deal with matters without solicitors but, at this point, Raymond had proven his commitment and gained knowledge and experience. He was a real addition to the team.

When the IHS executive committee met to consider its position, we still felt there was a possibility of being able to get some mileage from the tribunal. We knew it was not going to be easy, but equally felt very strongly that the circumstances of our members' infection should be investigated. We couldn't change public opinion and the department had washed its hands of us, but it might be beneficial to get into the process and try to get the tribunal to examine some of our concerns. A decision was taken to secure participation rights for the IHS, even if that meant taking our case to the High Court. In taking this decision, we didn't refer to Positive Action. We felt that they would understand our position and this proved to be the case.

The first step, however, was to apply to the tribunal to be allowed representation. This application was turned down on the basis that we were not included in the terms of reference. We consequently went to the High Court to have this decision challenged – what's known as a judicial review. While I had some experience of the law through the Hepatitis C Compensation Tribunal, going to the Four Courts was a different beast altogether. In the preliminary hearing, the judge granted us the right to challenge the decision. However, before it came to court, a deal was hatched on November 27, 1996, between our lawyers and those representing the tribunal. The solution was to allow the IHS to obtain what's called 'limited representation'. We were informed we could attend the hearings, apply to cross-examine witnesses and make a closing argument. This decision cleared the way for two other groups to get involved in the tribunal: Transfusion Positive, which represents men, women and children infected with hepatitis C through blood transfusions, and the Irish Kidney Association, a small number of whose members contracted hepatitis C mostly through dialysis.

Our next step was to meet the tribunal team and explain what we wanted investigated. We had a clear idea of what needed to be inquired into, but the problem was that the tribunal's terms of reference did not explicitly include our concerns. A meeting took place between the IHS representatives and the tribunal's legal team on the November 28, 1996. The tribunal had two senior counsel: James Nugent and Rory Brady – the latter would become Attorney General. Our barristers – Martin Hayden BL and Richard Nesbitt SC – explained what we wanted investigated. The atmosphere was cordial and, at the end, I felt we may have made some progress. Then we were sent what's known as the 'Statement of Facts' by the tribunal team, outlining what would be investigated. Our concerns were effectively excluded. It wasn't all that surprising but still depressed me.

I resolved that in future Raymond would be involved in any legal discussions pertaining to the IHS rather than leaving matters in the hands of barristers. If Raymond could negotiate with the Department of Health, why couldn't he negotiate on other matters? Raymond had been at the meeting, but didn't say anything. The legal protocol was that solicitors stayed quiet and barristers did the talking. This was ridiculous considering Raymond and I had a huge level of knowledge about the subject under discussion. It also jarred that any compromise agreement decided between the barristers was something I was going to have to live with. The senior counsel would move on to their next brief while I would be picking up the pieces if it all went wrong. This was a long-running tribunal and so the consequences of any compromise were going to be huge. I resolved that either Raymond or I was going to contribute in future.

So we found ourselves three days away from a tribunal in which we had limited representation and no expectation that the issues important to us were going to be dealt with. It was deeply disconcerting. It was driving me so mad that I started doing a law course at the Dublin Institute of Technology. I was spurred by a feeling that lawyers had a secret store of knowledge which I might become privy to by doing a course. After four weeks I came to the conclusion that they were just bullshitting.

There was no time to wallow. Two large boxes of documents arrived from the tribunal on Friday evening. My weekend was disappearing before my eyes. Raymond and I slogged our way through the documents on Sunday. Matters were complicated by the fact that our barrister wasn't available. Jeremiah Healy SC had been engaged, but was in the process of moving from Cork to Dublin. Raymond ended up briefing him at ten o'clock on the night before proceedings got underway.

On Monday, December 2, 1996, I went off to my first tribunal of inquiry. I felt mixed up. On the one hand I was conscious that this day belonged to the women of Positive Action, but at the same time I was yearning to represent people with haemophilia and make sure their voice was heard. It was an uncomfortable position to be in. The room where the Finlay Tribunal took place was very small with not much seating for the public. When I walked in, the women from Positive Action were already present. We shook hands, hugged each other and talked about how we hoped it would be a good day. It was good-humoured, but reinforced the feeling gnawing at me that the IHS should be keeping a low profile.

When the former Chief Justice, Mr Justice Thomas Finlay, commenced his inquiry it appeared to me that we were on a loser. He didn't seem to want to hear what we had to say and was extremely short with Jeremiah. When we sought to identify what we wanted the tribunal to cover, we were told to submit it in writing. Proceedings then quickly moved on. Our strategy of trying to push the tribunal into expanding its inquiry by our public presence didn't look as if it was going to bear much fruit. That feeling of being on the outside was accentuated by the facilities afforded to the IHS. Our legal team had not been allocated a table and ended up hassling others for places to put their folders. We were not provided with a room which meant that we had to load and unload our boxes every day. The thought of driving down, fighting for parking, carting in boxes of documents and then having no place to put them led me to only one conclusion: we were not welcome here.

Yet despite not having the red carpet rolled out for us, we persisted. Raymond sent a letter to the tribunal the following day stating that our team had not received all of the required Blood Bank documentation and so couldn't brief our experts. The following day there was a further rebuff when we were told by the tribunal that if we wanted to ask questions during the hearing they had to be submitted to them first in writing for assessment as to their appropriateness. The feeling that we were being frozen out was increased. By the second week, the scope of the tribunal became clear when we were informed that the section relating to the Blood Bank would be completed by Christmas. It seemed bizarre – we still hadn't received all of the Blood Bank documents, but the whole section relating to it was going to be completed within a fortnight.

Considering all the negative publicity caused by the Beef Tribunal, I felt this inquiry was also about restoring confidence. So, our objectives would be squeezed out as they would take up too much time. Our hope had been that by our very presence we could force some change in that plan. It was pretty clear now that our strategy was doomed.

Disillusioned, Brian, Raymond and I sat down to consider our options. We pondered everything from staying put to walking out, and the implications for everyone involved. This type of discussion was always productive and usually helped us arrive at a conclusion. In this case, the strategy was to give the tribunal one more chance but, after that, to walk out. With that in mind, Brian wrote an official letter to Raymond on December 11, 1996, to instruct him about what the IHS wanted. The letter said: "We are deeply concerned that the issues of major importance to our members, who are infected with the hepatitis C virus, are not being adequately addressed." The key points for us were to get access to Blood Bank documentation and play a fuller role in proceedings. The letter went on: "If these matters are not resolved by December 18, we will be instructing you to inform the tribunal that the IHS no longer requires representation, as continuing under the circumstances would be a waste of time."

Just as the possibility of a walk-out neared, the tribunal wrote to the IHS seeking someone to give evidence on behalf of people with haemophilia. It was a bit of a surprise, although representatives of Positive Action and Transfusion Positive had already given evidence. The tribunal team must have felt we couldn't be left out. It was decided I should give evidence. The decision to choose me as the witness was taken in a meeting between Brian, Raymond and myself. I argued it would be inappropriate for me to talk about other people's stories. I was also worried that I might be re-opening old wounds. To be honest, I also didn't enjoy the prospect of sitting in the box given the short notice. Brian and Raymond countered that it would be best for the IHS as I had more of an ongoing personal relationship with the members than Brian had. I would be in a better position to talk about the difficulties they faced.

Even though it was now more than ten years since our members were diagnosed with HIV and five since most found out about hepatitis C, there was no way anybody with haemophilia would have given evidence. The tribunal had arranged that a person could give evidence behind a screen, but it wasn't enough protection. There was still too much fear about being identified. Raymond wrote back to the tribunal's legal team to say that it was impossible for anyone to give evidence on the IHS's behalf by December 12, 1996. The letter resulted in a victory of sorts – the hearing was put back until the following day. It just happened to be Friday the 13th.

I'll never forget the night before. I didn't want to give evidence at all but, now that it was deemed essential, there was little time to prepare. It was unnerving to feel I was representing all of the IHS – the living and the dead. The preparation, in the end, amounted to less than three hours sitting with Raymond in the office in Eustace Street after spending the day at the tribunal. I went home with a few handwritten notes on a single sheet of paper. I didn't sleep.

Raymond and I arranged to meet at the Conrad Hotel near the tribunal at eight o'clock the next morning. He arrived armed with a Diet Coke and a Mars Bar which happen to be my preferred nutrition in times of crisis. I munched on my 'healthy' breakfast and went back through the evidence again. My strategy was to highlight the plight of people with haemophilia and explain the trauma. In some ways I felt, in just a small way, that the evidence might give the tribunal legal team some food for thought and bring about a change in how we were viewed. We walked from the hotel down to the tribunal. On the way up the steps, I was photographed and filmed which didn't exactly ease the tensions. Sitting in the witness box was extremely strange – I'd watched other people do it, but this didn't quite prepare me. I was the centre of attention and I felt distinctly uncomfortable. Sitting in my black suit, I could see all of the legal teams ranged in front of me. The public gallery was off to my right, but I tried to avert my gaze as it might put me off. The witness box was also uncomfortable with little leg-room which made concentration just that bit more difficult. At this point, I didn't really encourage my family to attend HIS events. I was probably being over-cautious, but I felt I needed to respect the members' fears about confidentiality. Sitting in the witness box, I wished I could see Arthur's face. Brian, however, was there to offer support.

The one thing that kept me together was the thought that Raymond would take me through my evidence. This was unusual as barristers usually do the talking in a court or tribunal. This change was made at my insistence. Part of the reason was that I trusted Raymond and this calmed me down, but the other aspect of it was that I didn't really trust barristers anymore. Raymond certainly wasn't thanking me for his lofty elevation as barristers were not particularly well disposed to solicitors addressing judges. So now there was a pair of us doing something we weren't at ease with but knew we had to see through.

My voice was very shaky at the start as I began tell the members' stories. Maybe it was nerves, but I ended up constantly clearing my throat. I kept my eyes fixed on Raymond throughout. Outlining the impact of hepatitis C on people with haemophilia, I told the tribunal: "This community has been devastated . . . It is very significant at funerals when you stand round and watch people. Really, they are wondering who is next, hoping it's not me." I also spoke about the culture of secrecy which still surrounded being infected: "People are absolutely terrified of being identified. We have a considerable amount of families who have not told anybody, even their extended families, about the infection. They are coping solely on their own . . . The fear of discovery by the employer is one of the major issues. This is very difficult when you want to attend clinics on a regular basis . . . Lies are being told about why they need to get time off work."

Thankfully, there was no cross-examination. Mr Justice Finlay asked me a couple of questions, but then I was free to stand down. My testimony took less than an hour, but felt much longer. Raymond told me afterwards that he felt I was holding back on the details of what happened to members. At the time, I felt he was probing beyond what I wanted to say. At one point he inquired about the yellow complexion of a person I was talking about. I answered the question. Raymond sought extra detail. I answered again. Raymond still didn't seem happy. I thought to myself: "If he asks me about the type of yellow one more time I am going to burst him."

After my evidence, I just wanted to get away. I was so wound up that I couldn't even consider giving an interview to the media. Perceptive as ever, Brian stepped in and ordered me off to the cinema. He put me in a car and I sped away. The movie was Neil Jordan's *Michael Collins*. Sitting in the middle of the then Virgin Cinema in Parnell Street, I tried hard to relax and unwind, but I knew that my mobile was clocking up messages by the second. Thankfully, I ended up engrossed in the film.

The hearings resumed after Christmas. Unfortunately, my

testimony didn't bring any change in the tribunal's approach. I had opened the door on the suffering of people with haemophilia but there was no change. It really galled me. The other issue which was infuriating was the question of documents. As we had only secured what's called 'limited representation', we didn't get full access to documentation. We were involved in a process, but in reality were only watching it through a glass window with our faces screwed up against it trying to work out what was going on. The other irritation was the knowledge that our members were expecting results and answers. I felt it was going absolutely nowhere from our point of view.

The process of leaving the tribunal began. I wrote a letter to it, explaining how some members contracted hepatitis C from blood products at a time when procedures were available to eliminate the viruses. I argued that our legal team had been unable to pursue this issue because we didn't receive any documents from the Blood Bank. The response I received was short: the issues I had raised were not in the terms of reference.

I also raised our concerns at a meeting with the Department of Health. Our approach was direct: if the tribunal believes our concerns are outside its terms of reference – then they should be expanded. We sought a meeting with Mr Noonan. The response said: the terms of reference could only be amended by the Dáil and Seanad and this was unlikely as the tribunal was due to complete its work in three weeks' time. We told the officials that we were going to tell the tribunal directly that unless they expanded the scope of their investigation we would be forced to walk out. They didn't seem too bothered.

Our fate had been sealed once the terms of reference were agreed. Before then, it was a political matter where astute lobbying might have got a result. But once the terms were set, the department argued it couldn't influence the chair of an independent body.

Our strategy of going into the tribunal, despite being outside the terms of reference, had been worthwhile to a certain extent. It certainly gave us an understanding of how a tribunal operated but, more importantly, where and when to fight. The public also knew something more about our problems.

The IHS executive committee met to consider our options on January 14, 1997. A unanimous decision was taken that we'd withdraw from the Finlay Tribunal. Our main objective now was to tell the public why we were taking this action and explain why our questions needed to be answered. Working out a media strategy didn't come easy. The morning after the decision I still hadn't worked out what to do when I heard RTÉ's reporter Sean Whelan being interviewed on radio about what was happening at the tribunal. After his interview, I rang him and asked him to tell the other members of the media to come to a lunchtime news conference at the Conrad Hotel. When I explained the purpose of the event, he was surprised. He warned me that this was perceived by the public as the best tribunal in modern times which, unlike the beef inquiry, was doing its job. Sean felt that I would have a hard time explaining why we were walking out. The conversation didn't do very much to calm my nerves. Getting the venue organised was also a problem. Thankfully the Conrad Hotel people were extremely kind and helped facilitate us. To their credit, the IHS was never invoiced which was much appreciated as, by this stage, we were heading into the red.

We sent out a press release before the news conference to make our position clear. We asserted that the terms of reference appeared appropriate in the beginning, but in practice our concerns about other infectious blood products were not taken on board. In fact, we were excluded. In what was fairly hard-hitting stuff, we claimed that the terms were "inadequate and unduly restrictive" to allow for a full investigation and, as such, "no useful purpose" would be served by our continued presence. It would amount to "a betrayal" of our members to stay on and also amount to a "waste of taxpayers' money".

Brian and I were now in the media glare. The journalists were not aware of our ongoing battle with the tribunal and the Department of Health as we had not gone public about it. They seemed initially sceptical about our approach. It was one of the most difficult situations I had ever had to face. Encountering tough questions and some confusion, I tried to simplify the matter. I explained our situation by saying the IHS had been "invited to the table – the party was on – but when we were at the table we were not allowed to eat". I can remember having a glass of water in front of me but not being able to hold it as my hand was shaking so much. When it was all over, I remember feeling extremely low. In the now empty room, I wondered: "Where in the name of God are we going to go from here?" I was also conscious of having raised our members' expectations. They now wanted answers to the questions about why they became infected. It was a very lonely place to be. It seemed, just at that moment, that all doors were closed to us.

As far as the press conference itself went, I was happy. We had thought carefully about what we wanted to say and delivered that message. I didn't believe that we were caught out by any question. One key gap was the fact that we didn't really have a working relationship with any of the journalists. I spoke to them individually afterwards and realised that it simply wasn't good enough to ask a reporter to inform his or her colleagues about a news conference. Our message could have been totally lost. I resolved that I would make more media contacts. And, despite my apprehension, the newspapers the following day indicated that our message had got through. One commented: "The decision yesterday by the IHS to withdraw from the BTSB Tribunal has to be regretted, but is understandable." Another said: "Health Minister Noonan should move without delay to allay their fears and assure haemophiliacs that their concerns will be addressed." The *Irish Independent* reported how I regretted giving evidence to the tribunal in the first place as I now felt it had been a waste of time.

We threw ourselves into a frantic round of media work and political lobbying. I recall one Saturday morning ringing a list of TDs. The aim was to see if we could persuade them to lobby Michael Noonan to extend the terms of reference or to set up another tribunal. I have had tough jobs before but this was one I really didn't relish as I was phoning people I had never met. I also knew that they wouldn't want to hear from me. As it turned out, most TDs were gracious. Even if they were not interested, they pretended to be. One Fine Gael TD was, however, both rude and dismissive. Maybe I caught him on a bad day, but his attitude was caustic.

This was a low ebb. We were campaigning for something which much of the public felt had already been dealt with. The IHS didn't have much money to initiate a high-profile campaign to convince them otherwise. Maybe we underestimated our power and position, but things looked pretty bleak.

One saving grace was that the issue of HIV-infectious blood became a hot topic once again within the Department of Health. This was due in no small part to what became known as the 'Kilkenny Health Worker' case. The case concerned a woman who had been given a blood transfusion which was contaminated with HIV in 1985. The Blood Bank, at a later point, realised that a particular donor had the virus but, incredibly, didn't have a policy in place where by it would check back on where the man's previous donations had gone. As a consequence, the woman, who was a health worker in Kilkenny, never found out about her condition until 1996, and then only by accident while on holiday. From a safety point of view, this was staggering. The woman had not just been denied treatment for her condition and therefore had her life put in danger, but she could also have been putting other people's lives in danger without her knowledge.

This woman's story became public in mid-December 1996. Fianna Fáil brought the matter to the floor of the Dáil at the end of January 1997. Maire Geoghegan-Quinn appealed to Mr Noonan to embrace "all the victims of this [contamination] scandal". She claimed the Government had "fled from accountability and rejected transparency. Even if they had to denigrate the dying and attack the advisers of the sick to do it, this Government lost sight of the victims, lost sight of the women, men and children whose blood the State had poisoned. It lost sight of the present pain and indeed the dark dread of the future that an infection like this brings with it". Michael Noonan's response was to pull a rabbit from the hat: he had been considering establishing a second tribunal to investigate the question of HIV infections through blood and blood products and would now expand this to include any matters which hadn't been investigated by Mr Justice Finlay. He would bring this to Cabinet.

The announcement came as something of a shock. I heard about it on the radio and while it wasn't totally unexpected, the timing was sooner than anticipated. Raymond was at lunch at the time, and I couldn't wait to tell him. Brian also arrived around the same time and we were all thrilled to bits. I was so excited that I had to jump up and down!

Looking back, it was fortuitous that our campaign for a new inquiry coincided with the Government's commitment to deal with the Kilkenny Health Worker case. Sometimes things just fall into place and this was one of those occasions. We now had a tribunal and, this time, we were going to make sure it worked for our members.

I remember making a list of priorities: a) IHS involvement in drafting of the terms of reference; b) ensuring IHS had full access to Blood Bank documentation; c) refusing to take 'second place' in the new inquiry; d) ensuring that IHS officers rather than barristers took decisions; e) demanding that Raymond be allowed to fully participate in any negotiations with the department. Members of the haemophilia community had died while we were fighting with the Finlay Tribunal. Next time out, I vowed to myself, we would be a lot sharper and far more forceful.

10

Back To The Future

My friend Austin was in the wars in 1996. He was meeting girls he wanted to form a relationship with. But working out when to tell them that he was HIV positive was a nightmare. It was a bit of a Catch 22 – if he told them in the beginning they would run away, but if he told them after the relationship had started then his silence would be viewed as betrayal. Either way Austin seemed to be doomed to being on his own. Outwardly, he was the life and soul of the party. He couldn't make it from one end of Temple Bar to the other without being stopped by ten people. Yet few knew the weight he was carrying on his shoulders.

Austin had thought he was going to die in the mid to late 1980s yet somehow he had avoided serious illness. He took a drug called AZT when it came on the market in 1987 on the basis of claims that it reduced the chances of moving from HIV positive status to full-blown AIDS. Some people who used it had survived, but many others died. Improved drugs were developed in 1991. However, the real breakthrough came in the summer of 1995. It was established that a person's HIV status could be stabilised by taking a combination of special anti-viral drugs. It became know as 'combination therapy'. By 1996, it was being widely used. The development was hugely significant, but it did come at a price. The drugs had side effects including panic attacks, vomiting and diarrhoea. If one set of drugs didn't work it was possible to try another combination. For Austin, the new medical treatment had meant he could actually contemplate a future. It seemed, however, that he was destined to remain single.

With combination therapy, Austin began to make plans. One move was to set up his own business. Part of the reason for this was a fear that if he went for a job the employer would ask him to do a medical and his HIV status would become an issue. The other reason for going out on his own was a deep distrust of big companies. Austin had become infected with HIV from a product made by a multinational firm and he didn't want to work for one of them now. Starting a business left little time for travelling to schools to give talks. The other side of it was that he now felt he had a future and the label of HIV was something he didn't want to carry with him.

Prior to combination therapy, Austin had some very dark times. As a teenager he had no plans. We spent many many nights sitting up talking and drinking Irish coffees, then wine and then whiskey – whatever it took to get through the night. The blackness of impending death is hard to deal with, especially when your friends see only life and happiness. When he moved into his twenties, however, he began to calm down and look a little to the future. In 1991, he received £70,000 compensation from the State and wisely bought a house. He might have drunk it, but someone told him that buying property would be the best thing to do. Money didn't mean anything to him at that time. Even the small bit of fun he had when awarded this substantial amount disappeared when the bank clerk viewed him suspiciously. He had to stand aside while the manager examined the cheque.

I saw the first signs of his revival in 1994, when I persuaded him to attend the Congress of the World Federation of Haemophilia in Mexico. While any IHS member was entitled to attend, twelve Irish delegates ended up going on what would be a memorable trip. At a 'get to know you' dinner before departure, I remember looking at two other delegates who were clearly in the final stages of AIDS and thinking: "Christ, these boys are not going to make it back from Mexico." In fact, I tried to convince one of them not to go. But he wasn't having any of it. The congress was a place where people with haemophilia from around the world gathered to get access to up-to-date information from medical experts. One of the other delegates was around Austin's age and also infected with HIV. I felt the bonding would do both of them some good. As it turned out, Austin took on the role of 'big brother' and really looked after the other young man.

The trip was great fun. I recall sitting in the back of a jumbo where we took up the whole line of seats. The airhostess just happened to have been a haemophilia nurse in the UK, so the drinks came fast and furious. In no time, we were all hand-dancing to awful music being pumped out through the armrest radio and into our headphones.

The reason I was travelling was to give a talk to the youth conference. When we arrived, it was with a bang: the conference was being held in a compound surrounded by Alsatian dogs. Delegates were not allowed out at night. Initially, we didn't understand why. It was certainly the main topic of conversation when the young people from all around the world gathered together for meals. After two days there was a revolution. The delegates had had enough and demanded they be transported into the capital's central square. We found out later that the dogs had nothing to do with HIV, but a fear among police officers that a youth conference could lead to political agitation and instability!

Austin certainly benefited from talking to other Irish people infected with HIV. The IHS organised weekends so people could gather together and feel safe when talking about their condition. While the seminars were in some way useful, the most important aspect was the social side. Men who were hiding terrible secrets got the chance to have a pint and talk openly in quiet corners. They could speak about their experiences and know that the other person both understood and would keep it confidential. One downside about establishing a bond is that if one person dies, those who remain often feel guilty: why did he die and I survived when we both had the same virus?

Austin had become very much part of my family. On New Year's Eve 1994, he came to Dundalk to spend the night with us and watch my daughter Aisling play the bagpipes at a dance in a local hotel. My father, being her mentor, was also present. At midnight, we walked into the main dance hall with the bagpipes roaring. I could see Austin acting as Aisling's bodyguard as she attempted to make her way through the packed room. One man foolishly robbed her cap. Austin turned around like a lion and said: "Would you ever fucking cop on?" His face dropped however when he realised he was facing a man about 6'4" tall and equally wide. Somehow we all managed to get through the night in one piece.

Because Austin was a firm family favourite, it came as a terrible fright when he got sick in the winter of 1995. He had taken great care of himself, but the illness took hold very quickly. Austin simply woke up one morning in horrific pain. His GP immediately sent him to Saint James's Hospital. I was up to his ward as soon as I heard. Lying in the bed in a room on his own, he looked white as a ghost. When our eyes met, I could tell he was scared. It wasn't just the pain which worried him, but the fact that he appeared to have contracted shingles, a form of herpes. It's possible to treat shingles, but what made Austin so frightened was that it could mean his status was moving from HIV positive to full-blown AIDS. It could mean he would deteriorate quickly and die.

My reaction was different from the way I assisted other members of the IHS. Austin brought out a strong maternal feeling in me and I set about fighting on his behalf. Due to our relationship, this was a role he was happy for me to assume. Over the next number of days, I was constantly in the hospital assessing the series of tests he was undergoing and constantly planning his homecoming. As it turned out, nothing sinister was discovered. Despite being weak, he was released after just a few days.

On the day he was due to go home, I drove to the hospital with my best friend Carol who knew Austin and how close he was to me. The atmosphere was very upbeat and lighthearted. Austin really wanted to go home to his own place, but I had been hoping he'd come back to my family home. He declined and I had to accept that he could make his own decisions. So we went up to his local shopping centre to get food with the aim of ensuring that he wouldn't have to go outside for a number of days.

True to form, Austin was trying hard to make everything as easy as possible. Sitting in the back of the car, he was cracking jokes and talking about everything other than the real issue. When we got to the shops, I tried to convince him to stay in the car, but he refused. So, we all trooped inside.

Carol and I didn't really know our way around the place and so we followed him. He was lucky to have us there at all as both of his helpers hated shopping.

At one point, Austin went to pick up something from a shelf and suddenly my vision went into slow motion. I wasn't looking at Austin through my own eyes anymore but through the eyes of one of the other shoppers. It was an image which stopped me in my tracks: a young but very frail man shuffling down the aisle; his body emaciated with seemingly no bum in his trousers. My perspective then shifted. Now I saw him with my trained eyes – free of emotion. In a second, I made an assessment: this was the look of a person on his way to an early grave. The reality suddenly hit me: Austin could die. When he had been in hospital, I busied myself. Now his frailty seemed so clear.

The emotional impact was so strong that I felt as if I had been hit by a train. I started to mumble: "Oh God, please don't let him die." My friend Carol grabbed me and said: "You can't let him see you like this. Cop yourself on." I walked the other direction for a few minutes just to regain my composure. I was scared stiff. What I'd hoped never would happen now seemed a possibility. The only reason that I didn't fall apart was that it would have been unforgivable to let him see me like that. I managed to pull myself together.

We drove back to Austin's house and put the shopping away. When we were finished, I tried to convince him again to come home with me. I used a bit of blackmail and said Aisling and John Joe would love to see him. This time he relented and we all returned to Swords. The children were delighted to see him but recognised that something was wrong. As I sat on my son's bed one night, he asked me simply: "Is Austin going to die?" My reply was equally simple: "I don't know, but it doesn't look good." For the next two or three days, the family rallied around. I think it helped bring back his spirit because he was interacting all of the time. Very quickly, he improved and his hearty laugh returned. I felt a dark cloud had been lifted. I allowed myself the luxury of believing that a cure would be found and Austin would be fine.

One of the depressing things about Austin's illness was the fact that he couldn't totally concentrate on himself as he was concerned about his mother. He knew that she was riddled with guilt about the fact that he had haemophilia because of its hereditary nature. Her logic went as follows: if he didn't have the haemophilia, then he wouldn't have contracted HIV. This meant that Austin was left in a horrendous situation where he was concerned that his illness would inflict great pain on his mother. He tried to persuade her to seek counselling, but she refused. He, therefore, continued to worry.

Every June 9, the day Austin was diagnosed with HIV, he sits down for a moment and says: "Yes, I've lasted another year." It is an ongoing struggle which other people can't really get to grips with. One problem with living with HIV is that you can be working normally and then suddenly become filled with anxiety that your future is short. A black mood can overtake and engulf you. Unfortunately, the people who are in the dark about your condition think you're just a moody bastard.

Even though the combination therapy allowed Austin to consider the future, it also reinforced the limitations on his life. One such bar was travel. From a physical point of view, he couldn't go to the Far East, South America or Africa. The reason was that if he became ill there wasn't a guarantee that there would be the expert medical treatment he would require there. The other problem was more insidious: countries such as the United States had a special visa requirement for people with HIV. This was difficult on two levels: in the first place, the special visa amounted to discrimination while, in the second, the reason why members had the virus in the first place was as a result of US-based pharmaceutical companies. On one occasion he travelled to a conference in Vancouver, Canada, and badly wanted to go and see his friend in Seattle, but it simply was impossible. He felt like a prisoner.

The greatest news I got in the mid-1990s was when Austin told me that he had met a special woman. He loved her. She knew all about him and still wanted to be there. However, Austin had to do an awful amount of soul-searching because of his health. One thought, which kept coming back again and again, was: he loved this person and wanted them to spend their lives together but was worried that he could put her at risk.

I met her in the very early stages of their relationship. I felt that Austin hoped that Emer and myself would become close. When, after a year or so, it looked as if marriage was on the cards, I ended up playing a pivotal role. An arrangement was made where Emer would come over for something of a summit. It would just be the two of us – Austin wouldn't be included. It was a bit bizarre as my daughter Aisling was extremely taken with Austin and thought Emer was taking away her future husband. My family were in the house when Emer arrived, but they let us get on with it.

Over a meal and several bottles of wine, we began to talk about what marriage to Austin meant. It was clear to me that she loved him to bits, but she was worried about what her parents' reaction might be. Despite my connection with Austin, this was something that I fully understood. Any mother would want to protect her child from the possibility that she might become a widow within a few years or risk infection as a result of a relationship. This is a problem which has led many men to keep the infection a secret from their in-laws. There is simply too much explaining to do and, at the end of it, many parents will never be able to either understand or come to terms with it. Emer's decision in the end was not to tell them.

Emer stayed with us that night and had breakfast with me the next day. She wasn't long gone before Austin was on the phone wanting to find out how it all went. I told him that he didn't need to worry about anything. From his point of view, it was important that Emer and I had now become firm friends. Austin married Emer. It was hugely important to me that he had found such happiness.

11

Come Into My Parlour

Between 1997 and 1998, another nine people with haemophilia died as the Department of Health prevaricated on establishing a tribunal to find out why they had been given a death sentence. Fewer members were dying from AIDS-related illnesses due to the introduction of combination therapy. Instead, hepatitis C was now the main killer. Eight deaths occurred in 1998. The only death in 1997 was as a result of liver failure brought on by the person's hepatitis-C condition.

Reg was a middle-aged, married man. He was a great man for the horses and we would often be on the phone to each other swapping stories. I knew that he was ill and began to call more regularly. It was one of those situations in which I was operating on two levels: on the one hand, I wanted to call to offer him support and yet I was also trying to establish whether or not he was nearing the terminal stages of liver disease.

The thing which I detected from Reg more than anything

else was a burning desire to protect his wife from the pain of knowing that he was going to die. The problem with this approach was that once he decided not to tell her how bad things were looking, he began to say virtually nothing at all. The difficulty was compounded by the fact that his wife knew he was dying but couldn't discuss it with him. She felt he didn't want to deal with it and thought it unwise to press him. Just to cap it off, his children were also aware that things were looking bleak but they couldn't talk to either their mother or their father.

With Reg clearly beginning to slip towards death, the strain on the family was intolerable. It was as if a huge elephant was sitting in the middle of the room but nobody was drawing attention to it. I talked to Margaret King about the situation and we decided that it was time to make the visit. Initially, our main concern was to ensure that Reg's family was aware of the body-bag situation. Our arrival signaled things were getting critical for Reg.

It was extremely uncomfortable walking into the house. Reg was spending all of his time in bed as he had no energy. This was difficult for him, having been an energetic person all his life. He would talk for a while and then fall asleep. I would have to wait for him to wake before resuming the conversation. He told us he knew that he was going to die soon. I asked him: "What do you want to do before you go?" He told me of some of the dreams which we all hope to achieve. I then asked him: "What do you want to do about your wife?" He stressed that that what he didn't want to do was to impose stress and strain on her. I tried to turn around his answer: "You might be causing just those emotions by not talking to her."

It was a conversation which lasted about an hour. In many ways, we were pushing an open door. Reg wanted to say things to his family before his death. He just needed to be helped along the road. He decided that he would open up. He first spoke with his wife and then separately with his children. Then the whole family gathered together in the bedroom. Margaret and I were present. It was terribly beautiful to see a family throw off their constraints and speak openly to one another. It was also terribly sad. There was a lot of crying and a lot of hugs. There were also a lot of laughs through the tears. Margaret and I stayed another day to help the family make the necessary financial arrangements and then slipped away.

Trying to get the Government to move on its commitment to establish a new tribunal involved going back to the Department of Health to meet Michael Noonan. For a man who had the reputation of being extremely tough, I found him to be friendly and reasonable. His bottom line was that he wanted the tribunal to be short – neither the public nor the Government wanted something to continue for so long that no-one could remember why it was set up in the first place. I told him that this was something we both agreed on as our members were dying and needed closure. What I neglected to tell him was that I wasn't prepared to curtail the tribunal without getting all of the answers. My list of questions was getting longer every day.

Mr Noonan suggested that the inquiry investigate anything which might have happened after December 31, 1985. This would mean the tribunal would examine whether Blood Bank-made Factor IX infected people with HIV or if foreign-made products were responsible – these were the latest HIV infections to occur and our society wanted them investigated. It would also establish why people with haemophilia became infected with hepatitis C in the late 1980s when a means of eliminating the virus was available. However, an investigation with a cut-off date of December

31, 1985, was simply a ridiculous proposition for people with haemophilia. The reason was simple: ninety-seven of the more than one hundred members to become infected with HIV were already positive by this date. There was no way the IHS could agree to an investigation which would not provide them with answers. Such a tribunal may have been expedient, but to our member it would have been simply a waste of time.

We knew from the Finlay Tribunal that the only way we could secure the answers we felt were needed was to have an input into the drafting of the terms of reference. The IHS also demanded that our solicitor, Raymond Bradley, be directly involved in the discussions. Apart from trusting Raymond implicitly now, I also wanted to ensure that I had legal backing when dealing with officials. I knew from past experience they were not going to have the IHS's best interest at heart. Our demands were agreed to.

As well as putting the officials under pressure in direct negotiations, I also mobilised the membership to lobby their local TDs if they felt this would not impinge on their secrecy. I didn't care whether it was by phone, letter or visits to their clinics, but everyone was expected to pull together. I told the members that their negotiators could only do so much. Their input was needed to ensure we got what we wanted. Even family connections were used: my father's close relationship with the Fine Gael TD Brendan McGahon was utilised. A subsequent meeting yielded an introduction to Richard Greene, the Minister for Health's programme manager. I wasn't sure what to make of this new form of political animal, but I knew he should be cultivated. Richard Greene had already been approached by one of our members whose child had been infected with hepatitis C through contaminated blood products. She simply sought him out and outlined her personal circumstances. I felt it made an impression on him.

Once a person had been informed of the situation by someone directly affected, it made it far more difficult to ignore their petition. I made a mental note to employ this strategy again.

Some of the meetings with Department of Health officials went off on very interesting tangents. I remember one official looking across the table at me and asking: "Why are you demanding that the tribunal look at matters prior to 1986?" I gave him the stock response: "Because most of our members were infected before that date." He asked me: "Have you considered the consequences of such an inquiry?" I said nothing. With a gap developing in the conversation he went on: "Because I am afraid it's going to lead to a situation where no one is going to want to ever work in the Blood Bank again." After attempting to scare us, the official then suggested: "When you put things into the hands of lawyers, they go all over the place." That last part I could sign up to, no problem.

Our main aim was to get the department to write up draft terms of reference for the new tribunal and then give them to us. This request was sent to the officials in February 1997, but nothing really happened. Initially, we'd thought the terms would emerge after the Finlay Tribunal report was published. However, the former Chief Justice's report came and went and no meeting took place. One reason we made little headway was because the lifetime of the Rainbow Government was running out. In mid-1997, there was a general election. A Fianna Fáil and Progressive Democrats coalition took power. The new Minister for Health was Brian Cowen. In reality, we had few direct dealings with Michael Noonan during his term in office. We had two meetings about a new tribunal, but the rest of the time was spent dealing with officials. Ultimately he has to accept the responsibility for failing to deliver.

157

A meeting with Mr Cowen, my fourth Minister for Health, was arranged for September 1997. My approach had become cold and clinical: I knew I had to get him on side as he was in a position to deliver for the IHS. But, I had no inbuilt respect for either him or his office.

I had never met Brian Cowen before. I had heard that he was prone to throwing his weight around. In the back of my mind, therefore, I was ready for a fight when we walked into his office. I was wrong. He spoke in a low voice, exuded calmness and appeared very comfortable with his position. The minister welcomed Brian O'Mahony, Raymond Bradley and me. He stated at the beginning that he was there primarily in a listening capacity. Even though he was effectively playing catch-up, he still had a strong presence. What I liked was that he appeared to be listening and, in a limited way, was willing to assist our cause.

The focus of the meeting centred on what a tribunal might have the powers to do. For us, things were only going to work if we could prepare by getting full access to all department and Blood Bank internal documentation. We didn't know the full story. They most certainly did. The minister seemed amenable to asking the Blood Bank to voluntarily hand over all of their papers. He suggested that the tribunal's public hearings could get under way in the new year. Until then, the IHS and his officials could work on terms of reference.

Brian Cowen was also a Minister for Health who was not afraid to make decisions. At the same meeting, Brian O'Mahony made the case for switching all people with haemophilia to recombinant or synthetic products. As these new clotting-agents were made in a lab, they offered the potential of preventing infections like HIV and hepatitis C in people with haemophilia forever. Brian argued that it would surely be a recommendation of any tribunal that the safest possible clotting-agents be used. Brian asked the minister: "Why not carry out that process now in a proactive manner rather than wait?" The officials objected to the suggestion. However, the minister ordered that these products be introduced immediately for all people with haemophilia. Walking out of the meeting, we were impressed.

Later that month, we began another battle with the Department of Health. Our opposite numbers this time were Paul Barron and Gerry Coffey. Paul Barron was the more senior official. He never let you know what he was feeling. This was simply business which had to be transacted. Gerry Coffey was more expressive and down to earth. He appeared to respond to human stories. I remember that our first meeting with them was somewhat unusual as Brian O'Mahony had to play the role of teacher and give the officials an explanation of what blood products had been used in Ireland from 1950.

By December 1997, things still weren't moving. I wrote to the department saying we hadn't received anything and we needed the tribunal's terms immediately so that our January AGM could consider them in detail. The letter, addressed to Paul Barron, stated: "There is a perception abroad that we have lost interest or are not pursuing our members' interests. This perception could be damaging to the profile of the IHS." This was a real concern. Paul Barron said they were "working" on the terms and were "committed to consulting the society" before the terms were finalised. No date was specified. To me it simply wasn't good enough: we had had the clear understanding that something was going to happen, but now we were being fobbed off.

By January 1998, I was becoming more direct. Paul Barron was receiving letters and phone calls from me demanding that we see the terms. I told him I was virtually under siege from members who were constantly asking about the tribunal. Paul and Gerry's response was similar. A regular gambit would be: "Do you know, Rosemary, that there are things which have to be done other than work for people with haemophilia?" They'd then change tack to claim that they were working extremely hard but there were only "so many hours in the day". The last resort was to appeal to my better nature and say: "We're getting there, just hang in with us." While I was busy attacking, I decided against involving the media too much at this stage. I didn't want to create bad feeling and endanger the chances that something might be achieved through discreet lobbying.

Gerry got back to us later in January and told us the terms were definitely going to be ready within a matter of days. To be honest, I didn't believe him, but hoped it might be true. One of the things Raymond taught me was to write back immediately when such offers were made. Memory of a phone call didn't constitute proof that an offer was made, but a dated letter could be used as evidence.

I felt it was time to try to push the political line by writing a strong letter to Brian Cowen. The letter expressed disappointment that a commitment contained in the Programme for Government and subsequent assurances hadn't been fulfilled. I wrote: "To date there has been a dearth of progress and we await receipt or even an indication of what is likely to be contained in the terms of reference for discussion purposes. We are disappointed that the commitments contained in your Programme for Government and the assurances received . . . have not been fulfilled." In essence, he was the person with whom the responsibility lay.

He hit back. Two days before our AGM in January 1998, he wrote back to say he was "very disappointed" with us as he'd devoted "a great deal of time" and "achieved a considerable amount of progress in a relatively short period". He then went on to list his achievements. Taken together it was certainly a body of work: introducing safer products and changing the compensation tribunal in 1997 to ensure it was there for as long as was required.

To be fair to Brian Cowen, I had been impressed with his speed on the new clotting-agents. He certainly struck me as a man of action. But the fact was that in relation to the terms of reference he, like his predecessor, hadn't delivered. I felt my criticism was valid. He clearly didn't, considering the progress made in other areas. I came to the conclusion, however, that political negotiations were a game. If things were going well, one was courteous. Yet if any minister or official didn't meet a deadline then you had to push them. The ultimate weapon was to go to the media and criticise them in public. While I now understood how things worked, it still drove me mad when things went off track. Engaging in a media campaign ate up time, energy and focus. At the end of it, we were all going to end up around the table again.

The meetings, phone calls and correspondence continued until the end of April. We decided that, in order to apply more pressure, we would hold an EGM on May 6. The day before the meeting, Raymond and I had further haggling with officials over what might be investigated by the tribunal. It was a very tense meeting – I knew we'd see the members the following evening and we still didn't have anything to show them.

The meeting was due to take place in Cork at eight o'clock in the evening. I got a call from Paul Barron to say that a fax would be sent sometime before seven. I sat in the hotel waiting for it to arrive, but nothing came. I became agitated as the minutes ticked away. Then, just fifteen minutes before the meeting, the fax finally arrived. I remember collecting it from hotel reception and bringing it to my bedroom where

Brian and Raymond were waiting. It was a one-page letter listing what was going to be included in the terms of reference. We scanned it for five minutes. Raymond and I looked at each other at the same time – it wasn't bad but wasn't good enough either.

We wrote to the department and outlined our problems, again. Our letter said the State had to be explicit about what the tribunal would investigate and, as it currently stood, some of our concerns did not seem to be covered. We said their document needed to state unambiguously: a) the list of organisations which would be investigated, the Department of Health being one of them; b) the possibility of investigating the US pharmaceutical firms which infected most of our members; c) the procedures which the new tribunal would operate by; and d) that any finding from the Finlay Tribunal report be deemed not relevant to the new inquiry. The last point was important. The fact was that we hadn't been allowed to participate in the Finlay Tribunal in any meaningful way. On that basis, we wanted to ensure that any finding of the Finlay Tribunal wasn't used as a pretext for blocking any avenue of investigation that we felt was necessary.

This time I didn't lose my head. It all just seemed to be part of the tortuous negotiation procedure in which the Department of Health habitually engaged. The officials must have known it wouldn't be enough. Prior to this, I used to question myself as to whether I had communicated our needs well enough. Now, I knew that they knew: they were simply engaging in brinkmanship.

The anger began to well up as I walked into the well-attended EGM. Some members had been worried about a tribunal and the ensuing media interest, but the prevarication by the department made this disappear. We decided to get even more aggressive and hold a news conference in Dublin the following afternoon. We informed the officials that the news conference would be held at four o'clock in the afternoon. The hope was that they would bend to our demands before then. Brian, Raymond and I left Cork before dawn. We were all very animated in the car, talking about what strategy to employ. So much so that no one realised, including Brian who was the driver, that we were drawing close to Waterford! It was a bit of a disaster as the point of leaving early was to get to Dublin as quickly as possible.

We met officials at the Department of Health at two o'clock, told them what was required and left the building feeling that a deal was on the cards. However, we didn't have it on paper as they needed to draft the document and get it passed by the minister. They told us that it would be brought to nearby Wynn's Hotel where we were due to hold a news conference. Raymond, Brian and I walked across O'Connell Bridge to the hotel and waited, again. We were late arriving for our news conference and I had to send down a member of staff to try to keep the reporters from walking out. It was a tense wait – would they finally give us the document we required?

The document finally came by courier. By this time, I was sitting in the room where the news conference was to be held, trying to stall. Thankfully, the document was a written commitment to all we wanted. We were extremely pleased as it seemed the tribunal we had long fought for was going to be able to do the things we wanted it to. We were also exhausted. One thing which we did do before going on a holiday was to send letters of gratitude to both the Minister for Health and his officials. Brian Cowen wrote back that day: "I am pleased that agreement has been reached on the issues of public importance that the society wishes to have investigated. I will now proceed to refer these issues for the consideration of the Attorney General."

Like so many other occasions, it wasn't the end of the road as the terms of reference had to be drafted by the Attorney General and then passed by the Dáil. While this was happening, we became involved in rows with the department over wording. These were the types of negotiation I found extremely frustrating. They continued for months without ever getting anywhere. The slow pace led to several more letters to Brian Cowen appealing for intervention to move things on. I believe it should and could have been expedited far more quickly. We eventually secured the terms of reference in May 1999. Over the period negotiating the terms, there had been fourteen official meetings, dozens of informal discussions and weeks wasted on preparing when I could have been actually helping people.

The main stumbling block had been our desire for the tribunal to investigate not just what happened in Ireland but also the international drug firms believed to have caused most of the infections. In his final statement on the matter, Brian Cowen said: "The proposed terms of reference include a provision which would enable the tribunal to investigate anything arising outside the State that it considers relevant." This sounded very good. However, there were qualifications. The international dimension would be examined only " . . . in so far as the tribunal considers it to be practicable, appropriate and reasonable to do so and considers that the procedures adopted for the purpose can be carried out without unduly delaying the completion of the inquiry and with a substantial expectation of being able to obtain the evidence necessary for the investigation". It was clear whoever was appointed to head the tribunal would decide whether or not this would happen. One crumb of comfort came from the minister. In an interview with RTÉ's *News At One* programme on May 14, 1999, he said: "We are looking into the products of the pharmaceutical companies, not just the BTSB." We would see.

One of the people who died while this prevarication continued was Gerard Healy from Cork – the first person with haemophilia whom I had ever met. He was the man who went public about his HIV status when few others felt they could. Gerard also tried to continue with litigation against the State, but eventually felt he had to settle so as to provide for his children. I was in Glasgow on holiday when the news of his death came through. The person who called was Gerard's father, Joe. It was August 15, 1998 – the day of the Omagh bomb on which twenty-nine people were killed. Gerard had not had an easy death. The deterioration in his health had been very difficult for his family. I managed to travel back to Dublin the following morning. I met up with Margaret King and we made the journey to Cork. When we arrived at the chapel, Joe was standing outside greeting people. My heart went out to him. He had done everything that was humanely possible for Gerard. He had gone public, lobbied every TD and was well known by medical professionals. I had seen him at so many other funerals offering support and comfort. Now, despite all that effort, he was finding it difficult to be the person receiving support rather than giving it to others. I gave him a hug and said: "I've no words for you." After the burial, I met Gerard's wife Antoinette and his children. They had supported him in every way over the previous ten years and were having to be strong again. Over a drink after the funeral, I learnt that soccer star Roy Keane had been a great help to Gerard when his health was failing. They had been friends for years and Roy always made sure he could have a seat at any game in Old Trafford and was looked after. It was much appreciated. While I had been focused on the tribunal, the staff at the IHS had also given considerable assistance to the Healy family.

Gerard's death was shocking not just because he was gone but also because HIV deaths were now becoming unusual. One other person died as a result of an AIDS-related illness in 1998 – six others who died were infected with hepatitis C. I was trying to do the impossible: help negotiate the terms of reference, provide assistance to those who were dying, keep up with all of my other responsibilities within the IHS and be there for my family. By this time, Margaret Dunne was playing a pivotal role in supporting Margaret King and me as well as providing the important services to members who had not been affected by HIV and hepatitis C. However, I had stretched things to breaking point.

12

The Question

"Fuck you and your tribunal! Let every goddam barrister you've ever sucked up to take a running jump, for all I care!"

I still shake when I recall Arthur's voice, shouting at me across our supposedly cosy breakfast-bar table. It was only weeks after it had been announced that the haemophilia community was going to get a tribunal after all – a tribunal we all so desperately wanted. However, the interminable late-night meetings had brought my marriage to breaking point.

"What was it this time that had you out all hours? Some overpaid barrister wanted to be briefed?"

I had never seen Arthur so angry and so aggressive before. Later he would explain that it was frustration; a frustration which had slowly taken hold of him after the Finlay Tribunal. Arthur had endured the long absences and intrusions into our family and private life without ever complaining. He had supported me through thick and thin as members, many of whom had become family friends, began to die. He understood how much they needed my assistance. Arthur had never complained when I disappeared into the night, sometimes not returning for a week or more. His calm response was always: "I'll look after everything here". He was a never-ending well of emotional support which I drew on constantly. Now things were different. Very different. It wasn't just the late-night meetings which gnawed away at Arthur but the inevitable drinks afterwards: gin and tonics at the local pub.

Sarcastically Arthur asked me: "Whose life were you saving in Ryans' at midnight last night?"

Arthur had more than a point. Increasingly I found myself resenting the mundanities of home life. I would find myself down in the shopping centre only to receive a call from the media or lawyers. I felt angry and put-out that I was away from the office, doing things which seemed unimportant and completely removed from what was becoming my whole goal in life – namely a tribunal which could provide answers to a community which desperately needed them. I was changing. So was Arthur.

While I didn't recognise it immediately, my husband had begun to withdraw his support over the previous months. His unbelievable capacity for support just couldn't stretch anymore. Arthur's changing attitude was at first manifested in small simple ways, but had become more deliberate. For example, he refused my requests for him to seek swaps at work and changes of duty which he had always done without question. Inevitably, rows and arguments became more tense and bitter as he refused to break appointments with friends or wouldn't ferry Aisling and John Joe from A to B.

Arthur's strategy had been to shock me to bring about change. Instead, my response was an unstated: "Well, fuck you!" Rather than confront him about the issue, I simply chose to side-step the problem. My father and closest friend

Carol were roped in to act as chauffeurs and home-help in order to take up the slack. Initially it seemed to work out well as Arthur could get on with his own life and I could return to what seemed the most important thing to me, the tribunal. In reality, however, we were drifting further and further apart both physically and emotionally. The after-work drinks and meals became a replacement for the empty void left by Arthur's increasingly obvious absence in my life.

This was a new departure. Having started dating each other as teenagers, we fell deeply in love and were married. He was twenty and I was nineteen. We put off having children for the first four years together and enjoyed a wonderfully carefree and exciting life. Even after our children were born, I don't think either of us felt trapped by the relationship. We did have arguments and sometimes fell out over certain matters. Some things were just forgiven and forgotten. Other times we just agreed to disagree. What was different about this morning was not that we were hurling abuse and accusations across the breakfast table at each other, but my realisation for the first time that there would be no respite from the bitterness and rancour which had dogged almost all of our arguments of late.

It was Arthur's sarcastic question about whose life was I saving over late-night drinks which finally made me understand what was driving his anger and frustration. He had given his complete support when the tragedy of HIV infection turned to illness and death. No task was too much and no absence was too long. What I had overlooked was that this was in fact conditional on the belief that by supporting me he was assisting some of the people who were infected. We'd often lain awake talking about how extremely lucky we were, with two beautiful children and a great family. We both felt that any small sacrifice we made was nothing compared to the suffering which many families within the haemophilia community were now going through. But with an inquiry about to commence, and after his experience of the Finlay Tribunal, Arthur no longer believed in what I was doing. He wasn't prepared to make the same sacrifices he had made before.

In something of a taunt, he said: "You and the lawyers are never going to find out anything that they don't want you to find out. No-one is going to be held responsible."

There was then a pause. Arthur looked down at his plate before looking back up at me. This time in a quiet but imploring manner he asked me: "Is this more important than your family?"

The question left me dumbstruck. I loved the man deeply, but couldn't escape the fact that I felt compelled to secure the answers the haemophilia community needed. It was a burning feeling inside me which would only be quenched when the tribunal had happened. In my heart of hearts, I wanted to respond to Arthur and say: "The answer is yes. Just now and for the next while, yes." But I knew that could end our relationship. Instead of saying what I felt, I answered Arthur's question with a straight: "No." Maybe it was the way I said the two-letter word, but Arthur didn't seem convinced. He had good reason, but wasn't in a position to say anything else. We left it at that. We'd talked, but resolved nothing.

I began to feel increasingly unhappy. The meetings I was attending were often long and fractious, with little achieved at the end except a date for a further round of discussions. I felt constantly guilty that I was missing out on things at home. Despite the intensity of those feelings, I still continued to put the job first. Arthur did try to rebuild our relationship. Occasionally we managed to get out for a quiet drink, but even then there was tension when my mobile would ring and I would spend maybe half an hour discussing the latest twist in the tribunal with lawyers or journalists. On returning to the table, the phone would ring again after only a few minutes. He would end up looking at me and saying: "Why did you bother coming out at all when you're still working?"

The whole issue really blew up one morning in October 1998. I'd woken up feeling particularly bad after yet another round of talks which went nowhere. I was at a low ebb. Arthur saw I was distressed and offered to bring Aisling to her bagpipe lessons, something I usually did. I was extremely thankful and promised to get home early. It was yet another promise I didn't keep. Arthur's patience finally snapped.

When picked up the phone to make contact I knew he was going to be furious. What I wasn't prepared for was his ice-cold voice and slowly delivered words: "I think it's best that you don't come home now. Stay away tonight." Things might have been different had I heeded his warning, but that's not my nature. I wanted to get home immediately. I wanted to see Aisling and John Joe. I wanted to sort it out now. In one way, I felt I was the person who was wronged as he was the problem. I simply said: " Arthur, I have to come home." I hung up and headed for my car. I drove back to Swords and rang the house just as the car turned on to our street. Aisling picked up the phone and, realising that I was close by, ran out the door. She had made it to my car when I saw Arthur coming up the road after her. It was a horrendous situation. I simply drove off with Aisling sitting beside me. I could see he was angry and I didn't want to have a screaming match in the middle of the street.

Arthur and I had always kept any difficulties between ourselves and away from the children. On this occasion, we failed. I lost it, he lost it and Aisling was caught in the middle. The fact that she was part of our row – something I caused–

is still a reason for regret. At the time, however, I believed that right was on my side. I drove to the Great Southern Hotel at Dublin Airport and set about getting a room. When Arthur called the next day, I informed him in my official voice that I was too busy to talk. Once again Arthur was thinking for the family. He suggested that he move into an apartment and I stay at home with the children. After three days, he packed his bags and I moved back home. We had separated.

I still went back to work the next week. However, things were very different for me. Even though I had been increasingly living my life independently of Arthur, he was always 'there'.

Arthur gave me such a sense of emotional security that when he was no longer around, I felt vulnerable. Friends and family were all extremely supportive, but there was a yawning chasm in my life.

I did have contact with Arthur, but it was very infrequent in the beginning. We spoke over the phone, but the conversation was limited to practical issues around him getting to see Aisling and John Joe. We were both still seething and simply couldn't be in the same room together. Days would pass before contact was established again. The first time we spoke about our separation was when Arthur rang and asked me: "What happened? What's gone wrong?" It led to us meeting for the first time since that awful night. We decided to meet in a bar so that our conversation wouldn't end up in a screaming match. Arthur looked destroyed emotionally and it provoked a response in me. While previously we had been hurling abuse at each other, now I wanted to comfort him. We didn't resolve any of the problems which had led to our break-up, but something had been triggered.

We went on to have other meetings. There was an unstated desire to avoid rows. We were sticking to our guns in relation to what had gone wrong, but there was a need to ease the pain and a willingness to get to the bottom of things. In our discussions, we began to move away from the anger and hurt and instead talk about why things had gone wrong. As weeks turned into months we began to spend an increasing amount of time in each others' company and a feeling developed that we didn't want to be apart. It was strange as we began to relax again with each other. It also slowly began to dawn on me just what I was in danger of losing. I realised that I had taken Arthur and the family for granted. I had got it wrong. I had hurt Arthur and the kids. I had been stupid. The answer to the question about whether the tribunal was more important than my family was now an emphatic "No".

Despite our problems, our families stayed in touch. My father had been devastated by our break-up, not just for me, but because he loved Arthur so much. He maintained his relationship with Arthur in the hope that there could be a reconciliation. This was something which became a possibility, but Arthur and I had a fear about getting back together again in case it didn't work out. We couldn't put Aisling and John Joe through that again.

We reached a decision on our future. We would spend Christmas together as a family and, if it worked out, then Arthur would come home. We spent the festive period in Carlingford, County Louth, which was traditional. It turned out to be a new beginning which seemed impossible only a matter of weeks earlier. Our separation was over. I agreed that I needed to re-prioritise my life and not let other people dictate the way it was going to be run. It was a totally different perspective and a turn for the better.

Life returned to normal – a normality which entailed a tribunal and dealing with some of the most difficult and emotional times. Thankfully, my family was able to see me through.

13

A Difficult Birth

Margaret King decided it was time to retire in 1999. She had been in ill health for some time and was reaching retirement age, but it was still a shock. We were sitting in our new offices in Smithfield, Dublin, when she said: "I'm going to retire." Having heard this once or twice before, I responded: "But are you really going to?" She said this time she really was.

A special party was arranged for her in the office. As Margaret didn't want to cause a fuss, only a small number of people were invited. It was one of those affairs where you smile broadly but are breaking up inside. It had been Margaret who inspired me to get involved more than a decade before, and now she was leaving. Her leaving would inevitably cause a huge void.

Despite our age difference, Margaret and I had got on famously, mostly because of our similar sense of humour. I remember the two of us organising a fancy dress for the members. We wanted to get away from the notion that people seemed to only get together at funerals. I dressed up as

Margaret King. I got one of her uniforms and name-tags, but spiced it up by cutting three feet off the length of the hemline, turning it into a mini-skirt. Margaret managed to go one better by getting one of my small black skirts, a polo-neck and then rounding the whole thing off by wearing one of my red bras over it. She won the competition hands down. Margaret was brilliant at whatever she did. I couldn't even beat her in a fancy-dress competition.

There was no way I could have helped people in times of crisis without Margaret's guidance. She had shown me all the skills about offering support: quietly, gently and even anonymously. One thing I found astounding was her ability to never let her emotions show. After one particularly trying experience, I asked her why she didn't appear moved. She said simply: "I keep all that – it's not for now." The only time I ever saw her break down was when Jerome Stephens died. She'd been so close to him that it wasn't possible to hold back.

Margaret had such an impact on so many people that everyone wanted to get involved when her retirement became known. One idea was to make a book out of all the tributes paid to her. It was entitled *A Forever Friend*. In his introduction, Brian O'Mahony wrote: "She did not allow herself to be consumed by the death and despair which surrounded her. Instead she helped people immeasurably to cope. To quote Wordsworth: 'She was the nurse, the guide, the guardian of our hearts and soul of our moral being.'"

My small piece was entitled *Just Like An Eternal Flame*. I spoke about our first trip out of Dublin and how I booked single rooms but we ended up together talking all night. After that, we were inseparable. I said: "I will always treasure the sight, when I woke up in the middle of the night, of spotting a tiny dot of light in the darkness. It was Margaret, sitting up smoking and contemplating the meaning of life. She was just like the eternal flame, always there, always comforting. I always had a philosophy of 'it will do' whereas Margaret came from the old school of perfection." I finished off my piece by saying: "In my head, I will always hear the words: 'Attention to detail, Rosemary.'"

But life went on. The year 1999 had begun well as the Government had agreed to provide more compensation to people infected with HIV from blood products. This announcement was not just welcome, but also somewhat surprising as the provision of £8 million back in 1991 was regarded as "full and final". It was decided to expand the terms of reference of the Hepatitis C Compensation Tribunal so that members infected with HIV would be able to make a claim there. The next step was for the Government to bring legislation to the Dáil. With an unambiguous commitment, I was happy that a full, final but fair settlement would shortly be put in place. I could turn my mind to other matters.

My main focus was trying to get through some of the tribunal preliminary work. I had anticipated that while its legal team needed to retain its independence, it would work closely with the IHS. The Finlay Tribunal team seemed to have a good relationship with Positive Action and we hoped for the same. That hope was quickly challenged. The first indication of a problem was in November 1999 over a seemingly simple matter of computer software. Raymond's law firm had a package which could categorise thousands of documents and make it easy to recall them on screen. He offered it to the tribunal, but was rebuffed. Worse still, the tribunal declined to share its system with us. I phoned the company which made the tribunal's software package. But, when I told them who I was, the person on the other end of the line just sighed. Then he said: "I am sorry, but I have been asked by the tribunal's legal team not to sell this system to you or talk about it." Obviously, there was not going to be the close relationship I anticipated.

This was only one of a series of problems which developed. The IHS was already facing difficulty from the Blood Bank over access to their internal documentation. Raymond was being allowed into their office, but they seemed to be making it as difficult as possible for him. For a start, he was not given a set area to work from each day, but was placed in different rooms. On one occasion he had to operate from a lab. The more important issue was that he was being prevented from taking away photocopies of the documents he deemed important. Instead, he had to note the document, tag it, keep a record of its index and scribble notes on what it contained. The Blood Bank didn't afford him the opportunity of looking again at a document if, for example, a month later he found a detail in another paper which appeared relevant. The other issue was that the Blood Bank would photocopy any document which Raymond took an interest in. They could see what he was interested in and prepare a defense in advance.

With all this going on, it was therefore quite a surprise when medical journalist Fergal Bowers asked me: "How are you getting on with the documents from the Blood Bank?" I responded: "I haven't seen them." He then told me that he had seen a letter from the Blood Bank's CEO, Martin Hynes, to the Department of Health's Paul Barron which indicated that our solicitors were being allowed to remove copies of the files. I was astounded and dumbfounded. Was the Blood Bank trying to make itself look good with the department by making statements it would refuse to abide by? I raised the issue at a meeting between the IHS, the Blood Bank and the department. Martin Hynes stubbornly refused to let us remove the photocopies. It seemed that if the Department of Health couldn't compel the Blood Bank, we were just going to have to wait until all of the documents were circulated by the tribunal. The row underlined the fact that once more we were facing a battle.

While Raymond didn't get the chance to remove the documents, he was able to brief us on what he saw. Every now and again he would rush into the office with lots of paper and an excited expression on his face. The first thing he was able to tell us was that the Blood Bank had been informed in 1986 by Professor Temperley about his suspicions that Irish-made Factor IX was responsible for HIV infections. Raymond also told us that there seemed to be some discussion about the matter by the board of the Blood Bank. What still seemed unclear was why people with haemophilia were testing positive for HIV in 1986 when Factor IX was supposed to be heat-treated to eliminate the virus. It appeared our suspicions were founded in fact, but the full story had yet to come out.

The piece of information which most shocked me was the knowledge that both the Department of Health officials, Gerry McCartney and Gerry Coffey, had been on the board of the Blood Bank. Gerry Coffey, the man to whom Brian O'Mahony had explained the history of blood products at our initial meeting, was on the board in the 1990s. Gerry McCartney, who was the senior official negotiating the 1991 HIV settlement, was on the board in the early to mid-1980s, including during the meeting where it appeared the Factor IX HIV infections were discussed. I couldn't believe it. Was this the issue he wanted to raise with me years earlier in a Dublin hotel? Neither had ever said they were not on the board, but they didn't declare themselves either. Maybe it was possible to secure this information through Blood Bank publications, but I hadn't focused on such appointments prior to the tribunal.

I thought back to conversations I had with Gerry McCartney about the Blood Bank and the problems the IHS felt existed there. I felt embarrassed. What had I said? What might they have known but not informed me about? Unfortunately, Gerry was now dead and I couldn't get the answers I wanted. The other interesting detail was that the chair of the board in 1986, Noel Fox, still held the post in 1989 when the IHS began litigation against the State. I was very interested in the evidence he would give to the tribunal. Would he validate our suspicions that the board of the Blood Bank knew since 1986 about the Factor IX HIV infections?

Raymond was also able to inform me that the Blood Bank signed an indemnity in the late 1980s which would ensure that Armour Pharmaceuticals – one of the international drug firms – would not be liable if its product caused infections. This was around the time when blood banks around the world were introducing processes to eliminate hepatitis C from clotting-agents. Why did the Irish Blood Bank sign an indemnity? Why did Armour feel it was necessary to secure such an indemnity?

It astounded me: first we had Gerry McCartney on the board of the Blood Bank when it became known that people using Factor IX became infected with HIV; the same official played a key role in negotiating an out-of-court settlement in 1991 in relation to HIV infections for which the Blood Bank did not admit any liability; then we had Gerry Coffey negotiating the terms of reference of an inquiry which would investigate the actions of a board he was a member of; now we had an indemnity being given to a massive pharmaceutical firm.

The documents often led to more questions than answers. The one saving grace was that this preliminary work allayed my fear that there was nothing for a tribunal to investigate.

Up to this point, I had fretted that the public could turn on the IHS for having demanded an expensive inquiry where it had not been required. The information Raymond had brought dispelled that notion.

On September 27, 1999, the tribunal held its introductory hearing. The purpose was to establish who wanted to participate in the proceedings. It was the first chance I got to see the Tribunal chairwoman. Judge Alison Lindsay graduated from University College Dublin with a degree in history and politics but went on to the Kings Inns and qualified as a barrister in 1975. She engaged in general practice until 1996 when appointed to the bench. Judge Lindsay was known by many people with haemophilia as she sat for a number of years on the Hepatitis C Compensation Tribunal. When she was appointed to head the haemophilia tribunal, many of the wider public recognised her name because her father, Paddy Lindsay, had been Master of the High Court. At the introductory hearing, the judge said she would investigate and publish her report "as speedily, efficiently and economically as possible". The expectation was that full hearings could begin as early as December. However, this wasn't possible because the tribunal legal team and the IHS got involved in a further spat.

Two separate issues resulted in a stand-off. The first was a decision by the tribunal that it was going to examine all of the documentation submitted by the bodies participating in the inquiry. After an evaluation of the papers in relation to the terms of reference, the tribunal lawyers would exclude what it felt was irrelevant and circulate what papers it deemed pertinent. I couldn't believe nor accept that we were only going to be allowed examine some rather than all documents. The whole point of the exercise was to get to the truth, but here was the tribunal's legal team trying to decide what was in and what was out. The other matter related to our desire to commence the tribunal with personal testimony from those who had been infected with HIV and hepatitis C. We felt this was important as the public would have a greater understanding as to why a tribunal was necessary. I wanted the hearings to be anchored in the human tragedy of what had occurred rather than in statistics. It was also a factor that some members might have died by the end of the tribunal if they were not allowed to testify at the beginning.

On December 9, 1999, these issues became public when the tribunal sat for another preliminary hearing. The IHS argued that its clients should have full access to all documents and not just what the tribunal's legal team deemed appropriate. Our legal team also stated that the tribunal should grant it costs for the legal bills it had already incurred. The day sticks out in my mind because the hearing happened to take place on my parents' wedding anniversary. The proceedings only lasted a day, which prompted my father to remark: "That tribunal didn't last very long, did it? " He thought it was all very funny. I responded: "Do you think I was putting in all that work for one day? There's more to come."

Just ten days later, I was lying in bed listening to RTÉ Radio 1 and waiting for *Sunday Miscellany* when the phone rang. It was a neighbour from Dundalk. My father had taken a turn and was waiting on an ambulance. From dozing with the papers, I was suddenly wide awake. The fact that my father hadn't phoned me himself set-off alarm bells. I rang my brother who lives in Dundalk and he left immediately for the hospital.

A mad scramble ensued in my house as I tried to grab a few things. Arthur was getting the car ready while I asked Aisling whether she wanted to come. It was a bit of a stupid question considering their close relationship. As she was getting her stuff, I shouted out: "Bring your bagpipes." When she asked why, I said quietly: "Because I think granddad is dying," To this day, I still don't know where I got that feeling from, but deep inside me I knew I was right.

When we arrived at Dundalk Hospital, my brother Billy was waiting for us. The medical staff had established that my father had had a stroke. Thankfully, he was still conscious and so we were able to spend some time together. From my experience of working with people with haemophilia I knew that this stroke, which is a form of brain haemorrhage, was probably going to kill him. It was one time I wished I didn't have that foresight.

The only thing which gave me a real boost during my father's illness, apart from my family, was the sight of Austin walking into the foyer of the intensive care unit. I had just left my father so the nurses could attend to him when Austin turned up. He sat down beside me and held my hand. The funny and brilliant thing about it was that our roles had now been reversed: he was the person who constantly hovered offering comfort and support. Other familiar faces were there, including Margaret Dunne and Brian O'Mahony from the IHS. The numbers increased as time went on.

My father died after just two days in hospital. I had hoped to bring him home, but it proved to be impossible. For the next couple of days, I was in complete shock but somehow managed to muddle through. My defenses collapsed on New Year's Eve. It was the eve of the millennium and we were invited to celebrate at Arthur's sister's house. Aisling struck up on the bagpipes at the stroke of midnight. The wild sound, which my father had so loved and had nurtured a similar appreciation for in my daughter, brought home to me that he was gone forever. I was inconsolable.

I returned to work just over two weeks later. I couldn't

think of anything else to do. By this time, the tribunal had dismissed our demands: it would decide, rather than the IHS, on the order of witnesses; we would not have access to all documents; and our legal costs would not be entertained at this point in time. Raymond, Brian and I met to consider what our next move would be. One option was to see if our barristers could communicate with the tribunal's legal team and negotiate a compromise. I was opposed to this. I felt the only way to deal with this issue was to fight. We had tried the diplomatic route before in the Finlay Tribunal but to no avail. The executive of the IHS decided to support my recommendation that we go to the High Court in an attempt to overturn the tribunal's decision.

Before taking such a move, it was necessary to talk to the members and so a meeting was organised in January 2000. The venue was the Ormond Hotel in Dublin city centre. The scene was very ordinary with a hundred chairs laid out in a function room facing a stage with a table and microphone. What happened, though, was extraordinary. I was already seething with the way things were developing and got more and more angry as I worked out what I was going to say. The meeting was very well attended with more people than seats. Brian spoke initially about what had happened and Raymond detailed the procedures and protocols involved. My voice was in sharp contrast to Raymond's soft considered delivery. I barked into the microphone that Brian, Raymond and I couldn't do much more to progress things, apart from go to the courts. We had tried to get the tribunal to do what was right, but had been dismissed out of hand. What was really required now was for the people at the heart of this disaster to take over. I sat down and the meeting was opened to the floor. One man stood up and verbalised what I knew many others were thinking: "We've been pushed around too long and it's time to make a stand." If the tribunal didn't want to pay attention then the members were going to make sure it was as difficult for them as possible. There was surge of anger which led to a startling development: sixty-four people came forward and said they would be prepared to give evidence. This was dramatic as people with haemophilia usually shunned publicity, but now they were demanding that their stories be told. Up to this point only five members had indicated that they would give evidence about their personal stories. Now the tribunal was going to be faced with refusing dozens of people who wanted to articulate – from the beginning – just what a colossal tragedy had occurred to a tiny community.

Thankfully the issue was resolved the following month. In a U-turn which surprised many, the tribunal decided that our legal team would have access to all documents and our members would be able to testify at the beginning of the proceedings. I don't know why this happened, but I was delighted. I felt it was a vindication of a robust response to barriers being placed in our way. I resolved that a similar approach would be taken in relation to the issue of costs which was now in the hands of the Government.

However, before that, the IHS had to secure statements from all of the members who wanted to give evidence to the tribunal, outlining what happened to them or their loved ones. The process was extremely testing. Everyone came in feeling nervous and unsure if this was the best thing to do. Once this was overcome, they began to tell their stories. It invariably meant speaking about matters of immense pain and sadness which had often been bottled up for years. Fathers told us how they lost sons, while mothers spoke of the heartbreak of not being able to get over the loss. It cut me to the core. I was writing down page after page of living testimony to the incredible hurt inflicted upon this community.

One mother told me how her husband received a letter from their son explaining that he was HIV positive due to contaminated clotting-agents. He just couldn't tell him face to face. The father, who was elderly at the time, was devastated. When he died, the mother told me that she discovered the son's letter in one of her husband's pockets. It was worn away from having been carried around with him constantly.

Once we gathered the statements, Raymond and I tried to match the stories to issues which required investigation: several members appeared to have experienced a delay in being told they'd contracted HIV and hepatitis C; some spoke of the absence of counselling and other supports; there were also the people infected at a time when it appeared that safe blood products were on the market.

Once we had compiled a list, it was also important to go back to the people volunteering to give evidence. I spent a lot of time ensuring each person had considered what impact their evidence might have on other family members. Many had never spoken about this outside their family circle and it was now about to be relayed to the nation. The members knew they could remain anonymous, but I felt it was essential that they secure permission from family members to speak of the aspects of their lives which involved them. Each person was reassured that they would be able to pull out of the process at any time. They were also able to change their statements. It gave people a lot of comfort, but meant that I was dealing with up to thirty people at the one time as they considered what they wanted to say.

The gathering of statements also brought me back into communication with people from whom I had drifted apart. It was relatively normal, after the death of a person with haemophilia, that my contact with the rest of their family would be infrequent. Therefore it came as a nice surprise to meet people like Mary. Her husband, Norman, had been someone I knew well. Norman died as a result of HIV infection caused by Factor IX. The blood products he used, he believed, were made and distributed by the Irish Blood Bank.

Norman was an outdoors type during the day, but a person who loved to sing and dance at night with friends – a real live-wire. Unfortunately, in the last stages of his life he was suffering from AIDS-related dementia. One day we had gone for a walk in Dublin and stopped off at Bewley's Café when confusion overtook him. He was standing at the counter, but couldn't make up his mind what he wanted to drink. The people behind us were becoming impatient so I remember buying tea, coffee, 7-Up and orange juice to cover all eventualities. I guided him like a child over to the table as his ability to walk had also diminished. I just kept talking until the person I knew came back to me. A similar situation developed in a video shop with the staff staring at his odd behaviour.

Next we went to the bank as Norman felt he needed some cash. I had enough to cover whatever he needed but, as is common when people have dementia, once they get an idea into their heads it is very hard to persuade them otherwise. I stood at the wall as he queued for the teller. By the time he got to the desk, however, his memory had slipped again. He suddenly shouted from the front desk: "Rose, will you tell these people my name and tell them to give me my money?" Slightly embarrassed, I rushed up to help him as the rest of the customers looked on. I felt the staff were trying to evaluate if I might be manipulating this man who was obviously confused and yet taking out a large amount of money. The transaction was finally completed and we left quickly.

We walked along Grafton Street and stopped where an artist was sketching portraits. Nothing would do him but to have his likeness drawn. I stood back thinking: "This will be nice for his wife and family as he doesn't have long to live." Shortly afterwards, he had a brain haemorrhage. I spent many days and nights in the hospital with Norman and his family. It was horrible, as he recovered physically for a period of time, but his quality of life was severely reduced. Norman effectively lost all his dignity and had to be fed and changed like a baby.

So when Mary walked in through the door of the IHS and said she wanted to testify at the tribunal it was very emotional for both of us. We sat together and went back over the story of her relationship with Norman and how he could have taken an independent legal case against the State over his infection but chose to stay within the 1991 HIV group settlement to bolster it. What made it all the more depressing was that Mary was also HIV positive. She had known Norman was HIV positive before getting married but unfortunately became infected. Mary had to cope not only with her husband's diagnosis, illness and death but now had to cope with the realisation that she too had the virus. I hadn't met Mary for several months and was delighted to see that she had things under control. Once again, combination therapy had helped her to live her life to the full. She told me that she was giving evidence as she knew that if Norman was alive he would have done so.

Vincent was another person I regained contact with. He was a beautiful man who had already come through a nightmare by the time I first met him. In 1985 he had his appendix removed at Saint James's Hospital. However, the following day his surgeon informed him that his appendix had been healthy. He had actually been suffering from gastritis. What Vincent learned later was that he received a large amount of a clotting-agent for the purpose of the unnecessary operation. He found out in January 1986 that this clotting-agent had contained a virus. He was HIV positive.

By the time we met in 1989, he was living life like Austin – every day as if it were his last. When he came into the office ten years later, it was very clear that he wanted the tribunal to provide answers to what happened. His logic was: "I answer for my mistakes, so why shouldn't they?" What struck me while talking to him was that he would be better able to deal with his HIV status if he knew how and why it had happened.

The statements given to me by people like Vincent were extremely compelling, but they were not enough in themselves. A lot of time was spent securing each person's medical charts to verify their recollections. It wasn't an easy job to obtain the charts from hospitals and we needed to be careful about gleaning the required information from them.

The statement which stood out in my memory more than any other was that of Fionn – the missing man. Back in 1991, Margaret King had been sure that the IHS's figure of 103 people infected with HIV was wrong. She had tried to confirm her hunch that one other man had been infected, by checking with former colleagues in Saint James's Hospital, but to no avail. In the end, the mystery was resolved when the 'missing' man phoned the office in 1999.

The following day Raymond and I visited him at home. Fionn was a very shy, retiring person. My main concern was for his health and, as the IHS had not been in contact, to ensure that he could avail of State compensation for his infection. It came as a shock to discover that he had already received it in 1991. He told me his mother had helped secure the money and he had travelled to Dublin to collect the cheque.

He didn't know, however, who had helped to organise this. This really threw me. The other fascinating aspect of Fionn's case was that he seemed to only have ever used the Irish-made blood product cryoprecipitate. It opened the possibility that not only had Blood Bank-made Factor IX been infected with HIV but also 'cryo'. Considering the State had paid out compensation to him as far back as 1991, it seemed possible that the Department of Health also knew about this for nearly a decade. Fionn, however, chose not to give evidence to the tribunal and wanted to stay firmly in the background.

While I continued to help gather witness statements, I also got involved in intensive lobbying over legal representation. The reason was that the Department of Health and the Blood Bank were able to pay a team of lawyers on an ongoing basis. We didn't have the resources to do this. We suspected that several lawyers didn't want to get involved in our case because they would be forced to wait until the end of the tribunal before they would be paid. The IHS also didn't have the cash to pay for expert advisors to help interpret highly technical documents. This, we believed, was a serious disadvantage.

An offer was made by the State to pay some of our legal costs on an ongoing basis, but it wasn't enough. This was underlined when our accountant looked at the IHS books. His advice was that we could not participate in the tribunal as the necessary financial guarantees were not in place. The fact was that we already owed a lot of money to our legal team. The auditor insisted that the IHS was technically insolvent as the liabilities far exceeded the available assets. The problem was so acute that the staff, including myself, were placed on protective notice. If the IHS finances didn't improve – we would be let go.

This put me on a collision course with the new Minister for Health, Micheál Martin, who had transferred into the post from the Department of Education. Brian Cowen had moved on to the Department of Foreign Affairs after the resignation of Ray Burke. I remember my first meeting with the man considered by media gurus to be one of Fianna Fáil's bright boys as he was young but extremely shrewd. My first impression was that he was remote and somewhat unfriendly. Yet, by the end of the meeting he seemed to be more responsive to our demands.

The negotiations followed the pattern of old with promises made by officials that documents were on their way, but nothing then arriving. I'm sure the officials would argue the delays were understandable, but I found it unforgivable. Within a short space of time the Minister for Health did break new ground though. I was standing in the kitchen of the IHS's office one night making a cup of tea when my mobile rang. The voice on the other end of the line said: "Hello, this is the Minister for Health." I was sure that it was Margaret Dunne messing. Micheál Martin had a different style in which he would often communicate directly in the hope of sorting things out one-on-one. This particular call led to further meetings but, at the end of it, we still made no progress.

Our first row happened on prime-time radio and the exchanges got very bitter. I had prepared well for RTÉ's *Morning Ireland* and arrived at the station an hour early to re-read material in the car with Raymond. I walked into the building just after eight and headed for the waiting-room where tea and coffee was available for interviewees. It came as quite a surprise when I was informed that the minister was inside and didn't want me join him. I was thrown – I had expected he would be interviewed on the phone from Cork but, more importantly, hadn't ever before come across this type of behaviour. I went to the smoking room where business journalist Geraldine Harney kindly gave me a cigarette and chatted until it was time to go on air.

I was extremely nervous when we went into the studio. While I never like confrontation, this appeared to be the way we were going. Mr Martin was very aggressive and I decided to fight fire with fire.

Once on air, the minister said that he would try to do something for us, but that he didn't respond to deadlines. I snapped back by saying our members operated under a different type of deadline – life and death. I argued that people with haemophilia could end up paying for an inquiry into how they were infected unless he gave a written commitment that this would not come to pass. We spiralled downwards. Mr Martin tried to suggest the row was about money for lawyers – something which would not garner much public sympathy. I responded that while in opposition, Fianna Fáil condemned the legal approach used against the late Brigid McCole, but now, in power, was employing the same tactics. The minister was clearly irked: "What I will not do from now on is to be subjected to the gun-to-the-head approach." I interjected and said: "Our members might die tomorrow." I managed to add: "Death is calling them, minister" before the presenter, Richard Crowley, brought hostilities to a close.

Afterwards, I was in a furious state. I felt Micheál Martin hadn't understood what the IHS was trying to say or else was hiding behind legal advice. I refused to shake his hand. I don't actually remember the moment. I was incandescent with rage. An RTÉ reporter later reminded me of the episode.

Later that night, the subject would dominate the *Questions and Answers* programme on RTÉ. The minister detailed that his department had come up with a package of £600,000 which would cover historical legal costs, preliminary work for the Lindsay Tribunal and also funds for expert witnesses. This was certainly true, but it didn't get away from the fact that if the ultimate bill was higher, then we could be liable. We wanted him to write a letter specifically stating that they would pick up the bill in that eventuality.

The journalist Eamon Dunphy took up our case with his usual combination of flair and aggression: "The citizens of this State want those people to be protected and to be given a fair chance." Micheál Martin responded: "So do I." Eamon came back: "Then do it – give them the guarantees!" Mr Martin said the Government's approach was in line with the previous tribunals. Ivana Bacik, the Reid Professor of Law at Trinity College, who was also a guest, asked him: "Why don't you just give them a comfort letter or some other form of written assurance – given that your department is dealing in good faith, given that they are the victims?" Micheál Martin said: "They are not going to be caught in any shape or form unless their own solicitor sues them and I think he has said he won't do that." Frances Fitzgerald of Fine Gael said: "You've said it in words that they are not going to be out of pocket – what's the problem?"

The chairman, John Bowman, increased the pressure: "Why not give them a letter?" This time Micheál Martin explained: "There's a difficulty in terms of two issues." The first concern of the minister was that he could not be seen to be writing a blank cheque for any party. The second point was an apparent concern for "the conduct of the tribunal, in terms of the chairperson of the tribunal's authority being undermined". Micheál Martin said he had very strong legal advice on the matter. However, this contention was challenged by Ivana Bacik: "You're hiding behind the issue of the chairperson's authority . . . I think that's disingenuous because . . . her authority is not going to be diminished by a written assurance or some letter."

The row was kicked around for twenty minutes. It was good to see Mr Martin being put under pressure. However, the most telling moment came when the man who asked the question identified himself as having hepatitis C. He told the programme: "You're talking about 240 people's lives deteriorating every day of the week. We're not getting the priority we should be. And, it's over to you, minister." There was just one dissenting voice in the audience who expressed the view that the Minister for Health was being "held to ransom" by the IHS.

Our next strategy was to publicly call for the tribunal to be postponed while, behind the scenes, putting on more pressure so that a deal could be hammered out and proceedings would get under way on time. It didn't get universal support. The *Irish Examiner* editorial stated: "There is something unseemly about the IHS getting hung up on the financial rewards for expert witnesses. The society is demanding a blank cheque for its lawyers and witnesses, while the remainder of society is expected to follow due procedures." The paper concluded by arguing: "The minister has been more than reasonable and is perfectly justified in withholding a blank cheque. Indeed, it would be irresponsible of him to do otherwise." *The Sunday Business Post* took a different line. Emily O'Reilly wrote: "Micheál Martin sounded depressingly like his departmental predecessors – obsessing on costs in the very week that the Government announced record revenue levels. Is it too much to ask, that those who have suffered, and will suffer, awful, premature deaths through the incompetence of a State body, at least be told why they had to die?"

The next step in our campaign was to arrange a walk-in on Mr Martin's Cork city constituency clinic. I travelled to Cork, but the people who were going to apply the pressure were members from the Munster region. My aim was to make it as difficult as possible for the minister to say 'No' to our demands. The best way forward was to put the pressure on, both locally and nationally. The reason I was able to do this now, rather than before, was that the members had become militant. They were no longer prepared to sit back but would risk their anonymity to express their fury at the way things were going. A meeting between a member and the former Minister for Health's programme manager, Richard Greene, had yielded a result – maybe this would bring similar progress.

When we arrived at the Orchard Bar, Micheál Martin had yet to arrive. We sat in this old-style pub with tea and coffee and waited. When he did turn up, I stayed downstairs while the members went up and pressed their case. On the way out, he did acknowledge me. He also happened to be on the flight back to Dublin. He quipped: "Are you following me?" I responded: "No, I'm haunting you." While we had our differences, at least the atmosphere had lightened.

Our next meeting ended up being quite bizarre. The venue was Leinster House. The IHS delegation included members of the executive committee, a number of members who had been infected with HIV and hepatitis C as well as Raymond and myself. The room was quite crowded as the minister had brought along some departmental officials and the Attorney General, Michael McDowell. It felt a little strange as it was the AG rather than Micheál Martin who was running the meeting. Mr McDowell introduced himself as the Attorney General and 'protector of charities', a title I didn't realise he held. Within a very short space of time, he was quizzing Raymond extremely closely about whether or not he had apprised his clients of the legal costs they were incurring. I was aghast. Was the AG was trying to undermine Raymond's credibility with the IHS? If that was his aim, it was a total waste of time. Raymond was forced to respond that he had honoured his obligations as the IHS solicitor. There were further questions from the AG, but Raymond fielded them very adroitly. If I had not worked so closely with Raymond over so many years and numerous difficult situations, the line of questioning from Mr McDowell could have caused a rift between us. Initially, I was just looking at the AG and thinking: "Dear Jesus, what is this all about?" I happened to be sitting closest to Mr McDowell and, at one point, he turned to me and winked. I didn't like it. I didn't like his approach. I didn't think he was 'protecting' the IHS. I also felt that Micheál Martin, although new in the job, would have been well advised to run meetings he had convened rather than to allow others to take over.

Shortly after this debacle, the department finally agreed a sliding scale of payment which was equal to what their legal team would get. Ray Kelly had taken a major part in the campaign to get this issue sorted. It was difficult to gain publicity and most journalists wanted to speak to people at the heart of the tribunal rather than a spokesperson like myself. This was where Ray came in – he decided to go public in order to help the other members. It was a brave decision as his baptism of fire was on the *Late Late Show*. He detailed what had happened to his son John, what his family wanted from the tribunal and why he was upset that the IHS was not being treated fairly. Pat Kenny asked Ray if he could understand why the minister couldn't write a blank cheque. Ray spoke for most members when he said: "Whatever went wrong, went [wrong] inside the BTSB or Department of Health or both. And they seem to have the power to limit what our legal team can do within this tribunal. And they're the people being investigated!" Pat Kenny said: "You feel you've had enough stress, enough pressure, enough loss." Ray responded: "And I can do without being here, I can assure you." I remember watching the show and getting angry again that somebody like Ray had to display his pain in public to get a political result.

When the issue was finally resolved and the tribunal was back on track, Ray was asked by RTÉ to give his reaction. He told them: "I am very relieved that the tribunal is going to go forward and that common sense prevailed in the end. I suppose maybe now we'll find out who, what and when. And what exactly happened and who is responsible now that we have the resources to investigate. We didn't do anything wrong." The news report had focused on Ray's son, John, and featured several pictures of him. It also contained images of his grave which read: *Kelly – Precious Memories Of A Loving Son and Brother. John. Died 9th August 1994. Aged 13 years.*

I was now able to focus solely on the tribunal which was just under two weeks away. I realised it would continue to be a difficult process. IHS members were also increasingly uneasy as the date for public hearings got closer. Some members wanted 'heads on a plate'; others took the view that nothing was going to happen even if those responsible were named; another group was uncomfortable that Professor Temperley was going to be the only fall-guy despite the benefits he had brought to the haemophilia community. Personally, I felt that those responsible for the errors which undoubtedly occurred had to be named and held responsible. I was, however, feeling uneasy that the truth might not come out. It was therefore with a degree of hope and some apprehension that I prepared for the Lindsay Tribunal.

14

Day 1

On Tuesday May 2, 2000, the Lindsay Tribunal commenced. We'd been given a commitment that an inquiry would take place in 1997 and now it was finally happening. By this time, seventy-four people with haemophilia had died as a result of contaminated blood products.

The morning of the tribunal was sunny. It felt like a good omen after a fitful night. I'd struggled to get to sleep and when I woke up, just for a split second, I thought it was a normal day. Then it hit me: "Oh God, today is the day." When I turned on the radio it was headline news. Things were due to get under way at half past ten, so I arranged to meet Brian and Raymond for breakfast at eight. There was a giddy atmosphere: we had fought for years to secure a tribunal and now it was about to happen. As we munched our breakfast, a car pulled up outside the Brown Bag restaurant and out leapt Austin with a large bouquet of flowers for me.

The first witness was going to be Karen Stephens – daughter of Jerome. The other person to testify that day was

Ray Kelly. We chose them as they were both prepared to go public and speak openly about what happened to their respective families. I wanted to ensure that the nation would understand why we wanted an inquiry in the first place.

After breakfast, we all returned to the IHS office as it was just five minutes' walk from the tribunal which had established itself in the Distillery Building on Church Street. We were due to meet Karen and Ray at midday, as the morning was going to be taken up with procedural matters.

Karen was twenty. Tall and beautiful with long brown ringleted hair, she was very emotional about testifying on her father's behalf. It struck me as she tried to compose herself that many of her mannerisms were inherited from Jerome. Like him, she was able to be strong when required. When Ray arrived, he went into the kitchen. As always, he didn't sit at the table but paced around the room. Usually it took him some time before he sat down and joined everyone else. Today he was so uptight that he remained on his feet.

We had been in almost constant communication with Karen and Ray for the previous month. Raymond went back over their statements with them several times to ensure they contained everything Karen and Ray wanted to say. My advice was to explain exactly what would happen and to assure them of our constant support throughout the process. I tried to boost their confidence by saying: "You are the expert on your life. No-one knows your story better than you. Just tell it as it was."

Very soon, it was time to walk to the tribunal and get ready to give evidence. I was so nervous I thought I might be sick at any moment. We tried to lighten the mood with a bit of banter. The jokes stopped as we turned the final corner and braced ourselves.

With the photographers' flashes going off, it felt like

something from a movie premiere. The spotlight was on us. There were TV cameras and newspaper photographers all in a semi-circle which we had to walk through. It's very difficult when cameras are flashing as you feel you're supposed to smile, but that wouldn't be the appropriate picture the next morning. It didn't show on my face, but now that the time had come I was feeling excited.

Once inside, I brought Karen and Ray to the place where they would give evidence. It was a rectangular room on the first floor. At the back was seating for the public, in front of that the media, several rows of tables for the lawyers, the witness box and finally the bench for Judge Alison Lindsay. Afterwards we returned to the ground floor where Raymond's firm, Malcomson Law, had hired a room. It was a small but comfortable place with a long boardroom table, six chairs and plenty of shelves for documents. One of our staff, Michelle, was armed with the essentials: tissues, water and Diet Coke. We also brought along a counsellor, Una, as it was clear this was going to be an emotional roller-coaster. The tribunal staff could not have been more helpful in trying to be discreet, welcoming and comforting. It was a room where I would spend many hours with our legal team which consisted of Raymond and barristers Martin Hayden, Jim McCullagh, Martin Giblin and John Trainor.

The time finally came for Karen to testify. Her hands were shaking. We didn't speak but walked into the tribunal room from a small side door. I accompanied her to her seat. Karen was by now on automatic pilot, so I turned around to take my place at the back of the room. It was only then that I saw just how many people had crammed inside. My eyes flitted from suits to microphones, to televisions for displaying documents, to the packed public gallery. For a minute I thought: "What in the name of God have we done? Is this for real?" I walked away and left Karen on her own. Most of the four rows provided for the public were taken up by members of the IHS who wanted to give their support. While we waited for proceedings to get underway, Ray was still downstairs in the room with our counsellor. Waiting. He wasn't able to hear proceedings upstairs which was probably a good thing.

John Finlay, SC for the tribunal, made some opening remarks and, at one point, referred to the evidence which was about to be heard: "The persons who have volunteered to give evidence have shown great courage in coming forward to describe matters which are obviously deeply personal, private and sensitive."

Karen was taken through her evidence by Raymond. I found it heartbreaking to watch this young woman recount how her childhood was ruined by her father's illnesses and premature death. She spoke of how she bore the brunt of much prejudice from the age of six after it became known locally that her father had HIV.

"Somehow it got out. Like, if I was going to school, parents were telling their kids not to touch me. If kids actually did happen to touch me they'd run to the toilet as quick as possible to wash their hands. They'd just ignore me and call me names, spit at me and stuff like that."

For the next seven years, Karen's life was orientated around helping out at home and bringing medicine to her father. She didn't realise just how different this was from other children's homes until she was sixteen. "Each year that goes by, there isn't a night that I don't think about my dad and cry . . . It really wasn't a childhood for me . . . I tell you what I really really want is my dad back, but that's not going to happen. I want to know why he was taken away. I want to know why he isn't going to be there for my wedding. I went to my debs and he wasn't there. I want to know why I'm supposed to have these memories." Jerome had died in February 1993 when she was thirteen.

Listening, I was so glad that she knew she was doing exactly what her father would have done had he been alive. As Karen neared the end of her evidence, I slowly walked to the top of the room. When she left the witness box, I accompanied her out the side door again. I just hugged her and she fell in to me. In tears, she asked: "Was that alright?" I had no words to say how right it was. I took Karen down the backstairs to our room. She stayed with Una, while I accompanied Ray Kelly upstairs. As we went up the steps, I felt: "This is what walking to an execution must feel like."

Ray was very tense. The reason he was here was part of his mission to continue to do everything within his power to honour John's memory. The other major objective was to try to find out why his son had died at just thirteen. I listened as he told the story of how John began to be injected with concentrates, but Ray hadn't been informed about any increased possibility of his son contracting HIV and hepatitis C.

Ray didn't want John to know about his HIV status because of the stigma associated with the virus: "That in itself created tremendous pressures. I mean, you had to constantly have your finger on the button on the remote control of the television in case a news item would come up that would link haemophilia with the possibility of HIV and AIDS."

Ray said this secrecy was jeopardised by Professor Temperley at a consultation at Harcourt Street Hospital: "He discussed it openly with people standing around waiting for treatment and mentioned John's name. And my wife and myself were very, very upset that this could happen." It wasn't his only problem with the professor. On another occasion, Ray said, in January 1994, Professor Temperley came to

John's hospital bedside. His son had problems with his hepatitis C infection rather than HIV and it wasn't clear if he would survive. Ray said: "I wasn't in the room myself, but my wife was [there] with a nurse and Professor Temperley stood at the end of his bed and said, 'Well, he may recover from this and then again he may not', and left the room." Ray said he was so angry when he was told this that he arranged a meeting with the professor. Another member of the professor's team turned up instead for the meeting. Ray told them: "If that man ever does that in front of my child again, I won't be responsible for the consequences."

It looked as if he was finding it hard to keep control of his emotions when discussing his experiences with Professor Temperley. Ray had had a good relationship with the professor until John became seriously ill. Then things changed. Ray now wanted to have his criticisms recorded in evidence. His comments prompted Professor Temperley's lawyer, Brian McGovern SC, to cross-examine him. I knew this was fair under the procedures, but I didn't think that it was appropriate as these matters were going to be dealt with in some detail at a later date. A short comment reserving his clients' position would have been OK, but the more detailed questioning, I felt, was out of place.

According to Mr McGovern, Professor Temperley's recollection of the Harcourt Street Hospital consultation was that medical personnel rather than members of the public were around at the time. Ray's response was: "Absolute rubbish." Mr McGovern said the professor would contend that both he and his team "did the best that they could, not only for John but for all the other patients". Ray retorted that he found Professor Temperley "very lacking in humanity".

Asked to sum up his views, Ray said his son John had been " . . . infected by products brought into this country from

America. I want to know who brought them in, who made the decisions and if they knew they were contaminated or possibly contaminated, which I think they did. If they did, then they murdered my son."

When Ray was finished, I escorted him back down to our room. The grief that he had held inside him in the witness box just exploded. I could only hug him and cry.

A short time later, we left the tribunal and walked out to meet the media. Brian and I stood by the door as Karen and Ray answered questions. Karen was carrying a photograph of Jerome. I liked it as he had a cigarette in the corner of his mouth and his eyes were dancing with all that humour and boldness I remembered him having in spades. She told the reporters: "I hope it's the last time I have to say what happened to me, but if I had to do it again I would." I was bursting with pride at how well Karen and Ray were coping under this immense pressure.

This was my first interaction with the journalists who were going to cover the tribunal. Those who usually attended every day were Joe Humphreys and Eithne Donnellan of *The Irish Times*, Evelyn Ring of the *Irish Examiner*, Paul Melia of the *Irish Independent*, and Paul Cunningham from RTÉ. Other reporters who regularly attended the hearings were Fergal Bowers of *irishhealth.com*, Susan McKay of *The Sunday Tribune*, John Drennan of the *Sunday Independent*, Emily O'Reilly then of *The Sunday Business Post,* Catherine Halloran of *The Star* and Cormac Burke then of *Ireland on Sunday*. I viewed them as important as they would be informing the public on a day-to-day basis. My aim was to make myself available for comment or explanation, but I didn't want to be seen as pushy. But from our experience of the Finlay Tribunal I knew I needed to have their phone numbers in case we needed to call a news conference urgently.

Day 1

On day one, I just handed out my phone number, then stepped back and let them get on with it.

After the interviews, we returned to the IHS office. Many of the people who were to give evidence over the coming days came along as well. They had taken the opportunity to see how the process would work. While the atmosphere was jubilant, I slipped into my own room, closed the door and wept in private. The whole day had been extremely draining.

I returned to the office that evening. The legal team and I had to hold consultations with the people who were to give evidence the following day. I managed to speak to Arthur and the children on the phone. They had been watching the news and were extremely proud and supportive.

With all of the commotion I hadn't really had the chance to think about what I was going to wear. The staff in the office had noticed and bought me a series of summer tops to wear underneath the various suits for the rest of the week. I stuck them underneath my arm and headed for home.

On the way home, it struck me that my father hadn't lived to see this eventful day. He suffered the consequences of my absences during the battle to establish the tribunal but didn't see it come to fruition. It made me think of cherishing the family I still had.

15

Bad Blood

After two weeks of personal testimony, the tribunal began its investigation into why this tragedy had happened. Of the seventy-four people with haemophilia who had died over the previous fifteen years, only two had passed away as a result of their disorder. The other seventy-two died because of a medicine which was supposed to help them. I was extremely uptight as we'd spent months reading more than a half a million pages of evidence and now, finally, senior officials and doctors were going to have to take the stand and answer questions.

I was brimming with anticipation and not a little emotional, when the words "All rise!" reverberated around the tribunal and Judge Alison Lindsay walked in and took her seat. The process of standing on this command would become so normal that I now find myself having to resist standing to attention when a court sequence comes on television.

The first thing Judge Lindsay did was to deliver her interpretation of the tribunal's terms of reference which had been passed by the Oireachtas. While this was possibly boring for members of the public, I really was interested. The reason was that I wanted to see what she would say about investigating international pharmaceutical companies. There were fourteen terms of reference and then a paragraph which stated the tribunal could "investigate anything arising outside the State that it considers relevant". Judge Lindsay explained her thinking on the fourteen terms but didn't elaborate in relation to this international dimension. She also precluded further discussion by stating: "I consider that today is not the appropriate day to seek a further clarification . . . but should any person have a query, they should write to the solicitor for the tribunal." We had written to her about the matter in March, and now I made a mental note to take up her offer.

The first component of the investigation was an inquiry into the actions of the Blood Bank. The tribunal's legal team would bring each witness through the available documentary evidence. Then the other lawyers representing the doctors, hospitals and ourselves had the chance to cross-examine. The Blood Bank could ask questions at the end.

Judge Lindsay invited John Finlay SC to give his opening statement on behalf of the tribunal's legal team. It just so happened that John Finlay was the son of the former Chief Justice, Mr Justice Thomas Finlay, whose tribunal we'd walked out on. I could see that the opening statement was going to be a long one. The journalists in front of me began to scribble as Mr Finlay detailed what haemophilia was and how treatment for the condition had changed through the years. My attention slipped somewhat.

I was catapulted out of my torpor when he began to outline what evidence the Blood Bank would give. Mr Finlay explained that the deputy medical director of the Blood Bank, Dr Emer Lawlor, had gone through all of its documentation in preparation for the tribunal. She would provide an expert opinion on its behalf, even though she hadn't been working in the institution at the time when people were infected. Part of her examination was focused on the Irish-made blood product Factor IX. Suddenly, words fell from Mr Finlay's lips which had never been heard before. He said Dr Lawlor concluded that as "a matter of probability these [seven] persons were infected with HIV as a result of Factor IX produced by the BTSB".

I knew these seven people and their faces came flooding back into my consciousness like a video montage. I remembered Jim's lovely, quiet unassuming manner and the guilt I'd felt when I touched his hand in hospital and inflicted pain. I thought of his son who was only a small boy at the time of his dad's death and how he was deprived of his father's love, support and comfort. Norman came back into my mind – the two of us laughing as he raised his pint. Picture after picture flicked through my mind.

Mr Finlay continued with his statement and I began to get angry. The reason was that he appeared to heap praise on the Blood Bank. He declared that Dr Lawlor's "straightforward acknowledgement" had "greatly assisted" the tribunal. He added that the Blood Bank had undertaken "very considerable work . . . in organising and making available a large volume of documents". I found this very hard to take. Why was the Blood Bank being praised for acknowledging that its products were infectious? This was 2000. The product had been used in 1985 and 1986. It had taken fifteen years to in any way acknowledge responsibility. Five people had died without knowing how they were infected with HIV. And now they were being praised? Furthermore, why was the Blood Bank being thanked for making documents available when this was an obligation on everyone?

This issue relating to Factor IX would become possibly the

single most important aspect of the tribunal's work. It was something both Brian and I would be questioned about when it was our turn to give evidence. The details which would emerge would shock the country and horrify the haemophilia community as they realised that some of their friends and family members could have been saved.

Even though I had viewed some of the Blood Bank documentation in the run-up to the tribunal, this public acknowledgement was a watershed. There was no more doubt: the Blood Bank had been responsible for infecting seven members with HIV and one of them had infected their partner with the virus. The disclosure led to many questions: How long did the Blood Bank know that its products had infected people? Who knew? Why didn't they tell the people they'd infected about this information? The horrible fact was that five of the seven had already died by the time this first public declaration of responsibility was made.

Over a number of weeks, the tribunal investigated the issue. It identified how many people with haemophilia who used Factor VIII imported from the US were diagnosed with HIV in 1985. However, those using the Irish-made Factor IX didn't contract the virus. It seemed they had escaped the nightmare of AIDS as the new process of heating the clotting-agent to kill HIV was introduced that year.

However, in April 1986, Professor Temperley wrote to the Blood Bank stating he was "becoming very concerned" that some people using its Factor IX product were now testing positive. By June 1986, he told a medical conference in UCD, attended by a shocked Brian O'Mahony, it was "very worrying" that Irish blood products could be responsible. This was the conference where Brian had seen the initials of those infected put on a screen in full public view. A report in *The Irish Times* the next day carried the headline: *Blood products may still carry AIDS virus.* In the article, the professor was quoted as saying that four people who used Factor IX had tested positive for HIV in 1986. It was stated: "He emphasised that there was no proof that these four patients had been exposed to the virus through the administration of native [Irish-made] Factor IX. They had also received commercial blood concentrates in their treatment, but it was very worrying that native Factor IX might have been the cause."

The way the Blood Bank dealt with this news in 1986 was bizarre. Much of my focus was on Ted Keyes who had only taken over the job of executive consultant – effectively CEO – at the beginning of 1986. An accountant by profession, he was recruited by Gerry McCartney in the Department of Health to bring some financial order to the Blood Bank's affairs. He attended a meeting of the board of the Blood Bank in June 1986 and the minutes of that meeting really dumbfounded me. They recorded that Ted Keyes had informed the board: "The situation with regard to Factor IX was unsatisfactory and he was examining this as a matter of urgency." When this was read out at the tribunal I was amazed: it seemed a blood product which caused devastation and death was being described as "unsatisfactory". Asked at the tribunal to explain the way in which the board minutes recorded the discussion, Ted Keyes agreed it was in a very "coded form".

Later that month, the Blood Bank's consultant haemotologist, Dr Terry Walsh, wrote an internal memo following a meeting with Professor Temperley. The news was stark. Dr Walsh said there was "a very strong possibility" that Pelican House products were responsible. The screaming question was how they could have had major concerns in 1986 but for it to remain a secret until 2000?

What I couldn't understand was that the minutes of

subsequent board meetings in July, August and September didn't detail anything about what happened to this investigation or what the board's policy would be. There was discussion about heat-treating stocks of Factor IX and the financial implications. There was no recording of the fact that the Blood Bank had infected people as a matter of probability. Why? There were senior officials who knew of this situation – executive consultant Ted Keyes, chief medical consultant Dr Vincent Barry, and consultant haematologist Dr Terry Walsh. The board members knew something of the problem from June 1986, but the trail seemed to end there.

Ted Keyes testified at the Lindsay Tribunal that he was "almost certain" that the board was told that BTSB Factor IX caused HIV infections. The question of their state of knowledge was important as officials from the Department of Health sat on the board – including Gerry McCartney. This was also significant as, by 1989, the Blood Bank and the State were being sued by members who'd become infected with HIV. Their cases would have been stronger if it was known that they were infected with Irish-made products as opposed to imported clotting-agents. Compensation awards would have been much higher.

Given this, I found it baffling that the tribunal's legal team refused to call all of the members of the board of the Blood Bank between 1986 and 1989 to give evidence. I had a particular interest in Noel Fox who was chairman of the board in 1986 when the problem with Factor IX first came to prominence and still held the office in 1989 when litigation was under way. Considering the huge implications, I found it to be inexplicable, unacceptable and indefensible that he wasn't asked to detail what happened. The IHS wrote to the tribunal about this matter but to no avail. No reason for the decision was ever made public. It was another clear signal that this tribunal was not going to deliver the type of closure we'd hoped for.

The evidence seemed to suggest to me that the board of the Blood Bank, and therefore officials in the Department of Health, knew in 1986 that the Factor IX blood product was probably responsible for infecting patients with HIV. While a recall of the suspect Blood Bank clotting-agent occurred in the middle of 1986, no further action was taken. No one contacted the people who used the product and appraised them of the situation. People were left in the dark. Was a cover-up taking place?

That concern was underlined by an interview given by Dr Walsh to *The Sunday Tribune* on January 4, 1987. He was quoted by the paper as saying: "No Irish person ever got AIDS from a transfusion and they won't either." In February 1989, Ted Keyes was recorded at a BTSB board meeting as denying that Irish blood products were responsible for any infections and castigating the IHS for suggesting that might be the case. I wondered: "What is going on? How can Dr Walsh and Mr Keyes deny something which they knew, as a matter of probability, to be true?"

The Blood Bank's position was totally different. It argued that while its product caused infections, it felt that it did its best with the knowledge it had at the time to protect recipients. In its view, this meant that while the infections were regrettable, the Blood Bank had no reason to apologise to people with haemophilia. It also argued that there was no hard evidence to suggest that the board was informed of the infections. It was pointed out that while Mr Keyes' recollection was that he had told the board, he couldn't say when or where this had happened or point to evidence that he had done so.

I just couldn't accept this. Blood Bank officials clearly

knew something of the problem in June 1986. The board of the Blood Bank knew, at the very least, that something was "unsatisfactory" and an investigation was under way. Dr Lawlor explained the subsequent denials of a problem by saying that the Blood Bank had gone into a "form of denial" about the infections. This, I felt, was later countered in evidence by Professor Temperley who joined the board in the late 1980s. He told the tribunal that he was "becoming a bore" by his continual suggestion that the Blood Bank's Factor IX caused HIV infections. How could they not have known and realised the implications?

The haemophilia community had always been confused about how these infections could have occurred at all considering heat-treatment was available from the beginning of 1985. The Lindsay Tribunal threw some clarity on the matter. Blood Bank documents showed that while Factor VIII was being heat-treated from January 1985, non-heat-treated Factor IX continued to be manufactured and distributed by the Blood Bank until the end of that year. This was the product which had caused the infections. Brian O'Mahony, who used Factor IX himself, had suspected that the Blood Bank's method of heat-treating Factor IX had failed. Now it was revealed that there was no heat-treatment at all. Why this was the case would be investigated later. What was important was that documentation from the Blood Bank also showed that Factor IX imported into the country was heat-treated by February 1985.

The Blood Bank didn't appear to let the recipients know that it was not heat-treating its own Factor IX. One particular piece of evidence really summed it up. It involved consultant haemotologist, Dr Terry Walsh, giving an interview on RTÉ Radio on August 25, 1985. In the interview, Dr Walsh said all blood products were being heated in order to kill off HIV and make them safe. He made this statement despite the fact that he would have known that while this was certainly happening to imported blood products, the Factor IX made in Ireland was not being heat-treated at this point.

Dr Walsh was taken through the text of the 1985 interview by another lawyer for the tribunal, Gerry Durcan SC, whose style was quite different to that of his colleague John Finlay. Gerry Durcan usually leaned back on his chair when asking questions. If a witness didn't give the appropriate response, he would say: "Well, let's break it down." A series of questions would follow which would block off avenues of escape and force them into answering the hard question.

Because Dr Walsh suggested in the radio interview that all blood products were being heat-treated to kill HIV, Mr Durcan asked: "Would you accept that at the time, again, at least in general, the view was perhaps being put out in public that the products were safe?"

Dr Terry Walsh's response was: "It's very difficult to . . . just answer it. I would have to think in terms of what one was trying to do at the time. It was a time of huge problems for the transfusion service generally. There was a lot of very negative publicity, donations were falling. You have . . . to give a more positive view about the essential service. One tried to . . . be as comforting or as hopeful as possible. That is a human reaction."

Mr Durcan countered: "I can understand that, doctor, but isn't the problem that one might look at the interview as an overall and say 'there is no risk involved here' – whereas there was a risk?"

Dr Walsh answered: "Well, I would . . . take issue with you again on that. I think that if somebody had a condition and was being treated . . . like haemophilia . . . I wouldn't rely on something in a radio interview . . . they have a number of sources of information."

Mr Durcan asked: "Could we leave it at that, perhaps, it was an unhappy choice of words?" Dr Walsh responded: "I can accept that." Just to underline matters, Mr Durcan added: "At least?" The answer came back: "In looking at it in retrospect."

This type of exchange really annoyed me. It seemed clear that he had said that all blood products were being heat-treated when it simply wasn't the case. This meant that a person listening to the radio interview would think that the products were safe when they were not. His attempt to shift the responsibility over to people with haemophilia was astounding. The patients were supposed not to believe this leading Blood Bank official but get the correct information elsewhere. At one point he said counselling was one avenue for information – a strange suggestion as those infected had already spoken about the absence of such support structures.

One of the other major issues in this section of the tribunal centred on Fionn. It was established from his medical records that he had only ever used the other Irish-made blood product known as cryoprecipitate or 'cryo'. It was made from five donations whereas something like Factor IX was made from hundreds. While cryo was cumbersome to use, it was safer than concentrates as the fewer donations meant less chance of being infected with a virus.

The story really came to life when his treating doctor, Professor Ernest Egan, testified. He explained that his practice was to treat his patients with cryo. He always felt there was a doubt about concentrates because of the way they were manufactured. Indeed, in 1984, he wrote to what is now the Irish Medicines Board saying concentrates should be restricted to "critical situations" as there was a "significant risk" attached to them.

Professor Egan said that he was sure he informed the Blood Bank when Fionn tested positive for HIV in January

1986 after having only been treated with cryo. He said it was "inconceivable" that he would not have done so. He was already concerned about cryo because it couldn't be heat-treated to inactivate HIV. Yet the person Professor Egan would have told about this infection, Dr Terry Walsh, said he had no recollection of receiving such information. Dr Walsh went on to say that if such news was imparted, he would have investigated the matter, because if cryo was infected it would suggest that other blood products, like Factor IX, made from Irish donations could also be affected.

Later in 1986 there was another row between Professor Egan and Dr Walsh over Factor IX infections. Professor Egan wrote to Dr Walsh in September that he was "very disappointed" that he had heard about the HIV cases from a third party: "I feel it is your responsibility to communicate this sort of information to the likes of myself so that appropriate action can be taken at our end."

While this conflict of evidence was being debated, a series of questions ran through my mind: Did the Department of Health realise in 1991 that Fionn became HIV positive as a result of using cryo? Surely they must have known as they would have had to examine his medical records before issuing any compensation to him? His treating doctor, Professor Egan, said his records suggested he only ever received 'cryo' produced by the Blood Bank. Was this the second piece of evidence showing that the Department of Health knew Irish-made blood products were infectious? Was this the second example of a cover-up? The dispute was left for Judge Lindsay to rule on.

The Factor IX issue had thrown up concerns over how the Blood Bank responded to information that its concentrates could be infectious. Questions also arose over how it dealt with cases where donors tested positive for HIV. In the middle of 1985, the US medical authorities were advising that if a donor tested positive for HIV then the recipients of their previous donations should also be checked for the virus. The case of the Kilkenny Health Worker had shown that this had not taken place in Ireland – she had become infected in 1985, but didn't find out until late 1996 and then by accident. The tribunal showed that things were more complex than had previously been thought.

The HIV antibody test was introduced in Ireland in October 1985. By mid-1987, the Blood Bank considered introducing a look-back policy. Dr Terry Walsh compiled information that five donors had shown up HIV positive since the antibody test was introduced. While he submitted the report recommending a look-back policy, the matter was not pursued. A further donor tested positive in 1989. Dr Walsh was by now the chief medical consultant and he recommended to the board of the Blood Bank that a look-back policy begin. The decision of the board was to do a look-back on the new donor and all future donors. The board minutes recorded: "The board were seriously concerned about the potential legal and public relations aspects of this." It went on to decide not to introduce look-back on the previous contaminated donations. Bizarrely, a full look-back was only instituted in 1995 after files on the five early HIV positive donors were discovered in a safe, by the deputy medical director Dr Emer Lawlor. Why did the board not introduce look-back earlier? What were these legal and PR concerns? It was clear we were not going to find out because the board members who took the decisions were not going to be called to give evidence. Questions were going to remain unanswered at the end of the tribunal.

While this was dramatic, the issue which was of more interest to me concerned a person known only as Donor F.

This individual made a blood donation in December 1984. As there was no HIV test, the Blood Bank didn't know that it was infected with HIV. The blood was used to make Factor IX batch number 90753 which infected a number of users with HIV. The person came back to donate blood again in August 1990. This time Donor F was identified as being HIV positive. No look-back procedure was implemented in this case because the person hadn't given a donation within the previous five years. I thought they should have done so anyway as 1984 was a time when it was possible Irish donors had the virus. The critical thing the tribunal established was that the Donor F case was investigated by the Blood Bank in early 1991 in the context of the litigation people with haemophilia were taking. By this point, they would have made the connection between Donor F, the 1984 donation and Factor IX batch number 90753. This was fascinating as the IHS received an affidavit from the Blood Bank in March 1991, but there was no admission of liability in respect of Factor IX. The out-of-court settlement was reached in May 1991 without the Blood Bank admitting liability. I wondered whether the Department of Health knew anything about this. Why hadn't they simply put their hands up at this stage? We were going to have to see what the tribunal's final report said.

While a lot of attention was paid to the products made in Ireland which had caused infections, the fact was that most people with haemophilia who contracted HIV were infected by imported products. In her evidence, Dr Lawlor rejected any suggestion that by importing and distributing commercial concentrates the Blood Bank was responsible for the product. In her view, the Blood Bank was merely warehousing imported concentrates and was responsible only for those products it manufactured. However, Ted Keyes said his understanding of the Blood Bank's position was that it was liable for products it either supplied or manufactured. He did not see a difference, but added this was only his personal point of view.

The thing which annoyed me the most about the discussions relating to concentrates was the fact that the medical community – both doctors and Blood Bank officials – was aware of certain risks associated with the products, but these were not always relayed to the users. The argument from the Blood Bank and from treating doctors was that the quality of life for people with haemophilia drastically improved following the introduction of concentrates. There is absolutely no doubt about that. I recall the mother of two boys who had died from AIDS telling me that when concentrates became available it was "heaven on earth" because their lives were totally changed. The boys could go to school, they could plan holidays, and more importantly, their pain and the damage to their joints was greatly decreased. However, I felt she should have been informed as information grew about possible risks. She now describes these very concentrates as "hell on earth" because her two sons are dead. If she had been informed of the risks, would she have made the same decision? However difficult these thoughts, it was doubly difficult for those members of the IHS sitting close to me. I sat at the back of the room angered by the prevarication and recording points in my blue note-book. But they were listening to the details of how their lives had been destroyed.

One of those was Damien who contracted both HIV and hepatitis C. His brother had already died after being infected by both viruses. Damien was a strong supporter of the IHS. He attended every function, fundraiser and meeting. His car effectively became property of the IHS: Damien ended up transporting anything that needed to be taken from A to B. I didn't find it unusual that Damien was sitting at the back of the tribunal on the first day. I knew he was going to give personal testimony and would also want to show support for the IHS. But when he was sitting there day after day, I took a bit more notice. I spoke to him about it and he told me that he was giving up his job because he felt the proceedings were so important that he did not want to miss one single second.

Damien and I not only became close over the following months but he was also a gauge for me. Having been infected with HIV and hepatitis C and having suffered the tremendous hurt of losing his brother, his opinion was something I greatly valued when making tough decisions on how we should proceed. No matter how strongly I felt about people with haemophilia and their circumstances, I was always acutely aware that I didn't have the disorder. Moreover, I was not infected with HIV or hepatitis C, and thankfully had not suffered the loss of a family member. Damien was not just a clever man but also someone who had lived through the tragedy of contaminated clotting-agents. Over many cups of coffee in the evening, we would talk about what had happened at the tribunal – putting the personal back into what had often been reduced to numbers and cold statistics. One thing which maddened him was the way the barrister for Saint James's Hospital, Deirdre Murphy SC, regularly talked about the high cost of haemophilia products and how much money Saint James's Hospital had spent on them. Damien quipped on one occasion: "I am so sorry for having been born with such an expensive disease." It became a refrain. As the tribunal went on and the number of members attending dwindled, it was always a comfort for me to have Damien sitting alongside me. The public seating area at the back of the room could be a very lonely place at times.

Ray Kelly also acted as an advisor. He attended as many of the hearings as he could but, when it was not possible, he would always be on the phone. I was making decisions in relation to our strategy on a dáily basis. While I was always getting advice from the legal team, I also began to use Ray and Damien as sounding boards for what the haemophilia community would think. Many an important decision was taken with Damien and Ray, on the stairwell of the tribunal building.

HIV dominated the tribunal's proceedings for a lot of the time, but the infection of people with hepatitis C was also dealt with in detail. The critical focus was on the late 1980s, when HIV was believed to be under control, but hepatitis C was becoming a major concern. It was against this background on January 27, 1988, that the Blood Bank received a letter from Armour Pharmaceutical, the US-based manufacturer of its clotting-agents. By this time, the Blood Bank had a system with Armour in which the company would take Irish donations to its plant and manufacture the Factor VIII before returning it to Ireland. In its 1988 letter, the firm informed the Blood Bank that it had a new manufacturing process which eliminated hepatitis C. It said it believed the process "represents a significant advance in the treatment of haemophilia". It also happened to be far more expensive. As a consequence of developing the new product, Armour was no longer willing to continue production along the old lines. The only basis under which it would continue was if the Blood Bank signed a letter which stated: "The Blood Transfusion Service Board, Republic of Ireland, shall indemnify and hold harmless Armour Pharma and its affiliated Companies (Armour) and Officers, Directors, and Employees of Armour from and against any and all third-party liability." The company also demanded that the concentrate "will not carry any Armour trademark". The letter came just one month after the voluntary withdrawal by Armour of a similar product in Canada which was thought to be linked to HIV infections.

This document had shocked me when I read it in the run-up to the tribunal and I was very interested in hearing an explanation for the decision to sign the letter. In his evidence to the tribunal, Ted Keyes said the letter caused him "problems". He added: "An indemnity had all sorts of implications, but we did at some stage talk to our legal people and managed to get it watered down." Despite this reported watering down of the terms, the contract still meant that Armour's name was not carried on the bottles and it wasn't liable for infections.

When Mr Keyes was pressed on the fact that the board of the Blood Bank was choosing a product which appeared to be less safe that others on the market, he claimed the decision rested with Professor Temperley who was then both medical director of the National Haemophilia Treatment Centre and a Blood Bank board member. Mr Keyes said the board "discussed it, but it was ultimately Professor Temperley who said he wanted [the] product for his patients". Mr Keyes' evidence was supported by the Blood Bank board minutes of June 15, 1988 where the decision to go ahead with the Armour contract was recorded as follows: "After detailed consideration, the board approved the recommendation of Prof Temperley that Armour Pharmaceutical Company Ltd should be asked to continue to produce." The old Armour product continued to be used.

When Professor Temperley was asked about this issue, he was shown a letter he wrote on the June 14, 1988 which the board quoted when making its decision. In the letter, the professor said: "The board should understand that in the present period of financial stringency the hospitals could not be expected to meet a doubling of the cost of concentrates in 1989. Some balance will have to be struck between cost and the infection dangers associated with blood products." It was certainly true that the late 1980s was a time of severe cutbacks in the health sector and there was an embargo on staff recruitment. Professor Temperley said the haematology unit was under threat and he and his colleagues were "put to the pin of our collar". He added: "This was a very difficult time financially and I felt the burden quite strongly." However, the professor's letter went on to say: "Virtually all of our treated haemophiliacs have had NANB" [Non-A Non-B hepatitis or hepatitis C]." It seemed a crass statement to justify going with the Armour contract.

The manufacturing process which operated at this time involved Armour returning not just Factor VIII to the Blood Bank but also any plasma material left over. This was processed into Factor IX in Dublin – the clotting-agent used by a minority of people with haemophilia. The Factor IX made through this flawed system had a significant human cost: four people, three of them children, contracted hepatitis C. More tragically still, two of the three children were brothers. Their mother, Felicity, was someone I knew well.

Her boys were born between 1985 and 1987 and she treated them at home with products secured from Harcourt Street Hospital in Dublin. In 1991, she called in with her children for blood tests because hepatitis C screening had become available. The tests were carried out but she heard nothing back.

In October 1995 the youngest child, who had been a lively, healthy and happy boy, became depressed and suffered from fatigue. She thought he was being bullied at school, but after investigating her suspicion found this wasn't the case. Worried about the change in his behaviour, Felicity called me and I told her to contact the hospital.

She told the tribunal: "I rang and spoke to a nurse and said I was very concerned about him. He was very depressed. He had no energy. And I thought he was suffering from depression. And I asked her did she think it was possible for a child so young to suffer from depression."

Raymond, our solicitor, then asked Felicity: "What did she say?"

Felicity responded: "She said no, maybe it's his hepatitis."

Raymond asked her: "And what was your reaction?"

Felicity answered: "I said he does not have hepatitis." The nurse went off to check the records and came back to tell her even more devastating news – that three of her children had hepatitis C. Two of them had been infected by Irish-made Factor IX while a third contracted the virus from an imported product.

Felicity said: "I panicked. I rang the Irish Haemophilia Society. I don't know what I said but I was so alarmed and panicked that . . . but I think in the back of my mind I kept thinking she's after making a mistake."

The children's medical records show that all three were diagnosed with hepatitis C antibodies in December 1990. It was confirmed they had the virus by the end of 1991. She found out in October 1995. This meant that for nearly five years they didn't get any treatment for their condition and also risked transmitting the virus on to other members of the family through cuts and bleeds. She had been going to the hospital at least twice a year and nobody had said anything.

Felicity said: "That's unforgivable, because for the five years that they left me wandering around in the wilderness as happy as Larry, they [the boys] should have been at least registered with the hepatology clinic . . . for five years their livers were untreated, unmanaged, they could have died and I wouldn't have known why . . . I am very angry . . . I can't understand why I wasn't told. Maybe they never wanted to tell me."

I helped Felicity prepare her statement prior to the tribunal. She was extremely nervous but so driven in her desire to find out the truth that those substantial fears were overcome. Felicity's emotions swung from feelings of rage to incredulity. In the early 1990s, she had complete trust in the system, Professor Temperley and the products. In relation to the Blood Bank, Felicity also raised at the tribunal the issue of finance: "I hope that my children did not end up with hepatitis C because someone was trying to save money."

After Felicity's direct evidence, we were downstairs in our room where she regained her composure. A knock came on the door and we were informed that the National Children's Hospital wanted to tender an apology. Felicity was so upset at the time that she didn't feel that she could go back into the witness box. I told her: "Nobody has apologised for anything before. By your presence, it's drawn an apology out of someone." She thought about it and, somewhat reluctantly, decided to return. It had taken them more than a decade to offer an apology – and they got their lawyer to say it.

Mel Christle, SC for the Adelaide and Meath Hospital, incorporating the National Children's Hospital, said he wanted to "offer a humble apology on behalf of the National Children's Hospital on the basis that it is clear that you were not informed, your husband was not informed and your children, your three children, were not informed that they contracted hepatitis C as far back as 1991". This date of 1991 was used by the hospital instead of 1990 on the basis that confirmatory tests were required to establish the boys hepatitis C status. Mr Christle went on: "And I hope that this apology goes in some way, but not in any great way, to ease the pain that you and your husband and your children have suffered as a result of that lapse in communicating information."

When he said the word 'lapse', I thought to myself: "If you're going to apologise – just do it. Why try to minimise it?" But it got worse.

Mr Christle went on to ask Felicity: "And would it be fair to say that they [the children] are being properly treated and cared for since 1995?"

Felicity somehow managed to keep her dignity and answered: "The service has improved greatly, yes."

Why did the hospital have to elicit that piece of information? They should simply have apologised and sat down.

Professor Temperley had responsibility for patients attending the National Children's Hospital and so was asked to explain why Felicity was not informed. The professor had actually retired by the time she was told about her boys hepatitis C condition. His explanation to the tribunal was that they attended the in-patients department rather than the out-patients. He said the former did not lend itself to a discussion on the question of test results as the children would often be in the course of acute treatment.

He said: "The system . . . just failed . . . it was terribly unfortunate and we are truly sorry about this. And naturally we are very sorry that it happened, but it did happen, and so I can't really say much more about it."

The financial status of the Blood Bank was something the IHS fought extremely hard to have investigated. The Blood Bank was a statutory body which ran its own affairs and was expected to balance its books. One way it raised revenue was to charge hospitals for blood and blood products, although any price increase had to be agreed with the Department of Health. We wanted to establish whether or not its board decided to import concentrates into Ireland in the 1970s, despite the concern of its national director, because it offered two profit margins: firstly a discount on a bulk purchase from a pharmaceutical company and secondly in the price it charged hospitals for the product.

Financial records showed that from the late 1970s the

Blood Bank was in dire straits, caused to a major extent by a move from its Leeson Street office to Pelican House off Baggot Street. It was financial suicide as the organisation didn't have the money. The Lindsay Tribunal revealed that that the institution had been almost insolvent and this was reported in the newspapers. One man in particular was paying a lot of attention. His name was Edward A Ryan and he was a former accountant and personnel officer at the Blood Bank.

It came as a quite a shock to him when it was stated at the tribunal by the Blood Bank's expert witness, Dr Emer Lawlor, that there was no-one around from the time who could be called as a witness. The Blood Bank clearly thought Mr Ryan was dead. It led to a rather surreal atmosphere when a man thought to be deceased came walking into the tribunal room to give evidence.

He said he couldn't quite understand how his former employers thought he was dead as they were still paying his pension.

Tribunal lawyer Gerry Durcan asked Mr Ryan: "Have you had any contact with the Blood Transfusion Service Board since you left?"

Mr Ryan said: "I have had, in fact. I got an award even at one stage . . . about two years ago . . . for something or other."

Mr Durcan quipped: "It wasn't posthumously?"

Mr Ryan joked back: "I can only quote Oscar Wilde: 'A face once seen and never remembered.'"

The person who made the award was the chief executive officer, Martin Hynes. Nearly everyone in the tribunal was giggling at this point, although the Blood Bank officials looked mortified. They could obviously envisage the next day's newspapers were going to be filled with headlines like *Dead Man Walking*.

While the development was funny to everyone but the Blood Bank, there was also a serious side to the appearance of Mr Ryan. The Blood Bank had contended that the people involved in its finances during the 1970s and 1980s were either dead or not in a position to assist them. On that basis, it employed an expert witness, John McStay, to examine its financial records and give his observations. Now it had been proven there was somebody around after all. As Mr Ryan told the tribunal: "If they were sending me a pension I think they should have known I was around all right, that is true."

Mr Ryan's evidence was broadly in line with what John McStay had told the tribunal. He spoke of how the financial state of the Blood Bank in the early 1980s was disastrous. In 1981, the Blood Bank had an overdraft facility of £200,000 but was £1.1 million in the red. No employee tax returns were made in the early 1980s. While Mr McStay had maintained safety was never compromised, he also expressed the view that the cash crisis "permeated" decision-making in the Blood Bank.

Mr Ryan was in great shape and attended the hearing in a sharp blue suit, shirt, tie and clip. He said to describe the Blood Bank finances in the early 1980s as disastrous would be an "understatement". He revealed that once a creditor said they would pay a bill, a Blood Bank employee would immediately go and collect the cheque rather than wait for it to be posted. He also spoke to the media after testifying. He told them that while he didn't read in the papers that he was supposed to be dead, he realised that the Blood Bank believed that to be the case. He didn't think of making contact immediately as he felt the proceedings were only concerned with medical matters: "At that stage, I didn't see finance as a major factor in this whole operation. Then certain discussions were reported in the papers and I felt, well, perhaps I should present myself there."

227

However, the whole scenario over Mr Ryan's appearance left its mark on me. I found it increasingly difficult to listen to Dr Lawlor's evidence and the defences she was putting up. I recognised that was her job, but I didn't like it. In the early stages of the tribunal we always greeted each other, but by this stage there was no acknowledgement. Silly as it may sound, I began to ensure that I got into a lift on my own as I couldn't bear the awkward silences that would occur if we happened to end up travelling to the ground floor together.

16

Luke And Shirley

The admission by the Blood Bank that clotting-agents made from Irish donations had caused infections gave an added edge to the personal testimony heard by the tribunal in November and December 2000.

One person I was particularly close to was Shirley. I had been present at the death of her son. Shirley is as normal a mother as you can imagine. She has a great belief in God and particularly in the Blessed Virgin. I saw at first hand how her religious conviction sustained her through some very difficult times – both when her son, Hugh, was dying, and coping after his death. When Hugh died on the Feast of Our Lady of Lourdes, it was a great source of comfort for Shirley. She had gone with him to Lourdes on a pilgrimage. Hugh passed away at twenty minutes to six in the evening, which coincides exactly with the time the Virgin Mary is said to have appeared to the visionaries. It makes Shirley believe that She was present.

When Shirley came to give evidence, she was nervous, but

felt the public should know about the devastation which HIV-infected Factor IX caused. I brought her to the witness stand and then resumed my seat. It was a bit strange – she now seemed to be the confident one and I was worrying.

Shirley opted to testify from behind a screen. Initially she spoke about what it was like trying to care for children with haemophilia in the 1950s and 1960s. When bruises appeared on her first son as a baby, she went to the doctor, but he didn't know what was wrong. Eventually, after more bruises and a second opinion, she established that it was haemophilia. It did not come as much of a surprise when her youngest son, Hugh, banged his arms off the side of the pram causing a bleed which manifested itself as a bruise. The medical treatment at the time was to infuse plasma into their veins and then the patient would be detained in hospital for several weeks. She explained that going to the hospital all the time was "awful": "We'd have to walk there because we had no car at the time, you know, and . . . I was always saying I wished I had a house down at the hospital."

Hugh had certain difficulties. Shirley explained to the tribunal that he had a bleed into his brain at birth: "He was always slow – slow to talk . . . and so we thought we would never see him walk. The day he went over the floor walking I let out such a shout, you know, I frightened him I think." One consequence of Hugh's condition was that he was quieter than most other boys of his age and didn't like sports. Instead, he loved music and enjoyed the more academic side of school. Because Hugh wasn't getting knocks on the playing fields, it meant he didn't get too many bleeds. His visits to the hospital were few and far between. It was quite a comparison – while his brothers could be in hospital every other week, Hugh went only a couple of times in total. It was ironic, therefore, that Hugh would be the person to contract HIV when a young man. But finding out wasn't a huge shock. The reason was that the doctor didn't fully explain to them what the situation was. Shirley was attending Saint James's Hospital with Hugh. She told the tribunal: "We met this doctor and he didn't come out really that Hugh had HIV. He must have been hovering around it and he said that if he ever was sick or [there were] any body fluids or anything like that, we were to wash it with bleach . . . He told us that it was his last day working there as a doctor and I shook hands with him and wished him good luck. So he shook hands with us. We just left then."

Raymond asked her: "Did you understand the full consequences of HIV?"

Shirley said: "No."

Raymond: "Or what the future would hold for Hugh?"

Shirley responded: "No, definitely not"

When Shirley was speaking about this day, it reminded me about a visit I had paid to her home with Raymond in the run-up to the tribunal. We called one evening to take her statement but were greeted by the whole family. It was slightly overwhelming as we were accorded a welcome befitting royalty. When we came to discuss what Shirley would tell the tribunal, she was able to recount almost exactly what happened on any particular day. She kept a small diary which recorded moments of significance in her life. Shirley could therefore speak with authority. The diary also made it clear that they didn't realise either the significance of the HIV diagnosis or its consequences.

Around Hugh's twenty-seventh birthday, she travelled to Saint James's Hospital with him to get some test results. An infection was found in his lung and he was kept in for three weeks on a ventilator. Shirley hadn't realised what a bad condition Hugh was in. His weak state was really highlighted as they were leaving. Hugh hated lifts. This was unfortunate as haemophilia patients were treated on the top floor of Saint James's Hospital Number 1. It took a lot of effort to get Hugh down three flights of stairs. When he did get home, his condition deteriorated further.

Shirley told the tribunal: "He really got worse then, every day weaker and weaker and terrible looking." With the support of her family, Shirley was able to look after Hugh. Sometimes they would try to relieve the boredom by taking him out in his wheelchair to the beach. Like so many his age, Hugh didn't like people looking at him so they ended up travelling to remote parts of the country.

Shirley said: "I think he knew himself, you know, I think he overheard them saying in the hospital that he had AIDS, you know, so he kind of went down." As Hugh became progressively weaker, the IHS was able to help by providing a nurse. It was a huge relief as Shirley no longer had to get up out of bed several times a night. She became so wrapped up in caring for Hugh that she didn't really notice the further deterioration. In her evidence, she said she didn't really think that Hugh looked really bad – it was only when she looked at photographs after his death that she realised he was like a walking skeleton.

Towards the end of her evidence, Shirley was asked what products she believed were responsible for Hugh's death. This was the mother of one of seven people to have been infected by Irish-made Factor IX. Her answer was stark because it underlined how little those who were given the products had been told about them. Shirley told the tribunal: "Well, the only thing we were told is that it was contaminated blood and it came from America. That's just all we were told." Her answer provoked a feeling of outrage in me. Why was it that when the Blood Bank knew its products were almost certainly responsible in 1986 that it was only made public in 2000? Why did five of the seven people infected have to go to their graves not knowing the true cause of their infections? Why?

Professor Temperley was questioned about this issue by our barrister Martin Hayden SC. Asked whether he informed patients who used Factor IX of his belief that the Blood Bank material was responsible for their HIV status, the professor said: "I don't know whether I did tell patients or didn't tell patients that the BTSB [was] involved. I don't think I particularly disguised it." When pressed further on the matter, the professor said it was a "blank" in his mind.

Shirley's last piece of evidence was straightforward but spoke volumes about what her family had experienced. She said: "I'd just like to say that I am so sad about the way Hugh died. I think that we should have had a lot more counselling, you know. We had no counselling really at all at the time. We just had to do everything ourselves."

I was waiting for Shirley once she had completed her evidence. As she had spoken from behind a screen to protect her anonymity, it was easy for us to slip out of the building and disappear into the crowd. I remember walking beside her and observing that she was immaculately dressed for the occasion. Shirley was extremely emotional and anxious that she'd done the best for her son. I was able to reassure her that she had done Hugh proud.

The day had a big impact on me. I think Shirley's story was hugely important because of the fact that Irish blood products had infected her son. But there was also a personal reason: Shirley gave evidence on my son John Joe's twenty-first birthday. The loss of a son had a particular resonance: I was going to be able to celebrate a special occasion whereas she was going to be reflecting on what might have been.

Another story which had a huge impact was that of Luke. I first met him in the mid-1990s. We didn't just bump into each other. I was seeking him out because of his extreme reluctance to go to hospital and get his hepatitis C condition treated. I knew there was no way Luke was going to come to the office for a chat and so I went about tracking him down at the hospital where he was picking up his clotting-agents. Luke was a very angry young man. I knew he was dealing with a lot of worries, but that he was also hard-headed and not going to seek counselling. When I arrived there, it was crowded. Luke turned up in a leather jacket. He spoke with me, but clearly didn't want to. I tried to reach out, using my youth-worker skills, but the only thing I achieved was to get him on to our mailing list. We had infrequent communication running up to the tribunal, but, as it turned out, he was keeping up to date with proceedings in the newspapers. His anger grew at what he read every day and then, out of the blue, he rang me and said he wanted to testify. He couldn't stomach it anymore.

Luke used the Factor IX blood product but, as he had mild haemophilia, he rarely required treatment. He explained to the tribunal that he liked to play soccer and other contact sports and, while he picked up significant injuries, he didn't need Factor IX. In fact, it was only on three occasions that he required injections of concentrates. In 1991, he was visiting Saint James's Hospital on a routine visit about his teeth when he was asked to see Professor Temperley. Luke didn't know what the meeting was about and hadn't met the professor before, but duly went down to see him after conducting his scheduled business.

Luke told the tribunal: ". . . he [Professor Temperley] says – you contracted hepatitis C through an infected blood product that you received here. And he told me very, very briefly what hepatitis C was. He says – it's a disease that affects the liver . . . and it's a small percentage chance you have of it ever harming you, but there is a chance that it could. There is no cure for it, he told me. It's incurable, we cannot take it away from you. Once you have it, you have it and that is it. There is a very small chance that it will kill you, but it could kill you. And that is generally the gist. And he actually says that, we really don't know a lot about it ourselves at this present moment in time. I just said OK . . . It was five minutes I was in with the man."

Although I'd heard this type of story before, it still infuriated me. That was the extent of Luke's information about hepatitis C. No further appointments were fixed. Sitting at the back of the room, it confirmed to me that the lessons of HIV in the mid-1980s had not been learnt. Unnecessary mistakes were repeated. Unnecessary suffering was inflicted. It was heartrending to listen as Luke recalled his horror of learning he had hepatitis C. He said he was so afraid, that he didn't know who to tell. Two or three weeks later, he told his mother. He said he was still very confused, particularly because of the association between hepatitis C and AIDS.

Luke's story was all the more poignant because of what he found out after his diagnosis. It became apparent that he had contracted the virus in 1990. The date was important because at that time there was a blood product available which had been specially treated to kill off any hepatitis C. The tribunal showed how he was given two doses of the safe commercial product on September 19, 1990, after having had dental work. However, on October 25, 1990, he was given the older product after returning for further dental work. The older product was the one made by the Blood Bank during the period of the indemnity arrangement with Armour Pharmaceuticals. It had still been stored in the hospital. It was batch 9885 and it was infectious.

Luke told the tribunal: "It's just crazy. I find it totally crazy that they had good stuff, like, but they gave me the old unsafe product. It was just a lottery like that I didn't get HIV."

It was dramatic evidence. Luke explained that any thoughts of the future were tempered by the reality that he could go to a haemophilia clinic at any time and be told that his liver was collapsing. He said he could be in a hospital bed in six months' time. Luke's concept of the future was limited to one hour ahead. In fact, time had become so precious that he felt that to sleep was to waste it.

While most people can think of relationships and jobs optimistically, it's all a minefield for Luke. He wants to complete college but has to spend a lot of energy looking after his health. If he does get qualifications, many employers now demand medicals and his condition could create problems. Regarding relationships, he said he was at a loss as to when he could tell someone he was hepatitis C positive. It reminded me of Austin all over again. He told the tribunal: "I have had one relationship . . . and that has finished up because of . . . it. Unless I meet someone with AIDS or HIV or hepatitis C . . . I couldn't see myself . . . getting into a relationship. It would be just a waste of time for that person. I would probably be too difficult to live with anyway, you know."

Finishing his evidence, Luke said he wanted to find out who had infected him. The fact that he first received safe clotting-agents and then unsafe product, was something he was still trying to deal with: "You know, why, why didn't they throw that stuff out when they had definite stuff, because it was worth a couple of quid, like you know, is it money and like accountants, is that who was running the Blood Bank?"

Professor Temperley was questioned closely about this case. He said he had issued directions to the dispatch department of Saint James's Hospital on June 7, 1990 that no person was to receive the older product unless it was an emergency. One key flaw in the letter was that he only referred to Factor VIII but not Factor IX.

Speaking about Luke receiving that product in October 1990, John Finlay SC put it to the professor: "This should not have happened."

Professor Temperley said: "Well, I agree."

Mr Finlay said: "It was your job at the time to ensure that such a thing as this did not happen."

Professor Temperley didn't agree: "I couldn't be everywhere and, you know, I couldn't be in the ward at the time the treatment was given . . ."

Mr Finlay: "No, professor, but I have to put it to you: it was your responsibility to ensure that the doctors working under you in the haematology department understood sufficiently the importance and significance of the changeover in product."

The professor replied: "Well, I mean, of course you can say I'm responsible for everything and anything that happens in the centre or associated with the centre, but I mean, I'm only one man."

Mr Finlay pointed out that the professor was not the person who had prescribed the old product, but he also noted that he hadn't sent out a written protocol to his colleagues identifying that the old product shouldn't have been used.

Paul Lynam, the chief technologist at Saint James's Hospital, was also questioned about how the old Blood Bank product came to be issued. He said that a patient who had obtained a quantity of the old Factor IX in 1989, before going on holidays, subsequently returned it to the hospital. He said he didn't stop it from being used because the professor's letter of June 1990 only referred to Factor VIII and not Factor IX. He was asked whether or not he consulted with the professor on the basis that his letter indicated a clear preference for the new type of blood product. However, Mr Lynam said he didn't because it specifically referred to Factor VIII only.

The idea that a person would get infected from the old product when the safer clotting agent was available was shocking. In my view, it was unforgivable. In helping Luke prepare for the tribunal, we spent quite a bit of time together. I called him several times after he had given evidence to see how he was getting on. He promised that he would keep in touch with the IHS and avail of counselling. Of course, that never happened. I knew that that would be the case, because he'd always done things his own way. I understand and respect it. He does, however, know that help and support is available.

17

The Medical Response

Rory and his girlfriend were discussing where they might go on their honeymoon when I dropped into Saint James's Hospital one afternoon. They were very much in love and, in that irresistible way, refused to believe that anything could separate them or interfere with their plans. It was a difficult discussion for me to listen to because, while I longed for them to enjoy their dreams of paradise islands, in my heart I knew that Rory would never recover enough to get married, let alone fly off on an exotic holiday. Rory had contracted HIV from contaminated blood products and had now developed full-blown AIDS. He was going to die.

Margaret King and I visited Rory quite often as he suffered a lot of infections. This meant that we were able to monitor his condition and ensure he was taken home when he slipped into the terminal stages. I was not able to join Margaret and take care of Rory as my mother was seriously ill at the time. I remember walking into the house before the funeral and being greeted by his father. The grief and pain on the man's face was terrible. It was a normal country home filled with neighbours. I went into the bedroom. It was heartbreaking to see a young man, still beautiful despite the pain and suffering he had endured, lying dead on a bed in his best suit. My mind was screaming: "Why, oh why, did this have to happen?"

That question was something which also ran through the minds of his family and led to his mother giving evidence at the Lindsay Tribunal. Using the pseudonym Jackie, she explained how Rory was born in March 1973 and for the following nine years was treated with cryoprecipitate. While she knew that concentrates could mean less time in hospital for Rory, she was reluctant to use them as she had a phobia about needles. Then Jackie met Professor Temperley. He explained the advantages. Jackie told the tribunal that she remembered asking the professor would she be able to inject her son considering her phobia. His response was: "Yes, even you."

In August 1983, Rory was spending some time in hospital and his mother used the opportunity to learn how to administer concentrated clotting-agents. She was successful. The next month, she gave him his first treatment at home. The critical thing, she told the tribunal, was that at this time she was not aware of any risks. She said she had received no warning about AIDS during 1983 or 1984. This also meant that she didn't know cryo carried a lesser risk of AIDS because it was made from only five donations.

In January 1986, Jackie's world fell apart. Rory had been admitted to Harcourt Street Hospital for an operation on his knee but didn't recover well after the surgery. He was just thirteen. Rory had been diagnosed the previous year as having contracted hepatitis B. Worried about the operation, she asked Professor Temperley how Rory was faring and was informed that he was "OK". On that very same day, a nurse told Jackie: "You know we're not treating your son any differently because he is HIV positive." It was the first time she'd heard about the virus. Yet another family devastated by a bombshell disclosure.

Jackie told the tribunal: "It was like getting a kick in the stomach. I went speechless. I was unaware [of this]. I went home that Friday evening and I said it to my husband, and he said: 'It's a mistake.' So he came back up the first opportunity he had. He met Professor Temperley . . . My husband was questioning him to know what was wrong and why there were so many problems. 'Well,' he said, 'he has it' or words to that effect. And [my husband] said, 'What do you mean?' 'Well,' the professor told him, 'he has got the virus.' And he just disappeared down the corridor and we were left to deal with it as best we could."

Jackie said there was no further discussion with the professor concerning Rory's HIV status. The hospital had told her to take precautions regarding hepatitis B but not HIV. She told the tribunal that what haunted her was the fact that if she had kept her son on 'cryo' rather than concentrates he may not have become infected. Jackie felt that had she been informed about the emerging concerns associated with the concentrates in 1983, she might have taken a different decision. She said she was "only looking for an excuse" not to use them due to her phobia about needles. A test for HIV was not available until 1985, but there was an emerging understanding in 1983 in medical circles that an unidentified virus might have been causing major problems.

The question of informing patients about possible dangers associated with concentrates was a key issue for the tribunal. A statement by one man with haemophilia summed up the experience of most: "The only choice I ever got about concentrated clotting-agents – which arm do you want the needle in, left or right?"

Professor Temperley was questioned closely about Rory when he took the witness stand. Asked about Jackie's contention that she wasn't informed about the danger of AIDS from concentrates, the professor responded: "She could well be correct." When John Finlay SC suggested to him that Jackie would be the type of person who would rely on the medical profession for information, Professor Temperley said: "I probably didn't actually tell his mother the pros and cons of this. I just felt that it was essential to go on." He defended his decision to switch Rory on to concentrates saying it was an "essential move" as the boy's condition was "deteriorating" quickly. The professor argued he wasn't being thoughtless, but making a clinical decision based on the perceived risk at the time. He was at pains to stress that his medical team "put an awful lot of effort" into helping Rory.

The professor's answers summed up, to me, the manner in which the medical profession operated at that time. Patients or their relatives were not consulted but were told what was going to happen. Diagnosis was often conveyed in incredibly harsh ways. The way in which Jackie found out was far from unique. Nobody could suggest that Professor Temperley didn't care, but at the same time the method and level of communication was not good enough. His evidence left me cold.

As I listened, my mind drifted back to Rory. I remembered sitting one time with him in Saint James's Hospital trying to explain that a particular aspect of his condition could lead to him going blind. His response was to tell me that he still hoped to fulfill his engagement promise to his girlfriend. He then smiled – one of those smiles which lit up the room. He died at the age of twenty-five without fulfilling his promise.

Seeing Professor Temperley under pressure in the witness box was very difficult for many members of the IHS. They felt extremely uncomfortable as this was a man who had helped establish the organisation. He took an interest when nobody else did. Professor Temperley was a recognised treating doctor on the world stage and members were often in awe of him. It's not an exaggeration to say that some viewed him as a saviour – many would have died earlier but for him.

While this wealth of trust existed for many, it was accompanied by a profound sense of confusion over his decision to desert them in their greatest hour of need. He opted to take a sabbatical in 1985 when he knew that dozens of his patients needed to be informed that they had become infected with HIV through blood products. This caused immense hurt. I didn't realise the depth of anger until he was questioned about the matter at the tribunal.

Professor Temperley explained that the sabbatical was first mooted in 1984 and there was some documentation to support this. He had just established the bone-marrow transplant unit while also remaining the main treater of haemophilia. He felt he needed a break and the sabbatical had taken a lot of effort to put in place.

John Finlay put it to him: "By March of 1985, wasn't it clear that there was a very serious crisis facing your haemophilia patients?"

The professor responded: "That is true, yes, but I felt I had to get away . . . to regenerate, to come back and . . . I needed this badly . . . It became difficult to function without some break."

Mr Finlay then asked him: "Did it occur to you to postpone the sabbatical because of the problem?"

Professor Temperley responded: "I would never have got this [sabbatical] back if I had done. I mean, it was very difficult to set this up again."

However, he accepted that at the end of 1984 and the beginning of the following year that trial tests for HIV were done and he expected at least 50 per cent to be returned positive. By March 1985, the results had been returned from Middlesex Hospital. Of 133 samples, fifty-four proved HIV antibody positive. Some repeat tests were requested. Professor Temperley said he still went on sabbatical as his position was to be covered by a number of stand-in doctors, known as locums, and they were all competent.

Martin Hayden SC, for the IHS put it to Professor Temperley that he should have taken the responsibility for telling his own patients. The professor said that ideally this should have been so, but he had been in hospital with a stress-type illness and was all the better for going away. He was able to work much more effectively when he returned. Ultimately, I felt his explanation wasn't good enough. HIV in 1985 was the worst condition any person could have. Professor Temperley described his haemophilia patients as being like his children – how could he desert his 'children' when they were about to be given a death sentence?

Professor Temperley's absence was all the more important because Factor IX manufactured by the Blood Bank was not being heat-treated in 1985, despite his letter to Pelican House in December 1984. He told the tribunal that the Blood Bank promised him it would introduce the procedure in March and then again in April. This didn't happen. By the time he was leaving on sabbatical, the new deadline was September. Had he been around, it might have been possible to speed up the introduction of safe Factor IX, or at least ensure that the Blood Bank met its deadline.

One of the locums who filled in for Professor Temperley was Dr Helena Daly. She's the type of person I automatically like – straight-talking. More importantly, she was also one of the few doctors who I felt tried their absolute hardest to do the right thing – irrespective of the consequences. Prior to working in Saint James's Hospital, she had helped to treat a patient in Bristol who was dying from an AIDS-related illness. Dr Daly knew about the risks associated with blood products which had not been heat-treated to eliminate HIV.

On arriving in Dublin on July 1, 1985, Dr Daly learned that while Factor VIII concentrates were heat-treated from the beginning of the year, the Irish-made Factor IX still was not. She was extremely worried. While there had been concerns earlier in the year that heating Factor IX could cause problems for the patient, Dr Daly believed they had now been dealt with. She wanted all of her patients to be using heat-treated Factor IX. Her first move was to call a meeting with the Blood Bank's national director, Jack O'Riordan, and senior official Sean Hanratty in August. Her aim was clear: Factor IX needed to be heat-treated immediately. Unfortunately, the request was dismissed as "outrageous". Though she left the Blood Bank bewildered, her visit must have had an effect as it emerged at the tribunal that the following day a decision was taken to heat-treat Factor IX.

While Dr Daly had been told that she would not receive BTSB heat-treated Factor IX, she didn't know that the Blood Bank had a large stock of commercial Factor IX which had been virally inactivated. The Blood Bank never informed her of what it had in store. Dr Daly did accept, however, that some patients felt Irish blood products were safer because of the low incidence of HIV in this country and the fact that donations were voluntary. On that basis, they were reluctant to use the commercial material.

Dr Daly left the meeting with Blood Bank officials feeling "deflated". However, she still felt compelled to do something and so she phoned Professor Temperley. Shortly afterwards, she travelled to London where the professor was on sabbatical and outlined her concern in person. The professor in turn wrote to the Blood Bank. He said: "I thought that I made it plain that we would require all products to be heat-treated." In very strong language he said: "We would be failing in our duty knowing what we now know [about HIV] if we allowed anyone in the future to become infected." Unfortunately, rather than demanding that only heat-treated material be used, Professor Temperley gave them a new deadline of November 1, 1985, to stop issuing non-heat-treated Factor IX. He would later admit this decision was a mistake, but qualify the statement by saying: "It's easy to say that in hindsight."

Faced with an obstinate Blood Bank, Dr Daly consequently modified her treatment practice to minimise the exposure of patients to non-heat-treated Factor IX. She used heat-treated material as often as possible. Despite being in no doubt about her dislike for non-heat-treated Factor IX, Pelican House increased the amount it was sending to her hospital. In the month of July 1985, she received 20,000 units of non-heat-treated Factor IX. However, records from Saint James's Hospital showed that three days after the August meeting in which she stated her opposition to non-heat-treated Factor IX, the Blood Bank sent her 44,772 units. A week after that, they sent her a further 43,940 units. The total for August was 120,832 units – six times greater than the average monthly take. Mr Finlay asked her: "Now, were you able to find any special or particular reason for that supply of Factor IX?" Dr Daly said simply: "No." Listening to the evidence, I was dumbstruck. Was the Blood Bank attempting to dump Factor IX which would be redundant by November?

John Finlay SC suggested to Dr Daly that it would have been possible for her to order more heat-treated Factor IX from commercial sources or from the Blood Bank. Some hospitals did purchase concentrates directly from companies. But the usual way was to purchase directly from the Blood

Bank. Dr Daly said she felt powerless – the November deadline for the introduction of heat-treated Factor IX had taken the matter out of her hands.

With Professor Temperley on sabbatical, the duty of informing people with haemophilia about whether or not they contracted HIV fell to Dr Daly. She received a list with the results of the HIV tests of her patients. Dr Daly said she tried her best, but it wasn't possible to contact everyone between the time she took up her position in July 1985 and when she left at the end of September that year.

Dr Daly said she counselled proportionately more positive than negative patients. Those who were not infected still needed to be spoken with as they had concerns about how safe the products now were. To those who tested positive, Dr Daly's approach was to emphasise the danger of sexual transmission and she recounted to the tribunal her dealings with Brian O'Mahony. He'd made contact with her shortly after her appointment and pointed out that people with haemophilia were not being given their test results promptly or advised on the dangers of sexual transmission. They agreed that when Dr Daly gave test results, the people would then be sent out to meet Brian in the car-park where they would receive condoms to help prevent HIV transmission. The hospital could not do it as they would be in breach of the law. Dr Daly said she felt her counselling service was important as the only other source of information in 1985 was the media. She said she didn't think that was the best way to get information, given the hysteria at the time.

Dr Daly said that after finishing her three-month contract in Saint James's Hospital, she passed all of her information to Dr Fred Jackson. Dr Jackson had worked under Professor Temperley previously at Saint James's. She said she met him in the Central Pathology Laboratory and set out what she had done. She described the process as fairly detailed. Professor Temperley returned in November.

Obviously, I had no interaction with Dr Daly during the period under discussion, having only joined the IHS in 1989. However, the members spoke warmly of her. We talked a number of times during the hearings. I was particularly impressed when she walked into the tribunal room and came over to Ray Kelly saying she was very sorry about his son's death. As far as I'm aware, she was the only doctor to do that.

While Dr Daly came away with her reputation intact, it was different for Dr Paule Cotter, head of the Regional Haemophilia Treatment Centre based in Cork. In our dealings, I always found her gracious. She had been head of the centre since 1979 and looked after about forty patients. However, haemophilia only took up about 10 per cent of her work.

Prior to giving evidence to the tribunal, Dr Cotter sat in the public gallery for a number of days. I would acknowledge her presence and she would always say hello back. While giving evidence Dr Cotter turned her head away from the legal teams and the public and focused instead on the brick wall behind Judge Lindsay. From the back of the room, I could only see the back of her head.

Like Professor Temperley before her, Dr Cotter underwent robust questioning about her actions. Factor IX remained a central focus. We now knew that while Factor VIII was being heat-treated to eliminate HIV from January 1985, the Blood Bank continued to issue non-heat-treated Factor IX. The Blood Bank had argued at the tribunal that there were legitimate concerns that by heating Factor IX it could result in a patient getting unwanted clots. While Dr Daly felt these concerns were no longer valid in August 1985, some patients believed that non-heat-treated Factor IX was safer because it was made from Irish donations. That view was challenged in October 1985 when a HIV test was introduced in Ireland and a person tested positive within two weeks. I felt this should have resulted in the Blood Bank taking immediate action.

In her evidence, Dr Cotter maintained that she felt there was only a "small risk" from using the non-heat-treated Factor IX sent to her from the Blood Bank headquarters in Dublin. She accepted that, in hindsight, she should have sought heat-treated blood products. Things got very difficult for Dr Cotter when the tribunal moved on to analyse the medical records of various patients she had treated, in particular the case of Andrew who had only ever used Irish-made Factor IX.

In a forensic fashion, tribunal lawyer Gerry Durcan SC showed how Andrew had been negative for HIV in January 1985, but tested positive in November. In December, another test result confirmed he had been negative at the beginning of the year. This was crucial – Dr Cotter had the information that showed for the first time that the Blood Bank-made Factor IX blood product was infectious. No other product could have been responsible because Andrew used only Irish-made Factor IX.

Mr Durcan asked Dr Cotter: "Did you realise that this [result] was significant?"

Dr Cotter responded: "Well, I think that the huge significance of this didn't really . . . impress me at the actual time. As I say, we were getting a whole series of tests back."

Mr Durcan inquired from Dr Cotter if she contacted the Blood Bank considering she had information which showed that a Factor IX patient had become HIV positive from one of its products.

Dr Cotter said: "I have no recollection of doing that."

Mr Durcan put it to her: "So the position was that you

knew one of your patients had been infected by a BTSB product, but you didn't know which batch it was. And did it not occur to you that [the] BTSB product was out there in other hospitals being used and that it might infect other people?"

Dr Cotter answered: "I don't think that I realised this at the time in December [1985]. I think it was later, when we looked at the results and analysed them, that this became clear. I think that it looks very obvious retrospectively."

Despite having the critical information at the end of 1985, Dr Cotter did nothing. She did not inform the Blood Bank that its product was infective. She did not inform the Department of Health. She did not take any action that would have prevented the possibility of this product infecting other patients. Professor Temperley wasn't told in 1985. The material continued to be used in Cork after the definitive results came through. Andrew's brother was one of the people who used the Factor IX on December 8, 13 and 19, 1985. Thankfully, it didn't cause further infections there. Non-heat-treated Factor IX continued to be used nationally until February 1986. It caused a total of seven HIV infections – one of those people went on to infect their partner. Andrew was one of five people to die as a result.

This wasn't the only portion of Dr Cotter's evidence which was controversial. She had written to all her patients advising them that they should be tested for HIV. The first problem is that no copies of letters said to have been sent to the patients are still in existence. When the results came back, they were put on a handwritten sheet of paper which she kept in a drawer in her desk, but also, she said, in her head. Once a test had been carried out and the results arrived back, no letters of notification were sent out. Dr Cotter waited for patients to call into the clinic for their next check-up before giving them their results. Some claimed they were never told. As I listened to her evidence, it struck me that this method of informing people was extremely haphazard and unsatisfactory. It meant that individuals were unaware of their HIV status and family members were exposed to unnecessary and avoidable risks.

Dr Cotter defended her position by claiming her system was a means of protecting confidentiality – writing a letter inviting people to come in for results was inappropriate. I found it difficult to see how a letter which says "Please come in to discuss test results" could have any impact on confidentiality. I don't believe patients ought to have been informed of their test results by letter, but they should have been invited on a systematic basis to discuss the results. Furthermore, when patients were informed of their test results, no counselling was provided. Some patients who sought counselling received it from Cork AIDS Alliance. In many cases where re-checks were required, there was an unacceptable delay between the first and the second test.

Dr Cotter was questioned about a patient called Noel in relation to informing people of their diagnosis. Noel was tested for HIV in January 1985. Dr Cotter maintained he was informed that he was HIV positive later that year. However, a letter written by Dr Cotter in 1992 refers to the fact that Noel did not appear to realise he was HIV positive. Dr Cotter's side of the story was that while there was no record of him being informed, he was told in late 1985. When he emigrated in 1988, Dr Cotter maintained that efforts were made to contact him in England to ensure that he received adequate treatment. Her explanation for his surprise at being told he was HIV positive in 1992 was that people often go into a state of denial when informed of bad news.

At this point things erupted. Noel's brother, Fred, had

been sitting at the back of the room listening to her evidence. He was getting increasingly angry as he clearly didn't believe that his brother had ever been told.

Gerry Durcan SC was asking: "He [Noel] was under the impression that he hadn't . . . that he didn't know."

Dr Cotter responded: "Well, I think that you have heard earlier in the evidence from the social worker in Saint James's, that sometimes − if people are given bad news − they go into a state of denial, and I think she had evidence of many patients being told of a diagnosis, forgetting that they had been told or not realising that they were positive."

Mr Durcan responded: "I see. So you believe that it was one of those explanations. He was either in denial of what he had been told or had in some way blanked it from his − "

Fred couldn't take any more. He jumped up from his seat and shouted: "I'm Fred, right. That's my brother. He's dead. That is a lie!"

I took Fred outside as Judge Lindsay and Mr Durcan tried to work out what to do. Fred was absolutely furious and yet was apologising to me for causing trouble. I sat outside with him and explained that he didn't need to apologise to me − I understood. I had been with Fred at the time of Noel's death. They had been extremely close and Noel's death disturbed him deeply. As his anger began to ebb, I remember Fred asking me whether or not he should apologise to the tribunal. My feeling at the time was: "No! Why should you apologise in such circumstances?" Yet, being the gentleman he's always been, Fred took the appropriate action and an apology was conveyed to Judge Lindsay.

I found the whole affair deeply depressing. Noel had been living abroad around the time of the HIV compensation deal in 1991. A number of years later he returned to Ireland and I remember him coming into the office with his wife. Margaret

King, as always, was the person deputised to speak with them. I spoke to Noel subsequently and he was adamant that he was not told about his HIV positive status in 1985. I believed him then and believe him now.

After Fred's apology, Raymond Bradley cross-examined Dr Cotter. Raymond and I had met Dr Cotter previously at Cork University Hospital and it seemed to me that she liked him. If that was true, her admiration for our solicitor was about to be put to the test.

Raymond asked: "Dr Cotter, is there any documentary evidence to confirm the imparting of Noel's HIV diagnosis to him in or around November 1985?"

She responded: "I think that there is good circumstantial evidence and that it was my practice to follow up results to inform the patients [and] to keep in contact with them."

Raymond: "With all due respect, doctor, is there any documentary evidence in respect of Noel's HIV diagnosis in November 1985?"

Her answer was curt: "There is nothing in my notes."

Raymond: "Is there any documentation elsewhere other than in the notes that you are aware of?"

Her answer: "I believe that there would be the result of an HIV test and that would be on a sheet with the other HIV results."

Raymond re-directed her to his question: "Doctor, that is a HIV test result. I am talking about confirmation of imparting HIV diagnosis to a patient. Is there any evidence of that in terms of documentation?"

Dr Cotter's answer: "There is no documentation in the notes to say that but, as I have told the tribunal earlier, for reasons of confidentiality it wasn't our practice to write in the notes."

Part of the reason that the IHS pressed Dr Cotter about

this issue was because of a boy called Garrett. In 1985, Dr Cotter informed his GP that Garrett was HIV negative. In fact, Garrett was HIV positive. Dr Cotter's misinformation came from a handwritten list containing a result for Garrett. The list was inaccurate. Dr Cotter said she accepted that this was an unsatisfactory situation.

As the tribunal investigated the case, it emerged that Garrett's mother may not have been told of her son's HIV positive status until 1990 – five years later. His mother said she found out while attending Cork Regional Hospital to collect clotting-agents ahead of her son's departure to France for a holiday. Raymond explained why Garrett's mother was so clear about the issue – her son was re-tested for HIV in March or April 1990 and, up to that date, believed he was HIV negative. However, Dr Cotter maintained Garrett's parents knew of his HIV positive test shortly after she got the result, but couldn't remember the exact circumstances of how and when she told them. Raymond cross-examined Dr Cotter and stated that Garrett's mother was "adamant" that she was told in August 1990.

Raymond asked the doctor: "Do you accept that Garrett's mother was informed in August 1990 for the first time of his HIV diagnosis?"

Dr Cotter replied: "If that is what she says, I would not dispute it, but I believed she knew earlier."

Raymond asked Dr Cotter: "Do you accept there was a test in and around that period?"

Dr Cotter answered: "If she says so, I'm sure there was, yes."

The additional pain in this story was that Garrett found out his HIV status by accident when he read a letter addressed to his parents. He went through his Leaving Cert not telling his parents that he knew of his HIV status so that he wouldn't upset them. I only got to know Garrett well from the mid-1990s. He insisted on giving evidence at the tribunal and the articulate fashion in which he gave his testimony really impressed me.

Despite all the odds, Garrett is a fine young man who has gone on and pursued his further education and is living life to the full. Yet his difficulties with Dr Cotter didn't end with the issue of his diagnosis. She didn't refer him to Dublin in 1995 or early 1996 to avail of the new combination drug therapy which would have significantly reduced his chances of developing full-blown AIDS. I met him in July 1996 to discuss securing compensation and was extremely worried about his weak physical state. I tried to convince him to come to Dublin to get the new treatment. However, he was so weak by this stage that he felt like giving up. Thankfully, he did come in the end.

Listening to the evidence of the members, it was clear that they placed total trust in their doctors and believed that they would work unswervingly to protect them. However, it was a rude awakening for them to hear what was actually going on. In my view, they were badly let down – and not just once. The fact that they became infected with HIV and hepatitis C was bad enough: they were reeling from the shock that their medicine was probably going to kill them. But, what I found unforgivable was that they were further let down in the quality of care they got after diagnosis.

In relation to Factor IX, things were also becoming clearer. We now knew Professor Temperley told the Blood Bank in December 1984 that he wanted all concentrates to be heat-treated from the beginning of 1985. The Blood Bank had said the request in relation to Factor IX was receiving "urgent attention", but nothing seemed to happen. An intervention by Dr Daly in August 1985 had been rebuffed. However, Professor Temperley reached a compromise deal in which heat-treated Factor IX would be used from November 1985. Even then, the old non-heat-treated blood product was not recalled from patients or hospitals and continued to be used by one child until February 1986. This was despite the fact that the Blood Bank was aware just two weeks after introducing its HIV test in October 1985 that the Irish blood supply was not free from HIV. Dr Cotter hadn't told either the Blood Bank or Professor Temperley at the end of 1985 that Factor IX was infected, even though she had the evidence.

If this wasn't bad enough, the Blood Bank had been told by Professor Temperley that its Factor IX product was probably responsible for HIV infections in mid-1986. Three senior officials were aware of this fact yet nothing seems to have been done. Indeed, two officials subsequently went on to deny information they knew to be true. The board at the very least knew there was a problem with Factor IX but never followed it up. Somehow in 1991, the State and the Blood Bank were party to a settlement for HIV infections which did not specify that Irish-made blood products had caused infections.

It didn't add up.

While Professor Temperley, Dr Daly, Professor Egan and Dr Cotter were the central focus for the tribunal, the behaviour of other doctors was also called into question. Trevor gave evidence to the tribunal on May 4, 2000, and his story was typical of many others. He went to see an unnamed doctor about confirmation of a hepatitis C positive result at Saint James's Hospital. The doctor said to him: "Yeah, you've got it alright." Then he sat back in his big chair and yawned. Many members told me afterwards that their diagnoses was communicated in a similarly insensitive fashion.

Hospitals were also criticised for failing to provide necessary counselling when it became known that a third of the haemophilia community had become infected with HIV. When hepatitis C later struck, it didn't appear that the hard lessons of the mid-1980s had been learnt. Isobel, whose husband John had died at Saint Vincent's Hospital from liver disease caused by the virus, told the tribunal on May 4, 2000 that they had felt isolated and should have received professional help. In response, Deirdre Murphy SC for Saint James's said that from 1985: "Strenuous efforts were made by medical teams and administrations to get funding for additional social workers." However, when Ms Murphy said finance for two additional social workers came from National Lottery funds it drew a sharp response from Isobel. She said: "That is just about the size of it, isn't it? Lottery funds . . . and our community was being devastated."

It was now up to Judge Lindsay to make a judgment on whether the Blood Bank's introduction of heat-treated Factor IX in November 1985 was timely and appropriate. She would also have to rule on the fact that non-heat-treated Factor IX was used up until February 1986 because an effective re-call system was not put in place. The actions of Professor Temperley and Dr Cotter would also be assessed.

It seemed we were going to be left in the dark about the state of knowledge of the board of the Blood Bank in relation to this matter. I felt this was an inexplicable decision by the tribunal considering that a senior Blood Bank official had contended he did inform his board. There was no testimony contradicting his evidence – yet the tribunal would interpret minutes of board meetings to assess whether or not it knew. We believed that the Factor IX infections were known to the board and therefore Department of Health officials. While we wouldn't get the chance to question the board, we would at least have the chance to press this issue when previous Ministers for Health and their officials came to give evidence. Before that, there would be further battles with the tribunal's legal team.

18

In The Background

On the last day of November 2000, Joe Dowling's daughter gave evidence. Linda said she was coming forward because Joe would have – if he was alive. She was a quiet but determined person and those qualities reminded me of Joe.

Linda explained how she grew up in the knowledge that her father had HIV. She later learned that he had also been infected with hepatitis C. She detailed how Joe became involved in the political campaign in the late 1980s for compensation for those infected with HIV. She said he felt bitter that he had to waste two years fighting for something which should have been automatic. Linda said he was delighted when the Fianna Fáil minority Government collapsed in 1989 over the question of establishing a trust fund for people with haemophilia infected with HIV.

Towards the end of her evidence, Linda began to address what she wanted from the Lindsay Tribunal. Her focus, in the main, related to the pharmaceutical companies which exported blood products into Ireland in the 1970s and 1980s.

This wasn't all that surprising considering these were the clotting-agents which were responsible for infecting Joe.

She told the tribunal: "I would ask that they be questioned or investigated because ultimately they infected – one of them infected my father." Linda said this was something which should be pursued for all of the citizens of the country.

Yet when Linda attempted to raise another concern about the way in which the Blood Bank operated, tribunal lawyer, John Finlay SC, interjected and said to Judge Lindsay: "Chairperson, I think the tribunal has shown now considerable indulgence to this witness and what is, in effect, a speech."

I couldn't believe my ears: Linda was, in effect, being told to shut up.

Mr Finlay went on: "And I can understand her feelings and her wish to express her feelings, but I think now she is transgressing any reasonable limit at this point."

Linda looked bewildered as she looked from Mr Finlay to the judge. I was incensed.

Raymond said: "I think the witness wishes probably to inform the tribunal of her personal feelings in relation to many issues."

However, Judge Lindsay, sided with her lead tribunal counsel: "I have listened to them carefully and I think she has made her case, and she has made her points very adequately and I think she has done it in a very open and fair manner, so I think that is sufficient."

This was a defining moment in my relationship with the tribunal. It seemed to me, rightly or wrongly, that 'considerable indulgences' were being granted to other witnesses but the IHS was being treated as if it were a nuisance. This was Linda's story and she had the right to tell it. The use of the word "speech" really stuck in my throat. Wasn't it reasonable that a woman whose father had died as a direct result of an

imported blood product had the right to articulate her belief
that the manufacturing firms be investigated? Wasn't it fair
that she be allowed to complete her evidence? Was the use of
words "considerable indulgence" and "speech" not inconsiderate?
My mind drifted back to an interview which Joe had given in
1988 about his brother's death from an AIDS-related illness in
which he said: "I feel very very bitter about my brother dying
from the disease. I really feel that he was murdered by the
American pharmaceutical companies." Linda was articulating
what Joe had wanted.

Linda was also fuming that her evidence had been
curtailed. Afterwards she told reporters: "What I wanted to
say was that I felt my father spent two years working on the
compensation campaign which they [the Government] could
have stopped at any stage and forwarded compensation to the
people that were involved. Furthermore, I would like to see
the American pharmaceutical companies investigated because
we still to this day don't know who was responsible for
infecting him."

I felt the tribunal was saying to our members: "Come in,
stick to the script, take up as little time as possible and go
away." Maybe that's unfair, but it is what I felt. When I met
with our legal team at the end of the day's proceedings I was
still angry. I instructed Raymond to write a letter to the
tribunal and express our disgust at what we perceived to be
insensitive comments and an unfair approach. I believe that
a form of apology was later tendered to Linda Dowling. Part
of the reason I felt so strongly about Linda's experience was
that this wasn't the first run-in with the tribunal's legal team
on the issue of personal testimony.

An earlier witness, Damien, was asked a question by John
Finlay SC which I felt was not just irrelevant but was
offensive. Damien had just explained his story including the

fact that he had secured compensation from the State in 1991. Mr Finlay asked Damien what he did with the compensation. This was greeted with gasps of surprise from the public gallery. We all looked at each other and wondered what was the point of the question. Damien was sharp however. He replied: "I paid the mortgage and invested it. It's not like winning the lottery – you can't spend it and have a good time." It was unbelievable.

Another witness, Martin, was explaining how his son, Stephen, became infected with HIV through blood products when he was interrupted by Mr Finlay on two occasions. The first interruption occurred when he made a complaint about a hospital which had not been in the written statement he had furnished to the tribunal. Judge Lindsay upheld Mr Finlay's argument that Martin's complaint was unfair as it wasn't in his statement and therefore the hospital wasn't able to prepare a rebuttal. I felt that this was an unfair procedure because Blood Bank officials didn't appear to be tied to their statements. It was also a policy which was extremely difficult for those giving personal testimony. People sometimes recalled issues while in the witness box but were then blocked from stating them. When the first argument occurred, Martin said to Judge Lindsay: "I don't want to appear out of line or anything, but I'm almost sixteen years waiting to tell my story, you know?" The second interruption came as Mr Finlay requested Judge Lindsay to order Martin to ensure his oral evidence followed the chronology of his written statement. The IHS barrister, Martin Hayden, had changed the chronology because a date in the statement was incorrect. He was ticked off by Judge Lindsay for not forewarning other parties. It was ridiculous.

In December 2000, another row erupted between the tribunal's legal team and the IHS. This time the subject was the medical records of people with haemophilia who had been infected with either HIV or hepatitis C. The tribunal had decided, having received extracts of medical records, that twenty-five records were representative of the entire group. We felt that this simply wasn't a correct approach to adopt. We decided to ask the tribunal to examine all of the medical records of those infected.

On December 18, 2000, our barrister, Martin Giblin SC, told the tribunal: "It is felt that it is not possible to say those twenty-five cases are representative of all – unless a look is taken at the 210 cases. And the Irish Haemophilia Society believes that the tribunal itself should look at those cases; not necessarily in public session." The tribunal was due to resume hearings on January 11 and so Mr Giblin requested that this date be put back so the examination of medical records could take place.

The suggestion was opposed by Brian McGovern SC, for Professor Temperley, on the basis that it would place a "wholly oppressive burden" on his client who had hoped to give further evidence the previous week but had now been put back until the new year. The professor wanted to give his evidence "without delay" in order to refute certain claims which had been made against him. The National Children's Hospital also opposed the suggestion on the basis that it would "further delay the work of this tribunal". The Blood Bank also expressed concern about the tribunal completing its work in an economical manner.

Mr Finlay, for the tribunal, said it would have been expected that such records would already have been made available by the IHS. He read into the record a series of letters between the tribunal and lawyers for the IHS. His conclusion was that the medical records should have been produced "a significant period of time ago".

He stated it was neither "relevant" nor "appropriate" for the tribunal to examine such a volume of records now. His only concession was that the lawyers for the IHS maybe should be allowed to submit records it deemed relevant, providing that the person in question had given their consent.

Judge Lindsay ruled that the IHS would have to undertake the review of medical records. This, I felt, was crazy as it was a huge task involving hospitals in Dublin and Cork. It was, at any rate, surely the work of the tribunal? She also set a deadline for the work to be done by January 8, 2001. She was therefore giving us twenty-one days to review all medical records. And it wasn't just any three-week period – it was over Christmas and the New Year. As it turned out, the hospitals were not prepared to grant immediate access. We only began to inspect the documents on January 3, 2001. I felt we were being forced to do a job which should have been undertaken by the tribunal. So much for an 'investigation'. As we were working on the medical records, we were not in a position to complete preparation for another appearance at the tribunal by Professor Temperley – possibly the most important witness.

We were not only having running battles with the tribunal, there were also fights with other participants. One key issue related to the constitutional right of any party at a tribunal or High Court hearing to withhold any record relating to legal advice or litigation. This right is known as legal professional privilege. We felt, however, that it was critical that all papers be put before the tribunal so that there would no doubts hanging over us at the end. This was particularly important to us in relation to Factor IX.

We received polar responses to our suggestion that we would waive our legal privilege if all other parties did the same. I remember going with Brian O'Mahony to a meeting with the Minister for Health, Micheál Martin. Brian asked him to waive privilege over departmental papers. He said he would. The meeting was over after one minute. I was left speechless which was a rare event in itself.

He later told the media: "There's an onus on us to be as helpful as we possibly can and, in particular, to make sure there are no doubts out there." His suggestion was taken up by the Irish Medicines Board.

The documents released by the Department of Health were of some interest. In particular, there was a letter dated December 1996 from the then Attorney General Dermot Gleeson SC to the then Minister for Health Michael Noonan. The letter was drafted as the IHS prepared to pull out of the Finlay Tribunal. The Government had wanted to know whether or not the tribunal team would be prepared to expand their terms of reference to take account of the haemophilia concerns. Mr Gleeson stated that if Mr Noonan made such a request it would be met "almost certainly with refusal". The reason given was that an inquiry in Canada into the same matter had lasted two years. Mr Gleeson explained just how opposed one of the tribunal lawyers was: "In colloquial terms, Mr [James] Nugent would feel that he needs a second inquiry like a hole in the head." No wonder we didn't get anywhere at that time.

However, the Blood Bank, Saint James's Hospital, and the Adelaide and Meath Hospital, incorporating the National Children's Hospital, absolutely refused to follow the lead set by Mr Martin. They were fully entitled to take this position, but I felt it was appalling. After all, the Blood Bank had either manufactured or imported the contaminated blood products while the hospitals had been responsible for either giving the clotting-agents to patients to take home or injecting them on site. When the Blood Bank also refused a request from the Oireachtas Joint Committee on Health and Children to waive privilege, Ray Kelly was back on the TV again: "I find that very, very hard to understand. It makes you wonder what they're hiding – what they have to hide. You know, the whole country is asking them to release these documents."

Considering the pain caused in the past and the fact that these same bodies were going to be dealing with the haemophilia community into the future, I felt it was a deeply distasteful decision. Surely they could at least have shown the documents to the tribunal team to prove there wasn't anything untoward in them? Such an approach would have prevented them coming into the public domain but also proven that they had nothing to hide. I felt it ensured that a sense of distrust would remain between the patients and the medical community.

Considering that seventy-seven of our members were dead, we felt the tribunal should be as aggressive as possible in getting to the bottom of matters. Instead, I felt the IHS was, at times, playing the role of defendant.

This feeling that we were in the dock came to a head on the morning of February 13, 2001. The IHS sought assistance from the tribunal in trying to get the Blood Bank to provide more information about 611 documents which it was withholding. We argued that the Blood Bank had provided a list of the documents over which it was claiming legal professional privilege, yet it was impossible to work out exactly why the papers were being withheld.

In his address to the tribunal, our lawyer Martin Giblin SC decided to take the opportunity to raise a question over how the tribunal was operating. He said the IHS was "coming to the conclusion" that there was a reluctance on the tribunal's side to allow new evidence be introduced, or for the IHS to go back over a matter following a new development. He said the IHS accepted that it was natural for the IHS and the tribunal team to clash from time to time, but this appeared to be something more worrying. Martin went on to say that the IHS representatives found it "somewhat unusual to see their counsel interrupted on more than thirteen occasions [by the tribunal's legal team] in the course of a short reply [a few weeks earlier]."

This statement didn't go down particularly well, not that it was expected to. John Finlay SC said: "I am astonished, absolutely astonished by the submission that has been made by my friend." Professor Temperley's lawyer, Brian McGovern SC, also chimed in to claim that Mr Giblin seemed to operate from "the erroneous premise that somehow the rights of the IHS are superior to everyone else's rights". He went on to claim: "My clients and other parties have had to read in the newspapers [about] a representative of the IHS setting out their position on this and on that, and this should not be happening. It should not be happening outside this tribunal. The business of this tribunal should be conducted here and nowhere else." Mr McGovern's comments amounted to an attack on me as I was usually the IHS person quoted by reporters. I felt absolutely justified in what I had done in the past. What's more, I fully intended to continue with the same strategy. I had never said anything hurtful or derogatory about his clients. Did he feel that the media had no right to report or that we had no right to speak?

Judge Lindsay wasn't giving us any relief either. She said she noted Mr Giblin's comments with "great regret" as she felt she'd "always acted in a courteous and proper manner". She said our barrister had been stopped during his presentation on the basis that he was introducing new matters and this was something which he wasn't entitled to do.

I didn't expect our intervention would result in any great change. However, we wanted our feelings to be recorded.

Some critics suggested that the IHS was being cavalier by bringing so many applications to the judge. They didn't seem to consider that days of preparation went into them. On several occasions we held back as we did not want to be perceived as moaners. This was difficult for some members who became extremely angry when they felt their issues were not being addressed. At times I practically had to sedate them.

On the issue of legal professional privilege, however, we felt so strongly that we went to the High Court to be allowed to appeal Judge Lindsay's ruling. It was a major decision as there are always financial consequences when you go to the High Court. In the end, Mr Justice Peter Kelly ruled against our attempt to get more information about the 611 documents which the Blood Bank was withholding. He upheld Judge Lindsay's decision in totality. I was forced to accept that Judge Lindsay was right in her interpretation of the law, but it certainly gave no comfort to our members who were left wondering what the 611 papers were about.

One aspect of the case which deserves mention is the decision by the Blood Bank and the tribunal not to seek an order of the court which would force the IHS to pay their legal bills. Such a move was open to both parties as we had lost the case. However, the tribunal and the Blood Bank chose not to do so. We were thankful for not having to carry the cost of the entire proceedings.

To this day, I still don't understand why the Blood Bank would not waive privilege over the documents – especially considering the appeal by the Minister for Health and the Oireachtas Joint Committee. What was in those papers? What was so important that they couldn't be revealed? Was it that they were explosive? Or was it that the Blood Bank adopted a shameful policy in which it refused to give more ground than it had to? Either way, I believe it reflected badly on both the Blood

Bank and the hospitals. The content of the documents remains a mystery. That fact will ensure that suspicion will hang over the organisations no matter how many times they argue that they 'fully cooperated with the tribunal'. To regain trust they have to go the extra mile. How they can remain so secretive having been associated with so many deaths is something I will never understand.

Unbelievably there were other battle lines. The IHS was also pressurising Judge Lindsay to explain whether or not she was going to investigate the international drug firms whose blood products were responsible for most of the HIV and hepatitis C infections. A number of months after the tribunal commenced its work, we wrote letters seeking clarification about what it would do. By early 2001, the tribunal still hadn't taken a decision on the matter. We were informed that: "Given the state of the evidence which has been given to date, the tribunal believes that it would be premature for it to reach a conclusion at this time as to how it will exercise its discretion pursuant to the terms of reference." This seemed strange as the tribunal had by now been sitting for almost a year. Statements were also being taken from expert witnesses in Europe and the US. This made me feel uneasy as these experts were not being asked about the roles of the international drug firms. It seemed unlikely that they would travel to Ireland to give evidence on one aspect of the story and then be recalled at great expense to tell another part. It began to become apparent that we were going to have to make a formal application to the tribunal to get the issue resolved one way or another.

There were times during battles with the tribunal that I wanted to give up in exasperation. Maybe it's that I don't have enough understanding of the legal system, but it seemed we were continually fighting. It's difficult to continue doing that. There were many private meetings between our legal team and the tribunal's on a variety of issues. In many cases, they were subsequently sorted out. However, what never appeared to exist was an acceptance by the tribunal that we were there to work with them. They seemed to regard us as a hassle.

Not only were we fighting with the tribunal, but there was also a battle with the Department of Health over the Government's commitment to provide additional compensation to members infected with HIV through blood products. Legislation had been promised which would allow our members to apply to the Hepatitis C Compensation Tribunal. However, no bill had been brought into the Dáil.

This row led to one of the shortest meetings ever to take place between the IHS and officials from the Department of Health. It concluded so quickly that I didn't even get the chance to sit down. For convenience, the meeting took place in the Four Courts, in January 2001. I was walking in with our solicitor Raymond when my phone rang. I took the call and when it concluded after a few minutes I turned to walk into the room but bumped into Raymond walking out. While I had been on the phone, Raymond was informed of the ground rules which the department was laying down: talks would be between barristers and would not happen if solicitors, i.e. Raymond, or representatives of the society, i.e. me, were present; the meetings would not be interactive; and the State wouldn't indicate what it thought of the IHS submission. Raymond immediately walked out.

I wasn't willing to enter into discussions with such limitations and so immediately wrote to the minister conveying our dissatisfaction. The letter ran: "It should be noted that the IHS, through its legal advisors, has furnished numerous submissions, has had many meetings with counsel for the State and responded to all queries raised. We believe that we have exhausted our capacity to furnish additional relevant information to your legal representatives." The letter concluded: "We request your urgent intervention to honour your obligation to deliver." Mr Martin responded by saying he was "fully committed" to enacting legislation. Further letters and phone calls were required before things got back on track again. He did ensure the meetings were inclusive and interactive, but it took pressure. I didn't like adopting this hard-ball approach. It was only employed because it delivered results.

One thing which kept my spirits high was the stream of letters and cards from the membership. There were also phone calls urging us to keep up the good fight. At one point, these communications became a little bit difficult as people told me that I was looking haggard, worried and urging me to slow down. I knew this already and didn't particularly want to hear it from others. When cards began to arrive saying that a Mass was being said for me, I began to really make sure I looked the part. Another hassle.

No matter what was happening with the tribunal, I always ensured that I was at home on Sunday to cook the family lunch. John Joe would often come down to the dining-room, which was just off the kitchen, to play the piano while I prepared the food. It was such a common event that John Joe composed a happy ditty entitled 'Peeling Spuds' which he would play and I would hum along to. He was pretty adept at picking up the signals when I was stressed. Instead of joining in, I would continue cooking while mulling over in my mind the latest legal strategy. When this would happen, John Joe would call me over and demand that I sit at the piano with him and play a certain duet. I had taught him how to play the piece as a young boy and now he used it as a form of therapy for me. At the beginning I would usually hit the keys with an undue level of force. With his ever-calm manner, John Joe would just say: "Soft . . . gentle . . . relax." It always worked.

19

Gang

John Berry was one of those people who could be in the IHS office and yet go unnoticed. He was a quiet and unassuming man who didn't want to make any waves. A truck driver by trade, he always appeared happy with his lot. John would usually make a beeline for Margaret King's office and so it took a bit of time for me to get to know him. When we finally did become friends, he told me that he had contracted hepatitis C from a blood product. John knew that the virus could lead to liver cancer and it was something which haunted him. I came to realise that behind the happy face was a person living in terror of what the virus might have in store for him.

Given that John was a quiet man, it came as a shock when he told me that he would like to testify at the Lindsay Tribunal. Even more surprising was his desire to go public. This was quite contrary to everything I had perceived about John, who lived with his wife Rose in Athy, County Kildare. Going public would put him at the centre of attention.

I was concerned that they might not have considered the

full ramifications of going public and so spent many hours with them. I remember warning him that once a person goes public about their hepatitis C status, there was no going back. I also wanted to ensure that he'd considered the possible repercussions for his family. John and Rose thought about it for a while and then said they still wanted to continue. Up to this point he'd passively accepted what was happening. This was something which he could take control of. It was something *he* could do.

Their first public outing was on RTÉ TV's *Prime Time* programme, prior to the commencement of the tribunal. They spoke about what hepatitis C meant to their lives. Typically for the Berry's, it was filmed as they sat around a table with cups of tea.

John told the programme: "It's a death sentence, you know. I get very angry. I'm used to driving, but I can't drive or anything like that. I do get very angry . . . I had to retire because I couldn't drive a lorry and I was driving all my lifetime. I get terribly depressed."

During the run-up to the inquiry, I got to know John and Rose particularly well. I could see that the hepatitis C virus was impacting on John's health, but he retained a tremendous sense of humour. He was clearly deeply in love with Rose and was very protective of her. Unfortunately, Rose became ill and so wasn't able to travel with him when the time came to give evidence.

John was nervous about testifying. The fact that Rose was unwell made him even more anxious. His daughter, Marie, travelled with him to Dublin, but it was clear that he wanted to get back to Athy as soon as possible. Despite the turmoil, he appeared quite calm. We walked to the tribunal together on May 8, 2000.

He explained that he was sixty-two and married with three adult children. John discovered that he had haemophilia in his early thirties following a road accident. However, his condition was very mild and so he didn't require much treatment. Indeed, he required so little that he only ever received one injection of the concentrated clotting-agent – the rest of the treatments were with cryo. He got the clotting-agent in January 1979 at Saint James's Hospital to stem a nosebleed.

John was much later diagnosed with cirrhosis of the liver. He went into hospital for a biopsy in which a piece of the liver is removed for analysis. He also attended the National Haemophilia Treatment Centre. It was at this point that he believed he was told he had hepatitis C. It was something he wasn't prepared for.

Asked what his reaction was to his diagnosis, John said: "I was on death row – which I am now at the moment. That's the way I feel now. I have no future. My future – my family's future is gone. The whole lot is gone. That's all."

The IHS barrister, Jim McCullough BL, asked him: "In 1991 you were told you had hepatitis C. What did you think the story was?"

John replied: "I thought I had AIDS and everything."

Jim McCullough asked: "You were confused with HIV?"

John said: "I didn't ask questions like that."

Jim clarified: "You didn't ask any questions and nobody told you."

John said: "No-one told me."

It was awful to listen to John. The news had a seriously detrimental effect on his relationship with his wife as she also thought he had AIDS. It was only when Rose made efforts to find out more that it was established that he actually had hepatitis C.

John explained how he now suffered from a form of liver cancer which was untreatable. He said he wasn't suitable for a transplant and he was pessimistic about his future. Every time he got a pain or ache he thought: "This is it." He lost most contact with friends and acquaintances from work and the town. He retired from his driving job and could no longer even garden or DIY. Even meals had become devoid of any enjoyment.

He was asked what he wanted the tribunal to achieve. His answer was: "I went in with a nose-bleed and I came out with hepatitis C. Now, I would like to know, there must be someone responsible for that, that gave me that hepatitis C . . . I know how I got it, but why was it given to me when the blood wasn't right? There must be someone responsible for that and that's what I'd like to see."

While John had been composed inside the tribunal room, his nerves began to give way as he was subjected to the glare of the media outside. He had chosen not to speak to journalists, but the cameras were waiting. I remember standing behind him and watching him and his daughter. In some ways it was appropriate that he didn't say anything: he just wanted to know why he'd been infected. I think that was one of the things that endeared him to me: there was no bull-shit.

Through the course of the tribunal, we were able to piece together some of the picture. John was admitted to Saint James's Hospital on January 8, 1979, suffering from a nose-bleed. While the blood-flow had been profuse, it then stopped. John was kept in hospital overnight as a precaution.

Early in the morning his nose began to bleed again. Cryoprecipitate, the blood product made from a small number of Irish donations, had been prescribed. However, it wasn't used because there was an insufficient supply of sterile water on his ward to make up the treatment. It appears, rather than find more water or delay treatment, a concentrated clotting-agent was used instead – one made from thousands of donations which had been imported. This would kill him.

Professor Temperley told the tribunal that it was the policy of his haemophilia treatment centre to use cryoprecipitate because it was a national product. John Finlay SC asked him if sterile water was something that should be in constant supply at the hospital.

"Apparently it wasn't," came the reply. Then he developed the point: "Sterile water per se would not necessarily have been a common form of fluid on the acute ward." The professor also remarked that John's bleed had occurred "at an inconvenient and very awkward time of the day". Considering it was a hospital, quarter to seven didn't sound like an awkward time to me.

Mr Finlay attempted to establish if Professor Temperley would agree that cryoprecipitate was being given from a safety point of view. The question was important: did the professor opt for cryo on the basis that it was made from fewer donations and John was a person with little or no previous treatment? However, the professor said he felt it wasn't taken into consideration at this stage. Mr Finlay responded by stating it was well known in 1979 that there was a greater risk of hepatitis C associated with imported blood products. Professor Temperley answered: "I think it was known, but it was not taken on board in any major way."

If it wasn't amazing enough to establish that a man had contracted a virus because of an absence of sterile water on the ward, Professor Temperley said the decision to administer a concentrated clotting-agent instead was made following consultation with the registrar on duty. Our barrister, Martin Hayden SC, noted that the registrar was identified as 'Dr Lawlor'.

Mr Hayden asked: "Which Dr Lawlor would that be?"

Professor Temperley replied: "That's Dr Emer Lawlor, as far as I am aware."

So it appeared that the answers John was seeking had been

given. It was established that he had contracted hepatitis C from an imported clotting-agent. He was not scheduled to receive this product, but ended up having it injected into him because there wasn't any sterile water on the ward that morning. The person who ordered that he receive the treatment was Dr Emer Lawlor. This just happened to be the same Dr Emer Lawlor who was now the deputy medical director of the Blood Bank and their expert witness at the tribunal. It was often pointed out in the media that Dr Lawlor wasn't in the Blood Bank during the time under scrutiny by the tribunal. Now she was most certainly under examination.

The tragedy was that John wasn't around to hear her evidence. In August 2000, just three months after testifying, he called me to say that he was feeling unwell. John told me he'd visited his GP, but he still didn't feel right. I urged him to go to Saint James's Hospital immediately. Much to my amazement, he didn't receive the attention I anticipated. He was seen by a doctor, but then told to return home to Athy. The only advice was that he should return to the hospital if he didn't improve. It wasn't good enough. I immediately made arrangements for John to return to Dublin.

An appointment was made to visit the hepatology clinic based in a new building at Saint James's Hospital. When I arrived, John was sitting in the waiting-room with his wife and daughter. It was crowded predominantly with women who I assumed contracted the virus through the anti-D blood product. John was in a really poor state and was finding it difficult to sit up. I was taken aback by his colour because he was really yellow. I knew immediately that he was going to die shortly.

John asked me would I stay with him during the course of the consultation. I agreed. After a time I became worried about him and told the staff that he was too weak to remain in the waiting-room. Thankfully, they arranged for him to go to a room and lie down. When the doctor came in, I could see John was absolutely terrified. I also had the sense he was incapable of making decisions.

John was admitted to Saint James's Hospital. Despite the fact that it was a new era and a new hospital wing, some of the consultations with John's family took place in a corridor because there was nowhere else to go. It was a newer, nicer corridor, but still not acceptable. He spent a couple of weeks in hospital and I tried to visit him every day – usually when no-one else was around. I was always greeted by a smile. John would tell me that he thought he was getting better. At that stage his tummy was very swollen and he was most uncomfortable. It was a situation I had seen before with my friend Dermot and I didn't hold any hope of a recovery.

After a series of tests, the last hope of a liver transplant disappeared. John prepared to return home to Athy. It was at this time that we discussed the fact that he was dying. I always told him that I would be straight with him when the time came. This was that time. I can remember that day, sitting in the hospital in a small private room which was nicely decorated. His big eyes were looking at me. I was holding his hand. After a brief conversation, he simply asked: "Will you just do one thing for me? Will you tell Rose and my family that I love them?" I assured him that I would.

I paid many visits to Athy to see John. His deteriorating health was now obvious to all. Rose and Marie were determined to look after him, but they also had the support of the hospice team and the public health nurse.

On the day that John died I got a phone call early in the morning to say that he was deteriorating, and I drove down to Athy. It was September 10, 2000. I was feeling extremely lonely and upset. I desperately missed Margaret being with me as I had become very close to John. As with everything that John

Berry did, he passed away quietly and gently in the loving care of his family.

The media was informed about his death as John had given evidence in public. The tribunal had been due to resume public hearings after its summer break, but proceedings were adjourned as a mark of respect. It was welcomed and appreciated by John's family that John Finlay SC and Judge Lindsay attended the funeral. It was a little strange because John Berry was such simple man and yet there was a large number of lawyers in attendance.

It was more than a year later when Dr Lawlor returned to the tribunal to give evidence in relation to the matter. She explained that she was the haematology registrar on call in Saint James's Hospital the morning John was admitted. She was asked about the medical chart which recorded: "Insufficient water for reconstitution of required dose of cryoprecipitate. Dr Lawlor instructed use two bottles of Hemofil [ie concentrated clotting-agent] slowly as cover." She said it was important to take into account that John had a history of bleeding. She stated that, as a policy, cryo would normally be used as it was the national product. The only reason she became involved in his case was the absence of sterile water to make the 'cryo' – around 150 mls would have been required to make the dose, but it wasn't there.

Gerry Durcan SC asked if it would be unusual for sterile water not to be on the ward.

Dr Lawlor replied: "I think it's unlikely it was the first time it happened. I think it shows up, it's something we would be much more conscious of now . . . there needs to be systems in place to ensure . . . that there is water . . . but, obviously, this is twenty years ago."

Cross-examining, Martin Hayden SC, pointed out that John Berry was a borderline haemophiliac. Indeed, in 1976 an assessment of his body's ability to clot suggested he wasn't a haemophiliac at all. Dr Lawlor was asked whether John's nose-bleed therefore constituted a danger to his life. She contended: "He was exactly the sort of person who the textbooks would sort of say: these people need to be treated." She was asked whether it was not possible for treatment to be suspended for an hour to secure the necessary sterile water. Dr Lawlor was emphatic: "He could have collapsed within that hour and I certainly wouldn't have liked to have to be explaining myself to either his relatives or to Professor Temperley . . . doctors want to do what is right and what was right at the time was to stop [the] bleeding." It was a decision which would be upheld by the inquiry as "clinically justified". The question which would never be answered was why there was no sterile water on the ward that day.

A few weeks later I received a letter from John's daughter Marie. Inside the envelope, she'd attached three typed pages under the title 'Gang'. It turned out to be an essay written by her son Gavin about John for his Junior Cert English class. I sat back in my office and began to read. This wasn't about facts, figures or the medical appropriateness of treatment, but the raw impact of medicine which killed.

Gavin's description of John was something I immediately connected with: "He was a simple, ordinary man, a funny, humorous and jolly character and you were always sure of laughter once you entered his company. He was not tall, in fact, he was quite short and plump with pink cheeks and a deep, deep laugh, that once heard, would cause you too to succumb. A lorry driver, that loved the sight of raw wood, a keen carpenter, with a wide collection of tools at his disposal, the talent of taking a piece of wood and changing it into a masterpiece."

As his condition deteriorated, it wasn't possible to keep his grandfather's illness a secret anymore. His mother told him what was going on: "I remember the smell of the hospital and walking down the corridors to his little room, where he lay, sometimes unable to get out of bed or talk and my mother telling him stories, saying he was looking better, even though he was getting worse. His skin-colour was turning the most revolting and horrifying colour of an off-yellow I have ever seen and he always worried if it was noticeable. Of course we lied and said no, bringing him the little joy he'd have, no longer able to drive or do carpentry."

When it was clear that John was going to die he was brought home: "He wanted to be brought around the entire house, from top to bottom. His kitchen, his living-room, out into his back garden that he loved so much and worked on each summer, planting flowers and finally, to his beloved shed. All his tools so clean, still and now silent. He said his final goodbyes as he was brought up to his bedroom, got into bed and never got out again."

He died a short time later. Gavin's mother had left the room but John called for her to come back in. She held his hand and he drifted away: "The next week was so painful and heartbreaking, unforgettable. The sight of him on the news, alive and then the wreath at his funeral . . . 'Gang', a name we called him, adopted from my mother, a name she had called her grandfather when she was two years old, through mispronunciation, a mispronunciation that had survived over forty years, bestowed upon my grandfather."

Gavin concluded his essay by observing the pain inflicted on his mother: "Her eyes so dazed and sad and often if you look carefully into them, you can see into the very depths of her soul, feeling her sorrow, masked by her as best she can and that is what is so sad, memories and the knowledge, through the Lindsay Tribunal, that this could have all been avoided."

20

Ultimate Political Responsibility

The first politician to give evidence to the Lindsay Tribunal was Barry Desmond on May 23, 2001. He had been the Minister for Health between December 1982 and February 1987. I was interested in what he might say as he was in office during the critical period when the haemophilia community became aware that more than a quarter of its members were infected with HIV. To be honest, I wasn't holding out too much hope of insight. The previous day I had gone to the library and checked his autobiography *Finally And In Conclusion* – there was not one mention of haemophilia or the disaster which befell the community in his 24-page index.

One of the first things to which Mr Desmond testified was that a minister has ultimate political responsibility for what happens in his or her department. The assertion was, however, qualified when he added, and the tribunal legal team accepted, that it simply wasn't possible for a minister to know everything which was going on there. Listening to his evidence, I was worried. It seemed that an escape-hatch of sorts had been constructed: something terrible could go wrong for which a minister could not be held responsible. Was this preparing the ground for a cop-out?

Mr Desmond did offer words of condolence and express sympathy for the families of people with haemophilia. But the longer he gave evidence the less impact his expression of sympathy seemed to have. The reason was that the former Minister for Health accepted that he had been informed in 1985 that many members of the haemophilia population had been diagnosed HIV positive, but he did nothing about it. He explained that he was given an assurance by his officials that matters were being dealt with and so didn't inquire further.

This approach was questioned by tribunal lawyer Gerry Durcan, SC. He asked Mr Desmond whether or not he took any steps to address the crisis. The former minister claimed that while he regarded the matter as "extremely serious", he didn't believe it was incumbent upon himself to develop further strategies. He said the Department of Health already had a plan vis-à-vis control of the spread of AIDS.

Gerry Durcan asked him: "Did you enquire what was being done for haemophiliacs who had become infected?"

The answer: "No, I didn't have any role in that personally."

I found this incredible. My sense of shock came from the personal stories I had heard from people diagnosed HIV positive in 1985. Their overriding feeling was one of abandonment. As the Minister for Health, Barry Desmond could have made a difference. For example, sexual transmission of HIV to partners of haemophiliacs was a real possibility at this time. Yet it was only prevented by Brian O'Mahony handing out condoms from the boot of his car outside of Saint James's Hospital. Why didn't Mr Desmond try to legalise condoms or at least make them available through the medical system? Counselling for those infected and their families would also have been extremely welcome, had the minister taken an interest. I felt that he was passing the buck.

One issue which Mr Desmond spoke bluntly about was on the question of the heat-treatment of blood products. In 1985, he had said publicly that all blood products were being heat-treated to eliminate HIV since the beginning of the year. This was inaccurate. The tribunal had, many years later, established that non-heat-treated Factor IX continued to be used until February 1986. The clotting-agent probably caused infection after Mr Desmond first inaccurately commented on the situation. Mr Desmond said mutual trust existed between the Minister for Health and his advisors and so he considered it to be a very serious matter that a minister could say something incorrect. He said he was never told that non-heat-treated material was still being used in 1985 and only found out during the course of the tribunal. He said he was appalled that he could say something as minister which was untrue. In an interesting conclusion, Mr Desmond said he had absolute trust in the information that he had received from the department. He added that he could only presume that his department was receiving information about heat-treatment from a source it was happy with. Did he mean the Blood Bank?

He was followed into the witness box by his successor, Dr Rory O'Hanlon. While I had never met Barry Desmond because he held office before my appointment to the IHS, I knew Dr O'Hanlon reasonably well. I still could not get over the cold demeanour he had displayed during the HIV compensation settlement in the late 1980s and early 1990s.

May 24, 2001, was a difficult day because, on the one hand, I wanted to stand up and lay into him for what I felt were his failings. I wanted to avoid any chance of contact with him, but I was also very interested to hear more about how

Ministers for Health were given inaccurate information. I sat at the back of the room and gripped my pen tightly.

Dr O'Hanlon said that he had been shown a document drafted by one of his officials in 1989 about the State's perceived responsibilities to people with haemophilia infected with HIV from blood products. The document stated: "Heat-treated products only were used since 1985 – again, as soon as it was shown that heat treatment kills the virus . . . non-heat-treated products were withdrawn."

Counsel for the tribunal tried to establish what impression Dr O'Hanlon had formed after considering the document. He said he believed that Ireland had no case of blood-donation-related HIV or AIDS. He accepted that while this had now proven to be inaccurate, it was relayed not just to the Cabinet but also to the critical debate in the Dáil in 1989 when the IHS was seeking a £400,000 trust fund for members infected with HIV. Dr O'Hanlon said that at the time he spoke to oppose a Labour Party motion, he was not aware that Blood Bank Factor IX had infected people with HIV: "Had I the information that's available to the tribunal today, I certainly would have seen it as a reason why I should have brought different proposals to Government." So it now appeared the Fianna Fáil minority government called an election in 1989 based, in part, on information which was completely untrue.

This information continued to be the basis under which decisions were taken, including the 1991 £8 million settlement between the Government and the IHS members who were suing the State over their HIV status. Dr O'Hanlon said: "I still had the view, and the Government obviously had the view, that everything was correct in the Blood Bank at the time."

After he concluded giving evidence, I turned to Brian to see what he thought. He had so much to say that nothing came out. Eventually he said: "I remember going to meet that man in 1989 when we were looking for the bare necessities for members with HIV – money to cover the extra heating, special foods and trips to hospital. The only thing we got was a cold reception and a statement that he wouldn't make a special case for us. He said flatly that the State had no legal liability. Opposition politicians went to him and lobbied on our behalf, but they too were brushed off – he wasn't going to accept any compromise and forced a Dáil vote which led to the collapse of his Government. And now he's telling me he'd do things differently?" Brian obviously hadn't been convinced.

I felt like confronting Dr O'Hanlon. He may well have been given inaccurate information, but there still had been an opportunity for compassion and a humanitarian approach in 1989. Unfortunately, I never saw him show any of these qualities at any of our meetings. It was a one-dimensional political response. His idea of political responsibility, like that of Mr Desmond, appeared to be quite limited.

Officials from the Department of Health were also questioned about this "inaccurate information" which had led to the collapse of a Government and the IHS having to fight for years for a fair settlement from the State. Paul Barron stressed from the outset that he had no personal involvement in what happened in the 1980s, but had familiarised himself with all of the documentation from the time.

Referring to 1985 and Barry Desmond's tenure in office, Paul Barron said the inaccurate information was obtained from the Blood Bank. The Minister for Health then relayed it to a meeting of the Royal College of Physicians of Ireland in October, and repeated it in the Dáil in November. Politicians were told that, in accordance with the World Health Organisation recommendations, the Blood Bank had been using only heat-treated products since the beginning of the year.

The tribunal began to zone in on the communication between the Blood Bank and the Department of Health. We already knew that senior official, Gerry McCartney, had been the Department of Health's representative on the board of the Blood Bank. Gerry McCartney was on the board in 1986 when three Blood Bank officials knew, as a matter of probability, that Factor IX had infected people with HIV. The obvious question was whether or not Gerry had been informed about the issue. This had added significance as Gerry was the official we had negotiated with while reaching the £8 million settlement with the Government over the HIV litigation in 1991.

Gerry and I came from the same part of the country. We enjoyed similar things. We both smoked. When I joined the IHS, I had always felt that he was not only an effective official but someone I considered to be an ally. Yet while I was keeping him more than informed about the views of the IHS, he was keeping his cards close to his chest. Gerry never told me that he was on the board of the Blood Bank. Seeing his name listed on the board's minutes made me angry. I felt I had been used.

The tribunal initially examined the role of a departmental official who has a seat on the board of a semi-State company, such as the Blood Bank. It was contended by Paul Barron that there was a degree of discretion about reporting back to their department about what happened at meetings. Yet he said he believed the Department of Health's attention would have been drawn to a subject such as HIV-infected blood products. Mr Barron added that there was no record of this having taken place.

It appeared from the evidence that Gerry McCartney had an intimate knowledge of the Blood Bank. He was so familiar with its operations that he had been specially appointed by the Minister for Health to help resolve its financial difficulties. He was involved in hiring Ted Keyes as executive consultant to put the Blood Bank on a more professional financial footing. Gerry McCartney even retained control of the Blood Bank portfolio as he moved positions within the Department of Health.

Considering Gerry McCartney's familiarity with the Blood Bank, I couldn't believe that he didn't know about the Factor IX infections. The notes of the board meeting from June 18, 1986 stated that Ted Keyes informed the members that the "situation" in relation to Factor IX was "unsatisfactory" and the matter was being dealt with "urgently". He told the tribunal he was "sure" he told the board what this problem was, but couldn't say exactly whom he told or when. Gerry McCartney was at that meeting. It simply didn't add up that he wouldn't have subsequently asked: 'What is unsatisfactory about our Factor IX? Why are we dealing with this matter urgently? Is everything that needs to be done being done?' It also didn't make sense to me that Gerry McCartney wouldn't have discussed this with his colleagues. I wasn't convinced by Paul Barron's repeated contention that there wasn't any record of such a discussion.

There was some indirect evidence which appeared to back up my hunch that the Factor IX infections were known by the State. The critical document was what's called an aide memoire – a paper prepared for Cabinet consideration ahead of a decision being taken. Attached to an aide memoire in relation to the HIV litigation, dated May 4, 1991, was a news clipping from *The Irish Times,* dated June 9, 1986. The article quoted Professor Templerley's raising the possibility that four people with haemophilia who used Irish-made Factor IX had become infected with HIV. It said the professor "emphasised that there was no proof that these four patients had been exposed to the virus through the administration of native Factor IX. They had also received commercial blood concentrates in their treatment, but it was very worrying that native Factor IX may have been responsible." The date of the aide memoire was very significant as it was the period in the run-up to the £8 million settlement agreed between the Government and the IHS. Surely at the time it was published back in 1986, this article was cut out by the department's press office and circulated widely among officials? Surely it prompted an investigation?

Two other officials were asked to give evidence to the tribunal. Michael Lyons testified that he was working in personnel in 1986 and so wouldn't have seen the article when it was first published. He said it hadn't appeared on any departmental file from that year.

Martin Hayden SC pressed him on the question of the department's press office picking up the vital link: "Is it not inconceivable, Mr Lyons, [that] an article such as this, touching upon what it does, was not picked up by the press section in the Department of Health in 1986?"

Mr. Lyons responded: "Well, all I can say, chairperson, [Judge Lindsay] and I say it again, is that I didn't receive this document until 1991, and I can't comment on what the press section would or would not have done at the time."

Mr Lyons, along with his departmental colleague John Collins, was also asked about a document they drafted in relation to how the Government should respond in 1988 and 1989 to the IHS's request for £400,000 to assist those infected with HIV. Their view expressed by Mr Collins and Mr Lyons was that, other than on humanitarian grounds, there was no reason why special arrangements for haemophiliacs infected with HIV should be made. Mr Collins' assessment of the situation was that an adequate legal defence was available to support a decision not to provide compensation. This was supported by Mr Lyons.

In advance of the 1989 Dáil debate, Mr Lyons prepared a further document for the minister entitled: "Haemophilia, HIV/AIDS". He said that he had consulted relevant sections within the department, the Blood Bank, National Drugs Advisory Board and documentation from the IHS. I couldn't understand how he did not discuss it with Gerry McCartney and other department officials who sat on the board of the Blood Bank.

Mr Lyons said he hadn't been informed by Blood Bank staff, including its chief technical officer Sean Hanratty, that HIV infections had been caused by its Factor IX. However, Mr Lyons did make a reference to the possibility of being told by the IHS that Irish blood products had caused one or two infections. While our fears were noted in Mr Lyons' document, it didn't go any further. His document notes this was of "concern" but asks what other clotting-agents they used and says that their "lifestyle" would have to be explored. It seemed extraordinary to me that our concerns could be dealt with in such a fashion. It was clear that this should have been investigated, but it was not. I felt there were two possibilities – either the department had been guilty of doing nothing at the time or it already knew what had happened. Both were appalling. Mr Lyons' document was subsequently used to brief lawyers representing the State in the HIV litigation. He also agreed that much of the paperwork which followed on from his April 1989 document was flawed.

The Blood Bank was also evaluating matters. On February 15, 1989, the board met and the question of the IHS's political campaign was considered. The now chief executive officer, Ted Keyes, was noted as saying that HIV infections had been caused only by imported products. It was an incredible statement as Mr Keyes had been told in 1986 by his own staff that the opposite was the case. Yet there, in black and white,

Mr Keyes was recorded stating in 1989: "The particular concern is that certain statements have been made [by the IHS] which would indicate that some of our products were infected, whereas it is quite clear that the source of the infection was imported product."

Several of the board members at the table in 1989 had held the same position back in 1986 when Mr Keyes alluded to the "problem" with Factor IX. Despite this fact, no dissenting voice was recorded in the minutes to what Mr Keyes had said about the source of infection. While Gerry McCartney was off the board by this stage, he retained responsibility for BTSB matters within the Department of Health. Asked to explain why he said something he knew to be inaccurate, Mr Keyes told the Lindsay Tribunal: "I had no objection to people with haemophilia pursuing that claim. I was worried about the impact on blood collection and we do have responsibility for tens of thousands of patients every year."

When Professor Temperley gave evidence about his time on the board of the Blood Bank, he said he never sought to disguise the fact that Factor IX had caused infections. His testimony was amazing. Here was the main treater of haemophilia in the country effectively being ignored by his fellow members on the board of the Blood Bank which was supplying products to haemophiliacs. Professor Temperley said: "I'm sure I had reminded the board on a number of occasions, which probably were never minuted, regarding the question of the infection, unfortunate infection, of the seven patients with the board's product. And I can recall, I mean, it's very difficult to be absolutely certain at this time, but I can recall feeling myself in a way becoming a bore about this." Unfortunately, as no other board members were called it was impossible to find out why they hadn't listened to him.

I believe that Gerry McCartney must have known about

the Factor IX infections. I also find it impossible to believe that he didn't tell any of his colleagues about this fact. The main problem with the IHS argument was that it was circumstantial. We didn't have proof, but strongly believed that all indications pointed to the veracity of our case. When the Department of Health's legal team came to sum up its stance, I knew we were going to be attacked.

Ian Brennan, SC for the Department of Health, firstly argued that the board of the Blood Bank was never made aware of the Factor IX infections. He pointed out how Mr Keyes' evidence changed from stating the board "was told", to "almost certain" it was told, to "suspect" they were told but couldn't identify to whom or when. Mr Brennan said: "It's not credible that the board, the members of which were people of good standing and who did not have any material interest, would not have apprised the department had it been so aware. It stretches credulity even further that these members of the board would have conspired to have taken steps actively to conceal the matter." Listening to Mr Brennan, I wanted to shout up at him: "What about Professor Temperley's contention that he was 'becoming a bore' at board meetings talking about how Blood Bank products had infected people with HIV?" Somehow, I restrained myself.

Mr Brennan then went on to deal with our allegation that Gerry McCartney must have known but covered it up. Mr Brennan said: "Whatever the motivation behind that allegation, it is without foundation in any of the evidence before this tribunal. That an unsubstantiated allegation of that nature should be made in submission concerning the board in general and about a named senior civil servant, in particular, is monstrous and quite beyond any reasonable comment."

As Mr Brennan had his say, my mind returned to a quiet drink I had had with Gerry McCartney in a Dublin hotel shortly after the compensation deal had been secured. Out of the blue, he had said there had been "tremendous pressure" to agree a settlement with the IHS and it was a great relief in the Department of Health that the issue had been resolved. I felt he was hinting at more than he was saying and I tried to pursue it with him. However, the moment had passed and nothing further was discussed. [He may well have been simply referring to the question of getting a thorny issue sorted out for the good of all concerned, but I believe he was alluding to something else.]

I understand why Mr Brennan described the IHS claim as "monstrous", yet equally, I can't stop thinking what I feel was the true state of affairs.

21

In The Box

There have been several times I came close to strangling Raymond Bradley, but his life was never more in danger than the day I was due to give evidence to the Lindsay Tribunal. It was Friday June 1, 2001 and I hadn't slept a wink. Even though I had known I was going to give evidence, I had always put it to the back of my mind. This had been possible because other IHS witnesses were going before me and I was both attending the hearings and then helping people prepare by night. Now it was my turn and it wasn't a very nice place to be.

I got up early that morning and met Raymond for one last meeting. I had closely examined my written statement of evidence which ran to nineteen pages and considered what questions I might be asked. Raymond looked at me when I came into the office and I could tell he was clearly going to enjoy my predicament. He would start to ask a valid question, but then veer off into something extremely personal and explode laughing.

I walked down to the tribunal and the cameras were

waiting. This added hugely to the tension. I took my place at the back of the room as Brian O'Mahony was still in the witness box. I didn't really listen to him. The only thing running through my mind was: "Will I forget everything? Will I remember my name?" As Brian finished off, my mind began to race: "Oh God, I'm next!" It was the Friday of a bank holiday weekend which marked the beginning of a two-week break for the tribunal so I said to myself: "Just get through this and you can relax in style."

I was preparing to take the stand and then Raymond came over to me. He said Brian's evidence had taken longer than expected. If I took the stand now, it was probable that I wouldn't finish it that day. It didn't seem logical to begin and then have a delay for two weeks. He asked me to agree to adjourn giving evidence.

The only person who didn't quite see the logic at the time was me. My first thought was to place my hands around his throat, but I resisted. There had been such a build-up to this moment. It was like the morning of the big exam and I wasn't being allowed to sit the test. I felt very hard done by. Grudgingly, I gave Raymond the instruction to say that I would delay giving evidence. When he left to speak with the tribunal's legal team, I began to cry. Nervous that anyone might see my distress, I slipped quietly out of the public gallery, met Arthur and said: "I'm going." I knew I was being irrational and the postponement was correct, but I had prepared so hard. Now I didn't know what to do with myself. I was gripped by fear that by the time the tribunal resumed public hearings I wouldn't be able to remember what to say.

My instinct was to travel to Carlingford immediately, but Arthur, being Arthur, calmed me down. When we got home he just said: "Relax and change." I was still wearing my good suit and he knew it made me feel uncomfortable. When I came back downstairs, he insisted on driving me back in to the IHS. I didn't want to see anybody or talk to anyone. Arthur was insistent. I also knew that I had to congratulate Brian on the good work he had done. Arthur stopped outside the office, pushed me out of the car and drove off.

The IHS office was crammed with members when I walked in. It gave me a lift to see everyone. I also felt slightly envious of Brian on account of the tremendous job he'd done. He looked both happy and relieved his stint on the stand was over. I managed to let off some steam by cornering Raymond and, while I knew it was silly, I ranted for a while.

The tension I felt about taking the stand was not just a question of personally looking good or bad: it had the capacity to have a major impact on the IHS. When signing up to the terms of reference, we made it clear that we wanted to know what people knew at particular times in order to evaluate their response to the latest HIV and hepatitis C developments. It was underlined by one departmental official who specified that the state of knowledge of the IHS was also going to be put under the spotlight.

The international experience of inquiries into what happened to the world's haemophilia population wasn't always good for the representative bodies. In the United States, members of their Haemophilia Society ended up suing their officials because they felt the organisation had information about AIDS but didn't convey it to them in a timely manner. I sought assistance from the Canadian Haemophilia Society who had endured a tribunal which lasted over four years. They gave me some useful advice on what to do. The main strategy in Canada was to agree that if their officials found, during a trawl of documents, that they were at fault, then an apology would be tendered immediately to members.

When the IHS staff and executive sat down to consider the

upcoming tribunal, the first priority was to ensure that the organisation would be intact after the inquiry. We all recognised that it would be an absolute disaster if the society was not there to offer support and services.

Our examination of how the IHS had conducted its affairs over thirty years was commenced with some trepidation. We knew that everything we did was aimed at assisting the membership, but there were some worries that a different interpretation might be placed upon those actions. The other pressure was that the normal services of the IHS had to continue while the research work got under way. Initially I tried to sift through documents while also supporting the parents of newly diagnosed children and keeping members up to date. In the end it was just too much work. So I began to focus solely on the tribunal while the day-to-day running of the IHS was taken over by my colleague and good friend Margaret Dunne.

As the documents were examined and questions drafted, we also had to agree on who was going to give evidence on behalf of the IHS. It was decided they would either be former chairpersons or secretaries. The five to give evidence were Frank Bird, Shay Farrelly and Pamela Aldrich – who covered periods prior to my involvement – as well as Brian O'Mahony and myself.

Brian was the fourth witness for the IHS to give evidence and he began his testimony on Aisling's birthday – another family occasion I was forced to miss. One of his great abilities is his capacity to prepare. The amount of effort and energy he put into this job was something that I had never seen before. His attention to detail was impressive. It was a faculty he needed as he would get quite a grilling from the other legal teams at the tribunal, particularly from the Department of Health.

Brian's evidence lasted over a day and a half and he came

across as a sophisticated, articulate and intelligent person. I felt that he gave his evidence superbly and was always clear about what he was trying to say. I know it must have been very difficult for him: Brian had been lucky not to have contracted HIV, but many of his friends had died. Of the fourteen men who joined the IHS with him in the early 1980s, nine were dead due to contaminated blood products. In the witness box, he managed to separate the personal from the official. I felt he carried the day.

The key point in his testimony related to his state of knowledge about the Factor IX HIV infections: when did he know Blood Bank products were responsible? Asked when he first knew that this was the case, Brian said: "During the course of this tribunal . . . I had suspicions . . . but . . . I think it's taken this tribunal to put that into . . . reality." He was asked about the Professor Temperley seminar in 1986. Brian described it as "a tremendous shock to hear that there had been infections because we'd been using Factor IX for a considerable period of time with no infections that we were aware of".

When Gerry Durcan, SC for the tribunal, asked him if he had followed the matter up with Professor Temperley, Brian explained that he didn't as it wasn't clear what the source of the infection was and an investigation appeared to be under way.

Mr Durcan then referred to Brian's notes of a meeting of the National Haemophilia Services Coordinating Committee on January 30, 1987, at which he recorded that a number of patients using Factor IX had tested positive for HIV the previous year. He asked if those attending the meeting had talked about this fact, but Brian explained that the professor was only quickly giving an update on the latest HIV figures: "There certainly wouldn't have been a discussion." An IHS document from 1987 was next to be considered. It referred to the up-to-date statistics from Saint James's Hospital on HIV transmission, including Factor IX users.

Gerry Durcan asked: "Was an inquiry made or did you know at this stage at all how that had happened?"

Brian responded: "We could only have suspicions. We didn't know."

He was then asked about discussions with the Department of Health the following year where the IHS raised its suspicions that Irish blood products were responsible. Mr Durcan asked how strong the IHS views were. Brian said that the IHS believed it was "likely" that the Blood Bank Factor IX was responsible.

Brian had always been suspicious that the Blood Bank product was responsible but had no proof. The IHS executive and membership were always conscious of some question hanging over Factor IX because the infections occurred after the time it believed that heat-treatment was introduced. Brian continued to raise his concerns during negotiations with the Department of Health during 1989 and 1991. Yet, confirmation that the Blood Bank product did cause the infections only came with the tribunal – fifteen years after the fact. In a bizarre turnaround, Brian was now being questioned about what the IHS had done or not done about Factor IX from 1986 on, when the suspicion was being denied by the Blood Bank and the Department of Health at every opportunity.

The issue was later taken up by Ian Brennan, SC for the Department of Health. He questioned how Brian, as a user of Factor IX, could not have gone to Professor Temperley and asked him about the problem. Brian repeated: "I went home that day [at UCD in 1986] absolutely shocked." He said he didn't know if the blood product had been virally inactivated or not. The other thing which happened quickly afterwards was that the product was withdrawn.

Mr Brennan asked: "How did you learn of that?"

Brian answered: "The Factor IX I was using was withdrawn. I was brought back and given commercial Factor IX and told not to use Pelican House material again. And that tends to give you a suspicion that perhaps it was Pelican House material [which was at fault]."

This response ended that line of questioning.

Brian had been very supportive during the two-week break. He was constantly around to offer words of wisdom and make the all-important cup of tea when required. His jokes didn't get any better, but his concern for my welfare was clearly evident.

I always turn on RTÉ radio's *Morning Ireland* programme when I wake up. On the day I was finally to give evidence, the newscaster announced it on the bulletin. It felt like something out of a movie. It was the June 12, 2001 – just over a year since the tribunal began public hearings. As usual, I went into the IHS. I can't remember exactly what my routine was, but it must have involved smoking a lot of cigarettes and drinking Diet Coke. After breakfast in the office and one more talk with Raymond, I proceeded down to the tribunal in a grey trouser suit and black top with my mother's gold chain, ready to face the glare of the media cameras. Many members from all over the country had converged on the tribunal room to support me. It struck me that I had offered advice to so many friends before they gave personal testimony, but now my words seemed so hollow. I had told them there was nothing to be afraid of: "It's your story, relax and just answer the questions, take it easy." It all seemed a little stupid now.

I sat at the back of the tribunal and waited for proceedings to begin. I felt the members' eyes upon me so I tried to look nonchalant and give the appearance of being in control. I saw Raymond take his place at the table with the rest of our legal team. He looked back at me a couple of times, but I wasn't sure if it was to offer encouragement, enjoy my discomfort or ensure that I had not run out the door. Then the words "All rise" echoed through the room and we were off. I didn't start off very well as when I tried to stand up my knees knocked against the table. I looked nervously at the glass of water which had been in front of me to ensure it had not spilled.

I was sworn in by the registrar, Siobhan Hayes. When I had that Bible in my hand, I was so emotional. I prayed to God, my mother, my father and anybody else who would listen. I wanted to do my best. Like others I had supported before going into the witness box, I was overwhelmed by the feeling that I didn't want to let down the people I was representing. The faces I kept seeing in my mind were of those who had died.

In truth, I can't remember very much of giving evidence. I made a conscious decision not to look around the room as I would end up looking at lawyers, journalists and friends in the public gallery. Instead, I locked on to Gerry Durcan SC, who was taking me through the evidence on behalf of the tribunal. The testimony started on what my role in the IHS was, before moving on to subjects like the HIV compensation and my personal involvement with the members. I was at particular pains to mention the body-bag situation. I wanted to garner publicity and hoped it might influence Judge Lindsay to recommend the ending of this horrendous practice.

I described how the IHS only ever achieved anything after a battle. I said: "Sometimes the society is perceived as a nuisance, maybe a bit hysterical, a bit over the top in their demands. I can understand why people would have that perception. But nothing that has been achieved by the Haemophilia Society for its members has come easy. It's an uphill battle every step of the way. So if we behave like nuisances – it's a bit sad to have to go to those lengths – but that's what it takes."

Gerry Durcan's way of taking me through the evidence was

direct but not confrontational. When he concluded, Judge Lindsay asked the other legal teams if they would like to cross-examine me. This moment I can remember very well. I was wondering what sort of questions I would face and was bracing myself to be in a position to answer adequately. But each lawyer who was asked declined. As the answer "no questions" was repeated, I began to breathe a little easier. Of course it was too good to be true. Ian Brennan took up Judge Lindsay's offer. He said he just had a couple of questions. I stiffened my resolve as Brian had been given a hard time by the same barrister.

I had a certain admiration for this man. He had a deep voice which could have been brilliantly employed reading Conrad novels about adventures on the high seas. He was also quite abrupt – even in the way he introduced himself: "My name is Brennan." It wasn't Ian Brennan or Mr Brennan – just Brennan. He wasn't the type of person who said a lot, but when he spoke you were very conscious that he had. Now he was sitting at a table directly across from me and it made me feel a little uncomfortable.

Mr Brennan's main interest related to what I knew about the Factor IX infections. He wanted to know whether or not I knew it as a certainty that Factor IX was responsible for infecting seven members with HIV. He zoned in on our legal strategy in 1991 to prioritise the cases which involved Factor IX rather than those people infected with imported Factor VIII. He suggested that surely our legal team must have known. I explained that we had always had a suspicion but that related to the fact that people using Factor IX had become infected at a seemingly late date. We felt that the 'problem' related to the fact that the Factor IX might not have been heat-treated enough to kill off the virus. What we certainly didn't know for a fact was that the clotting-agent hadn't been treated at all.

Mr Brennan said Brian's evidence suggested there was a

suspicion about Factor IX from 1986 following Professor Temperley's lecture in UCD. However, he felt there had to be a reason for the IHS deciding to take legal action on the matter in 1989. He said to me: "The reason, as you have put it, is that there was some knowledge of the Factor IX being deficient with regard to heat treatment. How much knowledge was there and when did you get that knowledge?"

I responded: "As you know now, those cases didn't progress anywhere . . . the first time that any validation of these suspicions were proved to be factual was when I was sitting down at the back of this tribunal."

Mr Brennan wasn't finished yet. He said that as part of the litigation in 1991, the Blood Bank had released some of its documents to the IHS legal team. He described these papers as being "pretty close to the knuckle" in relation to mapping out what went wrong with the Factor IX blood product. He then went on to try to link the documents to me via our legal team: "If your legal team knew, well, then, it's clear that your senior counsel must have known. And if he was advising the society and principally Mr O'Mahony, Mrs King and yourself at this meeting of May 16, 1991, isn't it virtually certain that he discussed the disclosures?"

I shot back: "It's not virtually certain at all because I was there."

Mr Brennan said: "All right."

I continued: "And if I had knowledge of the documents that Mr Durcan had just opened to me I think I would have remembered that because I remembered the day in this tribunal when it became apparent . . . about our suspicions over the BTSB, and it was quite an emotional moment because we had been talking about this for over ten years."

Mr Brennan responded: "Alright, I accept that and I don't have any difficulty with that."

The fact was that while documents had indeed been released to our solicitors in 1991, the officers of the IHS did not get to see them. We were apprised of the litigation in general terms but, possibly due to inexperience, didn't seek to view the documentation. Our suspicion about what went wrong remained just that – a suspicion. In the lead-up to the tribunal we went back through the affidavit which was released to us by the Blood Bank in March 1991. It did contain a record of Donor F's 1984 donation testing positive for HIV, but it would have taken a genius to connect this with the Factor IX infections. The Blood Bank had made this link, but chose not to admit liability. The £8 million settlement was reached in June 1991 – our members agreed to it only because they couldn't wait any longer. It was a shameful state of affairs: the Blood Bank protected itself rather than going the extra mile for the people it knew it had infected.

Raymond brought me through some questions about the society's provision of care for members. I also told the tribunal how two of the seven people infected with HIV from Blood Bank-made Factor IX were children. I was very grateful, or relieved, when Judge Lindsay said: "Thank you very much, your evidence is now completed. We will resume again tomorrow."

I was so happy I could have leapt out of the witness box. However, I managed to control myself and walk straight down the corridor. At the end of it I saw my son John Joe standing by the door. He didn't say anything and we went downstairs to our little room to take a breather. Boy, was I relieved: I then glided my way down the street and back to the office. I embraced one member after another. The feeling of relief was immense – both the IHS and I appeared to have survived unscathed.

22

Unfinished Business

Dr Donald Francis is a quiet man, but he is also one of those people who has an aura about him. He doesn't seem to say all that much, but you get the feeling when he talks that there's much more. He came to Ireland to give evidence at the Lindsay Tribunal in October 2001 in his capacity as an "expert witness". Dr Francis had been employed by the US Centers for Disease Control or CDC for twenty-one years. His job was to keep track of diseases and recommend any necessary response. He worked at the CDC when AIDS was first identified. I'm not sure whether it was because of his experience, but the lawyers at the tribunal appeared to treat him with kid gloves.

According to Dr Francis, blood banks and product manufacturers in the US showed remarkably little concern about the health implications of AIDS. He maintained that they had an incredible ability to stare the data in the face and yet do as little as possible for as long as possible. He said that producers obstructed the introduction of new safety measures.

To a certain extent, most of this had already been reported

in Ireland. However, Dr Francis went on to make a claim which captured the headlines and shocked our members. The assertion related to the recruitment of gay men by two major pharmaceutical companies to make a vaccine for hepatitis B. Due to their sexual practices, gay men had built up a resistance or antibodies to hepatitis B. The drug firms wanted to avail of their blood to secure the antibodies in order to make vaccines for the virus.

This would have been acceptable but for the fact that the blood product producers wanted to maximise their profits. Instead of getting rid of the plasma after having extracted the hepatitis B vaccine, the producers used the residue to make concentrated clotting-agents for people with haemophilia. Dr Francis maintained this was "almost a design for infecting them with HIV".

The reason he said this was because gay men in 1982 were considered to be a high-risk category for transmitting the new mystery virus. The fact that the gay men also had hepatitis B, a marker of sexual activity, made them even more of a concern. Dr Francis was at pains to stress that it was the drug firms who were at fault. The gay men were donating their blood in the hope that it would help people. Yet their altruistic response was being abused by the drug companies. He said the practice of using these high-risk donations had only been revealed in the late 1990s, in the course of litigation in the US. Had anyone known at the time, there would have been a major outcry and the material would have been taken off the market. The doctor said he didn't believe that the producers were trying to kill people, but were not thinking through what would turn out to be a fatal mistake.

Dr Francis had been called to give evidence by the IHS. I knew something about what he wanted to say, but wasn't quite sure if he would get the opportunity. When it was the turn of the IHS to ask him questions, I became immensely interested and yet also very worried that he might be stopped halfway through. It was great that he did get the chance to speak freely.

Dr Francis' evidence had an incredible impact on Peter Scallan whose brother John was one of the first Irish people to use US concentrates and subsequently died of an AIDS-related illness. Peter knew his brother had probably become infected with HIV as a result of these clotting-agents. What he heard from Dr Francis compelled him to go public. In an article, he said: "My brother died seven years ago of AIDS, not of haemophilia, and he died because he used a treatment for haemophilia that he thought was safe. It wasn't safe."

It's sometimes forgotten that of the more than one hundred IHS members who contracted HIV from blood products, all but eight were caused by imports. It was for this reason that we wanted the role of international pharmaceutical companies investigated. To get to the truth of what happened, US-based drug firms needed to be held accountable.

While negotiating the terms of reference of what would become the Lindsay Tribunal, we stressed at discussions with officials from the Department of Health that there had to be an international dimension. After months of protracted negotiations, an agreement was reached between the then Minister for Health, Brian Cowen, and the IHS. He wrote to us stating: "I confirm, among other things, that the tribunal will investigate the source of the infections whether arising from BTSB-produced products or products imported from abroad." It wasn't totally without qualification. There had to be an expectation of getting a result and an understanding that it wouldn't unduly delay the tribunal's work. Judge Alison Lindsay commenced her hearings in May 2000, but chose not to state whether she would investigate foreign firms. The tribunal was taking evidence from "expert witnesses" like Dr Francis.

However, their testimony, in the main, was used to compare the actions of the State, the Blood Bank and doctors here with what happened in other countries. It did not examine the actions of the pharmaceutical companies in detail. After corresponding over several months, we decided we would seek a hearing from Judge Lindsay on the matter.

On July 20, 2001, the IHS asked the tribunal to investigate "the role and the state of knowledge" of the drug firms. We made particular reference to Armour Pharmaceuticals because its product was strongly linked to the infection of an Irish boy with HIV. Less than a month before the IHS application, the tribunal had heard from the New York-based expert, Dr Alfred Prince, who explained that Armour had three sets of results in October 1985 which suggested the method they employed to heat-treat their product and kill off HIV wasn't totally effective. Despite this fact, they went on to export the clotting-agent to Ireland. The tribunal had also heard the previous week from another expert witness, Dr Peter Jones from Newcastle, who was the first to express concerns about Armour, in February 1986, even though the company tried to block him. Dr Jones had documents about Armour's activities, but the tribunal said they couldn't be admitted as evidence as they were not in his possession in the mid-1980s. Armour was the company with whom the Blood Bank later signed an indemnity preventing them from being sued over any future infections.

In our application to the tribunal, our barrister, Richard Nesbitt SC, said it would be a failure on the part of the inquiry not to order the pharmaceutical companies to produce documentation about the products they sent to Ireland. He argued the tribunal should at least try to secure the information, even if it did not expect success. Mr Nesbitt highlighted the fact that a lot of litigation against the same drug companies had taken place in the United States. The documentation related to those cases was stored at a special depository in Pensacola, Florida. These cases had resulted in millions being paid out to people with haemophilia but always on a 'no fault' basis. This meant that the case had been settled before a determination was made by the court and so there was no admission of responsibility. Under the rules of the US courts, the documents involved in the trials remained sealed in the depository at Pensacola. Mr Nesbitt suggested that the tribunal could apply to the US courts to get access.

Once again, the tribunal's legal team opposed the IHS motion. John Finlay SC said that the tribunal wasn't entitled or required to examine the state of mind of pharmaceutical companies. He said the inquiry was interested in investigating communications made by pharmaceutical companies to relevant persons in the State, but investigating the companies per se would not be helpful or appropriate.

While it wasn't a surprise to me that the tribunal's legal team chose to oppose our suggestion, I still found it deeply depressing. I felt it was ridiculous to regard the issue as irrelevant. How could it not be relevant when so many people with HIV contracted the virus from products produced abroad? While I didn't believe it would happen, I desperately wanted Judge Lindsay to rule that matters outside of the State were important. I felt she could at the very least apply to get access to the Florida documents. It would be like an Aladdin's Cave to the IHS.

On July 27, 2001, Judge Lindsay ruled that the terms of reference did not permit an investigation of the source of the infections. She said that had the Oireachtas wanted her to include this in her inquiry, there would have been a specific term of reference instructing her to do so. The judgement was quite long, but I tuned out pretty quickly. I thought back to Brian Cowen's letter and our expectation that the international dimension would be covered by the tribunal. Once again, there was a divergence between what we thought would happen and what actually came to pass.

After feeling sorry for ourselves, we decided to keep fighting for the international investigation. As Judge Lindsay had made her ruling, the person who was first on our lobbying list was the Minister for Health, Micheál Martin. Our plan was simple – if the judge felt her terms of reference constrained her from examining the drug firms, we would try to get the Oireachtas to expand them. The IHS raised this possibility during the trouble with the Finlay Tribunal but was brushed off by departmental officials. This time we were a far more formidable entity. I felt our submission was pretty persuasive. We knew that the drug firms based in the US had collected plasma from prisoners, people living on skid row where drug abuse is rife and other high-risk donors, as outlined by Dr Francis. What we needed to establish was whether or not this material had made it to Ireland. We suspected it had, but couldn't prove it as the drug companies refused to give out any information.

A campaign from the IHS on its own probably would have had a limited effect. However in October 2001, RTÉ broadcast a TV documentary on the practices of US drug firms. It raised serious questions about the way companies recruited donors in the early 1980s and backed up its case with confidential documents. One woman, who used to live on skid row as a prostitute, said the plasma collection centres must have known that drug addicts were giving blood: "I know they could see the fresh needle-marks, but they were getting what they wanted – they wanted the blood." She explained that most of the people she knew at that time were now either dead from an AIDS-related illness or dying. She said: "I am not surprised that a lot of haemophiliacs became [HIV] positive because of the people that I knew and know that are dead or dying from AIDS. Because I knew a lot of them who gave plasma."

Another woman, who still lives on skid row, spoke of how she got around the scant safety checks employed by the donation centres: "At that time I was using the same vein they were withdrawing the plasma from, so I didn't have scars on my arms. Or I was shooting dope in my neck and wearing collars to hide the marks." While there were screening procedures, including asking donors to fill out a form stating they were not high risk – they were not questioned on a one-on-one basis. The woman said: "A drug addict is a manipulator – when [you] need drugs, you know what to do and what to say right then."

The plasma firms also collected in prisons, where safety was a serious issue. One former Louisiana prisoner was asked how drug addicts managed to conceal the fact from the staff at the donor centre that they were using needles. The response was stark: "Well, you didn't have to hide it. Nobody cared. You want to sell it? You got it? We want to buy it! Bottom line." Dr Francis also appeared on the programme and spoke about the abuse of donations given by gay men for the hepatitis B vaccine.

The drug firms themselves declined to participate and so the question of whether or not plasma from prisoners, people living on skid row or high-risk donors made its way to Ireland remained a mystery. Only they had the answers.

The following day, we demanded that the Lindsay Tribunal's terms of reference be expanded. The minister praised the programme and agreed to meet the IHS. The documentary also had a major impact on our members – many of whom were upset to hear prisoners talking about how safety protocols were routinely breached. The media continued to focus on the story. Raymond was interviewed by the *Irish Examiner* newspaper which reported how Canadian police had a well advanced criminal investigation into Armour Pharmaceuticals. Ray Kelly was back on the airwaves explaining how he simply couldn't comprehend why the pharmaceutical companies were not being investigated. He spoke about his son John. I knew the price Ray and Ann were paying as it led to pictures of John being published again in the newspapers and rebroadcast on television. Wounds were being opened. Ray was left wondering if the pain was going to be worth it – would the firms be called to account?

In a subsequent meeting, Mr Martin pointed out to our delegation that Judge Lindsay would have to agree to her terms being expanded. It wasn't something he could simply decide. I tried to impress upon him the need for the Government to be resolute. The minister subsequently asked Judge Lindsay whether or not she would expand her terms of reference. The request was conveyed through the then Attorney General, Michael McDowell. Within a matter of days, Judge Lindsay said, in part, that it wouldn't be appropriate for her to expand her investigation at this late stage. It struck me as ironic that we had been seeking clarification for quite some time but had been told such a move was "premature". Now part of the reason being proffered for not inquiring into the actions of these companies was that it was too late!

The decision prompted Roisin Hennessy, the sister of John and Peter Scallan, to say that she was "disgusted, hurt and let down" by the decision. Roisin stated: "My brother [John] used products from a number of US [based] companies. It's a matter of accountability. The other tribunals have had no difficulty about heading off to the Cayman Islands for evidence of financial wrong-doing. This is the only tribunal looking into how people lost their lives. People have been so brave about giving their evidence. They deserve better."

The Lindsay Tribunal concluded its public hearings the following month. The final day was concerned with costs, and so the inquiry ended with a whimper rather than a bang. In her closing remarks, Judge Lindsay said: "I think the first group of persons that I have to thank are those victims, those people with haemophilia, their relatives and friends. And in particular, those who came and gave evidence here over very many times and very many days and they were very brave. And I appreciate that. And I also can say that many of them and many of those voices, many of those cases, many of those stories will stay with me forever." After thanking her staff and tribunal participants, she said: "So that's it. Thank you very much indeed for your attendance."

Two of the people who gave personal testimony, Isobel and Damien, were sitting beside me. We felt we had to get out of the tribunal room as quickly as possible and so returned to the IHS office. While there was plenty of food and drink, this was no celebration. It was a bit like a wake: we were marking the occasion. I was delighted that it was over but felt very strange. Now we just had to wait for the report to find out who would be held accountable for the Irish dimension to the tragedy. In relation to the international pharmaceutical companies, the campaign for an investigation continued.

Our position was that the Mr Martin had to commit himself to establishing another mechanism to investigate the matter. He was obviously concerned that a second tribunal could be expensive, complicated and possibly still not get to the bottom of matters. His compromise proposal was that a senior barrister would inquire into what opportunities there were for investigating the international drug firms. It seemed like a reasonable suggestion. We agreed to the proposal but made it clear that even if the chances of success were small, the State was obliged to at least try. In particular, an application should be made to get access to the documents stored in Florida.

Paul Gardiner SC was the person appointed to do the job. He travelled to New York for a period of time and also had consultations with our legal team. He furnished his report to the minister in late spring 2002. Unfortunately, a general election was pending and our ability to lobby was diminished.

Days before polling, we received a letter from Mr Martin. It said that while Mr Gardiner had "set out many difficulties" in investigating the drug firms, he fully recognised "the concerns of your members". He added: "One of my major concerns is to ensure that an all-encompassing inquiry would occur in respect of these pharmaceutical companies and you may be assured of my continued endeavours in this regard." The caveat was that he wanted to ensure that "any inquiry that would be established would have a reasonable opportunity to be effective within a reasonable time period". He said he would also have to await the publication of the report of the Lindsay Tribunal before taking any further decisions on the matter. The campaign was put on hold.

23

Going Into Orbit

If Micheál Martin ever writes an autobiography, I will be first in the queue to buy a copy as he spent a lot of time working on haemophilia issues. A lot of that work was very worthwhile yet he could have saved a lot of effort if matters were dealt with quickly and definitively. The issue of providing compensation to members who were infected with HIV from contaminated blood products was a case in point. Prior to his arrival in the Department of Health, a commitment was given to allow these people to make a claim to the Hepatitis C Compensation Tribunal. It was a clear recognition that the £8 million given by the State in 1991 was inadequate. I knew this to be true as I had seen at first hand how financial burdens added to the suffering. Mr Martin gave a commitment that he would introduce legislation on the compensation matter, but he continually delayed delivering it.

At the beginning of 2002, we received a letter assuring us that he was interested in resolving the issue and hoped to introduce the long-awaited legislation in the next Dáil term.

He described this as a "major priority". I had heard this type of language too many times. The reality, which I knew only too well, was that sixty-four people with haemophilia had already died from AIDS-related conditions caused by contaminated blood products. The State was making promises as people were dying. I wrote back to Mr Martin saying we welcomed the news that the legislation was finally going to be listed for discussion in the Dáil. However we noted that not everything which made it to the Dáil list was necessarily enacted. We would be watching his progress with interest.

I couldn't face the death of another friend from contaminated blood products without adequate and reasonable compensation having been put in place. People needed to be able to live the rest of their blighted lives without the worry that their family would be in financial dire straits after their death. My major concern was that if the legislation was not passed by the Dáil before the upcoming general election, then it was likely it would disappear from the political agenda. I resolved that if I was going to have to be abrasive or to tread on toes to ensure this issue was finally resolved – so be it.

The first step was to brief opposition TDs. I wanted them to put pressure on the minister in the Dáil to ensure that he did what he said he would do. On a regular basis I would have meetings with the health spokespersons, Gay Mitchell of Fine Gael and Liz McManus of Labour. The next part of our strategy was to try to generate public support. I remember holding a meeting in the IHS office when it was proposed we hold a news conference about the issue. It seemed a bizarre suggestion to me. I remember asking: "How can we bring in the media when we're waiting for something to happen?" The response was quick: "That's the point." There was a lot of discussion about the idea. On the one hand, the minister was promising to do the right thing and we might antagonise him.

Another issue was that some members were becoming tired of haemophilia being continually linked in the media to HIV and hepatitis C. Despite these considerations, we felt that we had to keep the pressure on. Towards the end of February, we held a news conference under the banner: *Government Fails to Meet its Commitment to the Haemophilia Community in Ireland*.

By March, we had upped the ante. With the IHS annual general meeting pending, members infected with HIV announced they were initiating legal proceedings against the Minister for Health and the State over the absence of fair and final compensation. The media were informed that legal writs would be served every week up to the general election. I was to the forefront in this legal strategy. I felt the promises made in 1999 hadn't been delivered on, the minister had failed to meet his own deadline and so no quarter could be given.

Serving the writ was a memorable moment. At a meeting between the IHS and Department of Health officials on the issue of compensation, Raymond served it on Gerry Coffey, the senior official at the meeting. Looking across the table, the former Blood Bank board member looked less than happy when the writ was placed in his hand.

When the pressure is on, things can become quite bizarre. One particular day, I remember going to the office and then racing to catch a bus with staff members to attend our AGM in Portumna, County Galway. On the way, I had to direct the driver to RTÉ for a quick television interview. Once back on the bus, I ended up constantly on the mobile phone doing interviews with local radio stations. Then the traffic seemed to get in the way of an interview with RTÉ Radio's *Five-Seven Live* programme. The producer wanted me to talk to the programme on an ordinary phone rather than a mobile. With only minutes to go before the appointed time, I had to stop at Mother Hubbard's restaurant near Moyvalley, County

Kildare. With the assistance of the manager, I managed to run through the kitchen, up the stairs to his office where I got on his phone – just in the nick of time.

The other aspect of our strategy was to make HIV compensation an issue in the minister's own constituency of Cork South-Central. I believed this could really have an effect. I had used this before when members from Munster met Mr Martin at his clinic in Cork city in the run up to the Lindsay Tribunal. This time I was going to ensure that he knew exactly what was going on in the lives of people with haemophilia. The man who got things rolling was Joe Healy whose son Gerard was the first person with haemophilia I ever met. Joe knows virtually everyone in Cork and so I asked him to help set this up. I travelled to Cork and met the members in the Metropole Hotel on the night before. They were distraught at the lack of progress and needed to be briefed on exactly what had been going on. I wanted to make sure that they couldn't be surprised by any detail of the negotiations which the minister might raise.

The following morning, just two days before Saint Patrick's Day, we gathered to meet Mr Martin at his offices over the Orchard Bar. I was impressed that he had agreed to the meeting in the first place – doubly so that he was attending without any officials. It turned out to be one of the most emotional gatherings I ever attended. One of the men began to explain how his combination therapy, the concoction of drugs which helped people with HIV survive, was no longer working. The man said simply that there were no options open to him: he was dying. Looking at the minister, he said he would like to have the compensation issue sorted before that happened so that his family would be provided for. As he finished his story, it unlocked the floodgates and everyone in the group wanted to relate their particular circumstances. Mothers who had lost sons began telling him in painful detail of their anguish. A recurring sentiment was that they were from Cork and they wanted him to sort things out for his fellow citizens of the city. The man who had the outburst at the tribunal, Fred, was also there. He stood up and said to Mr Martin: "You knocked on my door for a vote. Now I am asking you for something." There is no doubt in my mind that the Mr Martin was moved by what he heard. Nobody could fail to be. He was compassionate in his response. At one point, a mother became so distraught at her plight that she began to lose control and he simply stood up and embraced her. It was right. At the end of the meeting, nearly everybody in the room was in tears.

I had been sitting in the corner of the room. I didn't say very much except to introduce members by name when I saw that they wanted to speak. I felt from the time the first man spoke, Micheál Martin listened carefully. He didn't shuffle papers, move or interject. Part of the reason why the meeting was so powerful was that the members attending hadn't told each other about their personal pain and fears for the future in such naked terms. As the emotion in the room intensified, I believed it was the first time a government minister had come face to face with the real anguish of the haemophilia community. I felt that Mr Martin could now understand why I had campaigned so hard, why it was impossible to take no for an answer and why to him I could appear unreasonable and excessive. At the end of the meeting, I stood up and shook his hand and said: "Now you know why I'm like I am."

Things started to move much faster after that. Numerous meetings followed with officials from the Department of Health. There was a clear urgency as time was running out with the general election pending. On April 11, 2002, things were looking so good that we held a news conference to state that agreement had been reached on what should be included in the legislation. Two days later, a meeting of our members signed off on the proposals.

However, on April 16, the situation took a real turn for the worse. At a meeting with departmental officials, a new clause suddenly appeared in the draft legislation. It said: "The [Hepatitis C Compensation] Tribunal shall take account of any award previously made by it or by the High Court on an appeal from the tribunal to the person." The clause suggested that people who'd obtained compensation from the Hepatitis C Compensation Tribunal for their condition would have it taken into consideration when their HIV award was being made. In other words, they would receive a reduced amount.

I went into orbit, not just because a new clause was being introduced at such a late stage, but it seemed that those infected twice were being penalised. It was unfair. I believed the clause had the capacity to collapse the entire process. This hour-long meeting took place shortly after midday. I didn't have the opportunity to discuss the issue in detail with Raymond as I had agreed to take Aisling for an audition to the School of Music. While she was preparing for her big moment, all hell was breaking loose outside as I got on the phone.

At four o'clock that afternoon I was contacted by the Mr Martin. I told him in absolute terms: "If the clause remains in the legislation, then the IHS will oppose it." An hour and a half later, he called me again to say the offending section had to stay. Subsequently we received a faxed copy of the draft bill. The clause was still there.

At a quarter to eight that night, I held a crisis meeting with our legal team. We found ourselves in a real dilemma. It was clear that the legislation would go some way to redressing the terrible imbalance which had been there up to now. We also feared that if we rejected the bill, then the members could get nothing at all. I had been screaming that no more people with haemophilia should die without fair and equitable compensation. Yet I was now in a position where I could be about to end the only opportunity to secure something for them.

Despite all that pressure, I still felt that the deal would have to be rejected. The issue needed to be resolved in totality – I didn't want to have to return to it in a couple of years. I left the meeting and rang Brian O'Mahony and told him the situation. He rang the other executive committee members to secure their views. At half past eight he called back to say they agreed with what I was doing. They would support a withdrawal of support for the legislation.

Just a few minutes later, RTÉ *News* rang my mobile phone. It was just before nine o'clock and they wanted to see if things were going according to plan. No one knew about the problems. However, now that I had the backing from both the legal team and the executive committee, I told the reporter that the deal was about to collapse. Ten minutes later, the report went live on the *Nine O'Clock News* and the nation was informed. The story also got extensive coverage in the newspapers the next morning.

I don't know whether it was the media attention or whether things looked different in the morning, but there was a sea-change in the attitude of the Department of Health officials at our meeting the next day. Where there had been outright hostility, suddenly there was an open door. A deal was clearly going to be done and it would be on our terms. Everyone in the room was tired. Micheál Martin was telling us that things would now happen. As I looked at him, I couldn't help but think that we had wasted the last twenty-four hours. It was the same old story yet again – you have to go through the same old uphill routine before things were delivered.

Nothing came easy with officialdom. Funny how negative media coverage before a looming election can concentrate the minds of an outgoing Government desperate to stay in power.

As a lobbyist, it is depressing to have to go through the hoops and effectively give politicians no room to manouevre before a promise is actually delivered upon. There was no bad feeling at the meeting. It was just that we'd reached the point where business was going to be transacted.

The bill went further than any legislation in the history of the State. It was groundbreaking in the first instance as it was a revision of a 1991 settlement described as "full and final". It also reversed 150 years of precedent, in which a family lost the entitlement to claim general damages when the immediate relative died. Under the new legislation, a family was not being penalised because their loved one died before their claim could be heard.

The media constantly wanted to know how much the deal was worth, but it simply wasn't possible to say as the provisions had never been brought to court before. The Department of Health's own estimate was in the region of €100 million. Many observers believed it would be much higher. It was a long way from the £400,000 we had so desperately sought all the way back in 1989. The bill finally went through on Thursday, April 18, 2002. The overriding feeling I had that night was simply one of relief. It was all over – finally.

24

Cop-out

On Thursday, September 5, 2002, I decided to go for a walk. It was around ten o'clock in the morning and I was enjoying what I thought was the last of the summer sunshine. As I reached the valley opposite our house, the mobile phone in my pocket began to ring. I know it would drive some people mad but I was used to such interruptions. I pulled the phone out and hoped it would be a short conversation before I continued my stroll.

I answered and recognised the voice on the other end as Michelle from the IHS office: "Rosemary, the Lindsay Report is here."

While I stopped in my tracks, there was more than a sneaking suspicion that my colleagues might be trying to pull my leg – they knew I was anxiously waiting for the document to arrive but didn't know when. I decided to sound less than impressed: "Would you ever get lost!"

Michelle's voice got a little more insistent: "No! Really, it is here."

Still concerned it might be a wind-up, I said: "I'm warning

you – if I come into that office and there's no report I'm going to kill you."

Michelle re-assured me that it was waiting for me. I hung up. It was lovely and calm in the valley but, after a second or two, I turned on my heel and started racing back home. Another roller-coaster ride had begun.

I crashed through the door of the house and rang for a taxi. Then, I ran upstairs and put a suit into a bag – if the report was out, then there were going to be interviews. There was still a tiny doubt in my mind so I rang Raymond's office and got confirmation: the report of the Lindsay Tribunal – all 577 pages – had just been published. My first reaction was not of anxiety but of anger. The IHS had requested that it be given a copy of the report, or at least notification of its publication a couple of days in advance. Our objective was to be able to give a considered response when the inevitable media questions began to flood in. More importantly, we also wanted to be able to talk things through with our members and ensure they didn't hear about it on the radio or TV first. That courtesy wasn't being extended to us – the media would be getting access to the report at two o'clock.

The taxi arrived and we sped our way into Dublin city centre from Swords. The first phone call I made was to Brian O'Mahony: "The report's in the office." It was a short conversation. Nothing else needed to be said. The next call I wanted to make was to Raymond, but this was impossible – he was on holiday in Thailand. Sitting in the back seat of the taxi I thought: "Lucky him." It left me feeling a little exposed as he had the greatest knowledge about what happened at the tribunal and now he wasn't here on the big day. I thought to myself: "If we had been given two days' notice, he would have been able to make it." We were just going to have to get on with things.

I phoned Raymond's office and spoke to his colleague

Terry. He said: "Rosemary, we only have one copy of the report." I was incredulous: "You must be joking. How are we all supposed to read that?" This was definitely not working out the way I would have wanted. Our barrister Jim McCullough had the sole copy. I rang him as he stood in the middle of our solicitor's room stripping the binding off the report and trying to get it photocopied as quickly as possible. My first concern was for the IHS. I asked him: "What does it say about us?" Jim said: "There's very little." It appeared we had been commended, if somewhat mutely, for the services we provided for our members which the State had not. I was relieved, however, to hear that there wasn't any criticism. It made me breathe a little easier as the taxi pulled into Smithfield.

When I got to our office, IHS staff Michelle and Marian hugged me. The ten-month waiting game was over. By this point, I was a bundle of nervous tension. I needed to get my hands on the report to find out what it said. Raymond's office was on the floor beneath ours. Brian arrived and we tried to begin getting to grips with the document, but it was impossible amid the photocopying chaos. It was a ridiculous situation. I called the Department of Health to demand extra copies and was informed they would be sent over as soon as they had them.

The farcical nature of the whole episode really came into sharp relief when journalists began to call me shortly after noon. Word was out that the report was going to be released. I was being asked for my reaction to a report which was in 577 pieces all over the floor of our solicitors' office. I was furious but had to control myself. I rang upstairs to Michelle and told her to start calling the members who had given personal testimony to the tribunal. I wanted them to hear about the report's publication from the IHS. I hoped it would be possible to protect all of them from the sudden shock of hearing the news on the radio, but realised that it probably wasn't going to be possible.

Additional copies only arrived at our office just ten minutes before the report went up on the internet. By this time, we had already managed to photocopy it. Brian, Jim and I then divided it into sections and tried to absorb what we could. Michelle was briefed to tell the media that we would have a news conference at half past four in the Westbury Hotel. We sat in Brian's office and realised we would have just over two hours to digest its contents.

The first thing I looked for was an executive summary. There was none. I then looked for the conclusions chapter. There was none. My heart sank. As I quickly flicked through the report it seemed relatively inaccessible as a finding in one area would then refer on to another chapter.

I started at the beginning. After a number of introductory pages, the tribunal dealt with the personal testimony. The report said: "Their evidence was at times sad, at times tragic and at times harrowing. It was the authentic voice of those whose lives had been touched and irretrievably altered by the infection which is at the centre of this inquiry. The tribunal believes a valuable function of this inquiry has been to provide a forum in which this voice can finally be heard." I agreed with this, but recalled the battle we endured to ensure this "authentic voice" was allowed testify at the beginning of proceedings. The issue now was whether the tribunal delivered for the dozens of people brave enough to come forward.

The divergence between the tribunal and the IHS began just one paragraph later. The tribunal stated that 104 people with haemophilia had become infected with HIV on the basis of records from the Virus Reference Laboratory [VRL] in Dublin. The IHS put the figure at 105 because of the man with haemophilia who had returned to Dublin from abroad for a hepatitis C compensation claim and was also found to be HIV positive. In relation to hepatitis C, the tribunal put the numbers infected at 217. It did say, however, that this was a "minimum figure" as the VRL had not conducted all tests in the State. The IHS figure was more than 250. People continued to be diagnosed with the condition during the tribunal hearings and after.

Yet rather than focus on the disagreements, we decided to identify areas in the report which had been of use and value. This was a tribunal we had fought long and hard for and we wanted to focus on any positives. From our initial examination, we saw that the tribunal found there were serious failures on the part of the State and its agencies in the care afforded to the haemophilia community in Ireland. The report was critical of the actions and policies of the Blood Bank, the Department of Health and some doctors.

While reading the report, we also began to draft a press release to be issued at the news conference. It included the finding that the Blood Bank had a responsibility in relation to the safety of the concentrates it imported. The report stated the BTSB had a duty around 1983 to "inform both treating doctors and persons with haemophilia of the risk of transmission of AIDS". The tribunal also found that while the BTSB was "not the only body with a responsibility", it should have alerted doctors to the risk of hepatitis. Unfortunately this was a duty "which it failed to discharge".

This principle was important as commercial concentrates were responsible for most infections in Ireland. The problem was that the tribunal didn't blame anyone for these lapses. There was a statement of fact, but nothing else. I thought of Jerome Stephens' daughter Karen and Joe Dowling's daughter Linda and realised that this type of language was not going to be enough to satisfy their yearning for justice.

In relation to the domestic Factor IX product, there were a number of findings. The tribunal report stated that by August 1985 the Blood Bank should have heat-treated Factor IX and stopped issuing the old product. Instead the practice continued until December 1985 and a recall was only instituted in the middle of 1986. The report stated that had action been taken in August 1985 "it is probable that most, though not all, of the seven persons would have avoided [HIV] infection". The tribunal said that even if the BTSB had taken no action in August 1985, then the identification of a HIV positive donor in October 1985 should have caused a recall of the old Factor IX product. The report said: "This was not done." What the report didn't do was to sum up these events and apportion blame.

I wanted to see what the tribunal found in relation to our belief that a cover-up had taken place over Factor IX. Lindsay took the view it was "probable" that the board of the Blood Bank was told in June 1986 that Factor IX patients were testing HIV positive but, critically, not what caused the infections. The tribunal also found that the board was not provided with the later information which indicated that BTSB non-heat-treated products were probably responsible. It came to this decision apparently because the board minutes of meetings in July, August and September 1986 made no reference to the issue. Accordingly, the tribunal found that: "Dr Barry [chief medical consultant] and Mr Keyes were principally responsible for the failure to bring the information to the board." I scanned the page again and realised that even this finding wasn't a straight statement – there was a qualification: "If the tribunal is correct in its analysis of what occurred." The report went on to say that the board wasn't "entirely blameless" as it should have inquired at its subsequent meetings about "the problem" with Factor IX which it was informed about in June 1986. The tribunal concluded that this state of affairs led to "an ambivalence and blurring of the facts within the BTSB" and that this "persisted in the dealings between the BTSB and the Department of Health".

I didn't have high hopes, but these findings on page 84 I found really offensive. Firstly, with so many questions to answer, why on earth were the board members not called to give evidence? The fact that they had not been called meant the tribunal was not just incomplete but seriously flawed. Secondly, how could the tribunal conclude the debacle over Factor IX could be explained away by the phrase "ambivalence and blurring of the facts"? The inquiry report was failing miserably to get to the heart of the issue of how information which was conveyed to the Blood Bank ended up being buried. The finding seemed to buy into the idea put forward by Dr Emer Lawlor that the Blood Bank went into "denial". The tribunal did describe the matter as a "serious failure", but this simply wasn't good enough for the IHS. Ted Keyes had asserted in evidence that he brought the matter to the attention of the board, but the tribunal found against him – even though there was no direct evidence contradicting this position. Professor Temperley said he repeatedly told the board about the Factor IX infections. Their evidence seemed to count for nothing because there was no record of such discussions in the board minutes. Oh dear!

As the tribunal didn't believe that the board of the Blood Bank was aware of the Factor IX infections, it found that the Department of Health couldn't have known either. Gerry McCartney had attended the June 1986 Blood Bank board meeting, but this didn't seem to register with the tribunal. The only criticism the department received in relation to Factor IX was regarding the Blood Bank's claim that it was heat-treating the product when it actually was not. The tribunal stated: " . . . the department should have continued to pursue the matter during 1985 and if it had, presumably it would have become aware that the BTSB was continuing to produce and to issue unheated Factor IX during the year."

The department was also criticised because its "supervisory actions were lacking in a number of respects" and that it should have "moved more quickly and more decisively to attempt to resolve staffing a – structural problem in the BTSB" once the HIV crisis became known. The Department of Health was chastised for its delay in responding to requests from Saint James's Hospital in relation to counselling facilities. But what about Barry Desmond and Dr Rory O'Hanlon? I flicked on to page 233 and found that they had both been absolved. Even though Mr Desmond was told that more than a quarter of the haemophilia community had been infected with HIV but never returned to the matter, the tribunal "does not think it would be reasonable to expect the then Minister [for Health] to have greater involvement in what was then just one aspect of a very wide portfolio of responsibilities". Similarly with Dr O'Hanlon, who had misled the Dáil: it found he was "acting on incomplete and unsatisfactory information, but the tribunal does not believe that he can in any way be blamed for this". The report did not go on to say who should be blamed.

The Blood Bank was criticised in other areas. In relation to the introduction of HIV-antibody testing, the tribunal decided there was "a lack of urgency" about the way arrangements were put in place. In relation to hepatitis C, there was a valuable finding which stated: "By 1987, the tribunal believes the BTSB should also have been seeking protection against the risk of transmission of Non-A Non-B hepatitis." While the report didn't criticise the Blood Bank for its subsequent decision to give an indemnity to Armour Pharmaceuticals, it said: "By June 1988, the board of the BTSB ought to have been distinctly unhappy and uncomfortable at the prospect of continuing to supply a product treated with a system of viral inactivation believed to be inadequate to destroy the Non-A Non-B hepatitis virus." Of course, as board members were never called to give evidence, it was not possible to find out how they came to take the decision or sign the indemnity letter.

Possibly the strongest criticism of the Blood Bank came in relation to look-back – the procedure whereby if a donor tests positive then their previous donations were checked to see if they were also infectious. Look-back had been considered in 1987. The BTSB's Dr Terry Walsh had even identified five donors who were HIV positive. However, for some unexplained reason, the policy was not implemented. The tribunal found that there was "no valid justification" for the board not introducing the policy at this time. The matter came back before the board in 1989 when another donor tested positive for HIV. Dr Walsh, who was now chief medical consultant, testified that he had called on the board to introduce look-back on all cases dating back to 1985. However, the tribunal had "doubts" about how clearly he had explained this. In the event, the board decided to introduce look-back for the new case and all future cases but not on the earlier ones. The tribunal found this to be "clearly wrong". The amazing thing about this decision is that the minutes record how the board expressed fear about increased litigation. The tribunal found that this was "not an appropriate matter to in any way influence" such a decision. When a full and complete look-back finally took place in 1996, it was impossible to link all of the donations to recipients. In some frightening statistics, the tribunal stated: "Out of six donations in the very high-risk period [for HIV], three were traced, two were found to have caused infection and the other one did not; while three remain untraced." In other words, it's possible for the recipients of those three high-risk donations to have been infected with HIV and still not know about it. This was pretty staggering stuff yet, once again, the tribunal chose not to take the matter further. Why not? If a decision taken by the board had "no valid justification"; if another decision was "clearly wrong"; if this decision could have been influenced by inappropriate matters; if, as a consequence, people might be infected with HIV and not know about it; then why was someone not held to account? The board should have at least been forced to explain why these decisions were made.

When I got to the section relating to treating doctors, I really blew a gasket. Page 188 particularly stands out. On the one hand the tribunal appeared to be intimating that unless there was absolute proof then it wasn't possible to make a finding, yet on the third paragraph of page 188 the tribunal seemed to me to break its own unwritten rules. The section related to grievances which members of the haemophilia community had regarding the manner of Professor Temperley. As the report recorded: "Some witnesses' perception of Professor Temperley was that he was unapproachable, arrogant or dismissive." I had expected the tribunal would not come down on one side or the other in relation to this question – how could it be otherwise when this happened years previously and there was no documentation to prove it? I never expected to see the following written in black and white: "The tribunal has had a considerable opportunity to observe Professor Temperley as he gave evidence and has also examined the records of his treatment of a considerable number of patients. The tribunal does not believe he is or was arrogant, cold or dismissive." I thought: "How in the hell was that conclusion arrived at? How could Judge Alison Lindsay make a finding based on a perception of a person who was giving evidence? How could she claim that medical records would indicate whether or not the professor was uncaring in his dealings with his patients? Just to rub salt in the wounds of the membership, the tribunal chose to continue in the same vein: "It is very sad that some of his patients perceived him to be so, sad for them because it would have added to their feelings of anger and hurt." I felt the paragraph was patronising – poor sad people with haemophilia whose memories are defective and they thereby end up hurting themselves even more. It filled me with contempt.

The report did make serious findings against Professor Temperley. It was concluded that he should have told Jackie about the risks of AIDS associated with concentrates when advising that her son be switched from cryo in May 1983. Rory subsequently contracted HIV. The tribunal found "very little evidence" that the professor put any arrangements in place in early 1985 to ensure his patients were informed of their HIV tests before he went on sabbatical. The report said: "He should have postponed the commencement of his sabbatical . . . and that he should himself have commenced informing patients of their results."

In relation to Factor IX, Professor Temperley was criticised for not having taken action in August 1985 when Dr Helena Daly expressed concern at the continued distribution by the Blood Bank of non-heat-treated material. The report stated that while such a decision would not have been expected prior to the professor going on sabbatical, the balance had shifted decisively by August. It stated: "The tribunal believes Professor Temperley ought then to have instructed Dr Daly to stop using unheated BTSB Factor IX and to switch all haemophilia B patients to heat-treated commercial Factor IX until heat-treated BTSB product became available." The tribunal didn't adequately deal with why Dr Daly received lots of non-heat-treated Factor IX from the Blood Bank when she had just stated her desire not to use this product.

The professor was further criticised for not having "turned his mind" to the risk of hepatitis C infections in 1987. In relation to Felicity, who wasn't informed for years that three of her children had hepatitis C, the report said: "The tribunal believes what occurred in respect of Felicity's children was something that clearly should not have happened and it agrees with Professor Temperley that it could not be explained or excused." In relation to Luke who received two infusions of safe product and then received the old BTSB Factor IX, the tribunal found that Paul Lynam, chief technologist at Saint James's Hospital, should have consulted Professor Temperley before releasing the old product. Professor Temperley was criticised, however, for not having delivered a clear instruction to Mr Lynam about not issuing the old BTSB product.

Dr Paule Cotter was also criticised over her handling of the Factor IX issue in which she had the first information showing Blood Bank material was infectious: "The tribunal cannot accept on the basis of her evidence that she took sufficient steps to stop the use of a potentially infected product in her own hospital or to inform the BTSB and Professor Temperley so that its use could be stopped elsewhere and a proper investigation take place." The tribunal also went against Dr Cotter in relation to her claims that she informed patients of their HIV diagnosis. Regarding Garrett, the report said that it was "likely" his mother only found out he was HIV positive in 1990 – five years after the information had become available. In relation to Noel, the report said that while it was "difficult to reach a conclusive view", the tribunal had "considerable doubt" that he had been informed.

Some time after three, I left Brian's room and walked to the kitchen to put on the kettle. Ray Kelly was sitting at the table. He was flicking through the report. I could see he was angry. I asked him: "What do you think?" He responded:

"There is nothing in this for me." It was a deeply unsettling verdict from a man who had acted as my informal advisor during the 196 days of evidence. If Ray was unhappy, then the membership were, in all probability, going to be unhappy as well. I went back to Brian's room.

There were lots of issues which we had hoped the Lindsay Tribunal would comment on but which were ignored. One course of action which we hoped the tribunal would recommend was an investigation into the pharmaceutical companies. This didn't happen. The other major issue for us was that we wanted the tribunal to say its report should be considered by the Director of Public Prosecutions. However, it only said: "It is not the function of a tribunal of inquiry to decide issues of criminal or civil liability. The tribunal is of the view that it is not appropriate in these circumstances to send a copy of the report to the director." There was no recommendation that the practice of placing people in body-bags be discontinued.

Instead it said: "The tribunal accepts that the use of such bags by Saint James's Hospital and the National Children's Hospital was believed by the hospital authorities to be a necessary measure of infection control." I wanted to continue reading, but time had run out. As I photocopied our press releases, my anger grew.

I changed into my suit and then ran down the stairs to the car where Brian was already waiting. It was half past four – we were going to be late. On the way to the Westbury, Raymond rang out of the blue to ask me what was going on. By this stage, I was so uptight that I couldn't speak to him properly. I was caught in two minds: on the one hand I wanted to tell him to go away as we were dealing with it, but, on the other hand, I was still wishing that he was here.

Because he had gone public already, we asked Ray Kelly if

he would come down to the news conference. He agreed. When we arrived, the room was packed with photographers and journalists. We sat down at the table and began to give our views and then conducted individual interviews with different reporters. Rather than talk in detail about the findings we kept things broad.

Brian said: "I think the State agencies, including the Blood Bank, need to learn from this and need to ensure that the catastrophic failures which led to so much death and misery for our members are not repeated. I would really be disappointed if we went through twenty years of misery as a community, six years of active lobbying as an organisation . . . and then not to have those lessons learnt from and recommendations complied with. That would be devastating." We did say that the report appeared to be short on recommendations, but left it at that. I was asked about the possibility of another tribunal into the actions of the pharmaceutical companies and said: "The IHS calls on the Minister for Health to ensure that the facts surrounding the pharmaceutical companies emerge through a full and rigorous inquiry."

When the initial rush was over, I was asked to do a live interview on RTÉ's 6:1 news from outside the Westbury. I heard that the Blood Bank had issued a statement in which said it: " . . . expresses its sorrow that blood or blood products made by the BTSB led to the infection of nine people with HIV [i.e. the seven who contracted the virus through Factor IX, Mary who contracted it from Norman and Fionn who became positive from cryo] and to hepatitis C infections in a large number of patients prior to the introduction of effective viral inactivation methods. The IBTS apologises unreservedly to these people and their families for the suffering and distress they have had to ensure." It was the first time an apology had been tendered by the Blood Bank. It was welcome – if several years late. The other thing which caught my eye was that the Blood Bank described the report as "fair and accurate". If the Blood Bank was happy, then it probably was going to mean that we were not.

The live interview was difficult. Rather than being in studio where I could see Bryan Dobson, it was conducted by a satellite link-up. This meant I had to talk into the camera lens which is disconcerting. On top of this, the Minister for Health was also on a satellite link-up from Cork. Before the interview took place, Andrew Kelly, acting CEO of the Blood Bank, was interviewed. He described the report as "very fair" which increased my concern. I was then asked for my views on the report, but was slightly evasive: "We have not had the chance to read the report in detail . . . but what the report does detail is that people with haemophilia in Ireland have been seriously let down by the State and its agencies." Asked about the recommendations, I zoned in on the seventh which stipulated: "Doctors should ensure that test results in relation to patients are given to them as soon as such results become available." I said: "Many [of our members] were not aware of their condition. In some cases for three of four years. This is something which is totally unacceptable and intolerable and shouldn't happen again in the State." I thought of the members, like Austin, who were not even informed that a HIV test was being conducted on their blood, but didn't get the chance to say it.

Micheál Martin said he was committed to implementing the recommendations. He was asked about whether it should be referred to the DPP, but avoided answering directly: "This report is being sent to the Dáil . . . so obviously we are going to debate it . . . and I think it's too early, to be fair to all concerned in the context of natural justice, to be making definitive conclusions at this particular point." I was asked the same question, but could only say that the report would be considered by our members and they would decide on what action should be taken.

By the end of the interview my head was buzzing. I had been talking non-stop for two hours with dozens of people and trying to keep to the script: this was our initial response. Just when it looked as if things were going to calm down, RTÉ's *Prime Time* requested that I go on that night. I thought to myself: "Jesus, things are bad and hectic enough without this."

We returned to the office where Jim McCullough had been joined by our other barrister Martin Hayden SC. They had continued reading the report in our absence and things were becoming clearer: after checking and rechecking it was now obvious that on most issues of concern to us, the findings simply had not gone far enough. The report appeared to highlight what went wrong but not follow through on those individuals who were responsible. Nobody seemed to be guilty of anything. A total of seventy-nine people had died and no-one was to blame. I didn't like the way the report was released to us. I didn't like the format of the report. Most of all, I didn't like what was contained in the report.

Donor F was a good example of what was wrong. This was the person who donated infected blood in December 1984 which went into Factor IX batch 90753. As there was no HIV antibody test, this wasn't picked up. In August 1990, the person donated again and their HIV positive status was identified. The Blood Bank didn't institute a look-back policy as the previous donation had been given more than five years previously.

In a finding I agreed with, the report stated: "Since the December 1984 donation was given at a time when the risk of infection was higher in the donor population, the tribunal believes that a look-back procedure to trace the blood products made from the December 1984 donation should have taken place."

The tribunal went on to state that "inquiries which were made in or around January 1991 by the BTSB in the context of information which was required for ongoing litigation revealed that product from the December 1984 donation had ended up in Factor IX batch number 90753." This was very interesting as it meant that the Blood Bank knew in or around January 1991 that BTSB Factor IX had infected people with haemophilia. The significance of the date was that litigation by members of the IHS infected with HIV was ongoing at this time. Nearly one hundred pages later, the tribunal came to deal with the litigation. It chose not to comment on the linking in January 1991 of Donor F to Factor IX 90753. It didn't comment on the Blood Bank's failure to admit liability at this time. Instead it said: " . . . the tribunal is of the opinion that it is unnecessary for it to make any further comments in regard to the [litigation] matter since the tribunal is aware that the present Minister for Health and Children, Micheál Martin, has reached agreement with the Irish Haemophilia Society in regard to the payment of further compensation to persons with haemophilia who have been infected with HIV." This was a total cop-out.

By eight o'clock I was driving out to RTÉ and was prepared to go further in my comments than I had in the afternoon. The minister was on a link-up from Cork again. I was joined in studio by the acting Blood Bank CEO, Andrew Kelly. Before the debate got underway, there was a report which featured Joe Humphreys of *The Irish Times*, who had covered the entire tribunal proceedings. He accurately predicted that there would be mixed feelings within the haemophilia community: "No-one has been held accountable. Specifically, there will be no prosecutions. There are people walking free from the tribunal, as they might see it – former ministers, former treaters, high officials in the blood transfusion service – and at the end of the day, no-one is being held accountable or being punished for what they [the haemophilia community] would feel as a wrong done to them." He finished by saying: "In terms of selecting a fall-guy, there is no obvious one in the report."

Presenter Miriam O'Callaghan began questioning Andrew Kelly who repeated the Blood Bank's apology and went on to say: "It is clearly a time when mistakes were made. And clearly actions which should have been taken, were not taken at the appropriate times." I said the report was strong in some areas, but I zoned in on the issue of Factor IX and how it fell short of what we wanted it to say: "In the areas of the Factor IX infections and the knowledge of what the BTSB knew in 1986 and how it communicated that knowledge internally and to the department it is not strong enough as far as we're concerned. The language [in the report] is that there was ambivalence. Well, ambivalence isn't strong enough. We believe that there was misleading information given and, at least, there was wilful misleading [of information] or a cover-up."

Mr Kelly said the tribunal didn't support this contention. Miriam O'Callaghan asked him how could the public believe in the Blood Bank when it withheld 611 documents over which it claimed privilege. I interjected at this point: "If we had had sight of those documents I think that things would have been much clearer." When Mr Kelly was asked why the documents were withheld, he didn't answer the question, but said: "We were of the view that the information which was necessary for the tribunal to do its work . . . was fully available to it." When pressed further on why the documents were withheld, he said: "Because we are entitled." It was a typical Blood Bank answer. What was the real reason? Why not come clean?

Asked to sum up and also to reassure the public, Mr Kelly spoke of how the standards of safety in the blood supply were now extremely high and he encouraged people to continue to come forward to donate. He drew in the IHS by stating that it was our policy to always support the donation of blood. While the statement is correct, I didn't like the way it was used in the context of what was being discussed. I interjected again: "It's difficult to have confidence when you refer to privileged documents. To keep your privilege you have lost [our] confidence because we still don't know what was in those documents. We support blood donations – absolutely. But if you want confidence in the blood supply, you must have openness."

I found it hard to be objective and not to vent my anger towards this unfortunate man who had only recently taken up this position. I didn't want to throw the apology in his face because I didn't have haemophilia, but I felt I knew what our members would think: too little, too late.

After *Prime Time,* I returned to the office to collect my bags. It was close to eleven o'clock, but thankfully Margaret Dunne and Michelle had waited for me and we had gin and tonics in our local pub. The rollercoaster which had begun at ten o'clock had finally ground to a halt thirteen hours later. I was absolutely shattered.

The next day I knew the report would still be of major news significance and so, even though still tired, I turned on *Morning Ireland.* Dr Emer Lawlor, the Blood Bank's expert witness at the tribunal, was on air. From what I could hear, it was back to the bad old days. The issue of the 611 documents was, according to her, "a red herring". She then went on to make an extraordinary statement: "There is no evidence that those documents impeded the judge in any way at making what is an extremely detailed and informative report." By now I was wide awake, and shouting at the radio: "Of course there is no evidence because no-one knows what's in the bloody documents except yourselves!" Fergal Bowers of *irishhealth.com* asked her to promise the public that there was nothing of significance in the documents. She answered: "I can say that there is nothing that would change what is already in the report." It was crazy – the Blood Bank of all people telling the public that their secret papers were not important to the tribunal's work. Whatever apology had been given the day before had, in my eyes, now disappeared.

The Blood Bank's decision not to introduce a look-back policy was another bone of contention. It was put to Dr Lawlor that the failure of the Blood Bank to adopt a policy of checking back on donors testing positive for HIV from 1987, as opposed to the partial look-back in 1989 and full look-back in 1996, amounted to negligence. Dr Lawlor stated: "It should have happened sometime in 1986 or 1987, as the tribunal says. I am not a lawyer . . . I think clearly mistakes were made and we clearly say that we don't agree with it and it shouldn't have happened." Once again, a mistake was made but culpability wasn't an issue. The interviewer, Cathal MacCoille, continued: "To a layperson, a mistake of that magnitude means negligence on somebody's part – somewhere. It doesn't just happen." Dr Lawlor responded: "In quite a number of countries it didn't happen [i.e. introduction of a look-back policy]. When something happens not just in one place . . . it always suggests that there is either an ideological problem or a system failure – that it is not simply a thing of individual negligence." It made my blood boil. Nothing seemed to have changed in the Blood Bank. Listeners could have been left with the impression that aliens had landed in their offices, messed things up and blame could certainly not be directed to any of the senior staff who worked there.

Sitting at the breakfast table later that morning, I felt as if someone had died. I know the feeling of grief better than most, having been present when so many people died in tragic circumstances. My mind turned to one of the people who threw off the cloak of anonymity and went public about his infection: Bernard Smullen. I remember him walking out of the tribunal after speaking about how he was exposed to the hepatitis C virus. The infection changed his character. He became estranged from his children due to mood swings. It was difficult for him to open up about what happened to him, but he had the guts to do it. When he walked out to the reporters after giving evidence he said: "There's a lot of people shifting the blame, but someone is responsible; someone has got to be held responsible." Sitting at the table, I didn't think anyone had been held to account. Bernard and all the other people whose lives were ruined had been cheated of closure.

My mood darkened further when I read the editorial of *The Irish Times* which said that the report was "most welcome", adding that "Judge Alison Lindsay has produced a detailed and comprehensive report and she and her team are to be congratulated". It accepted the approach of the tribunal without reservation: "Given the matters investigated by Judge Lindsay relate to matters which occurred up to twenty-five years ago, it has been difficult for the tribunal to reach clear-cut answers to the issues it examined." Whoever wrote the editorial obviously hadn't spoken to their own reporter at the tribunal. But *The Star* newspaper had a headline: "78 dead . . . and no one is to blame". The number was actually seventy-nine, but the sentiment was absolutely correct.

I went in to the office. We were still dealing with media queries, but I spent most of my time talking to members. Raymond had also returned. Any benefit from the holiday in Thailand was quickly washed away as he began to pore over the report. His face said it all – I could see that he was absolutely livid. I tried to brief him on what had happened over the previous twenty-four hours, but didn't get too much time. One thing which helped me focus my thoughts was writing an article for *The Sunday Business Post* in which I said: "Many sections of the report say the actions of the treating doctors at the time were unreasonable. This to me is unacceptable because it fails to explain why these actions were unreasonable. It does not appear to overtly connect unreasonable, unacceptable and inexplicable actions with the consequences of those actions. I fear this will mean many people who read the report, without a comprehensive background knowledge of what happened, will be at a loss to understand what the whole inquiry was about." I explained how every time a member had died, I found myself asking the same question: Why? Seventy-nine times. The article concluded: "From the brief reading [of the report] I have done to date, I still ask myself why."

The Sunday Tribune also phoned seeking a reaction. I told them: "There is grief over this report and there's been enough grief. Tears have been shed, when enough tears have been shed already. I've cried myself. People put their hearts on the line, and their hearts have been broken. This has been soul-destroying. People are shattered and they just feel they've nowhere else to go."

Brian told the paper: "Judge Lindsay just doesn't join the dots. We welcome her findings as far as they go, but they just don't go far enough. The language is weak and woolly. God, this report should have been so much better."

That evening, Brian went on Eamon Dunphy's *The Last Word* show on Today FM, along with Fergal Bowers of *irishhealth.com*. Dunphy was caustic in his views of *The Irish Times* editorial and stated that the *The Star* was far more accurate – Fergal and Brian agreed.

The major event for the IHS that Friday was Ray Kelly appearing on the *Late Late Show*. Years before Ray had waived his anonymity and spoken to Pat Kenny in order to put pressure on the Government to resolve the problem over the funding of our legal team. Now, he was returning to the show to give his verdict on the report. Brian and I went with him to RTÉ to give moral support. As he prepared to go on, I said: "It is like the day you gave evidence at the tribunal, but I am sure this will have much more value." Ray had composed his thoughts and let fly.

He was asked if he felt the tribunal, in any way, had been a help. Raising the report in his left hand, Ray said: "That, to me, is useless, absolutely and utterly useless." The key problem for Ray was that there were not enough conclusions and those that were there didn't go far enough: "Nobody is blamed. There are [only] some people slapped on the wrist."

Pat Kenny asked him how the evidence he gave to the tribunal was reflected in the report.

Ray responded: "I don't think it is. In actual fact, in the report by inference I am called a liar. In regard to Professor Temperley, I had disputes . . . [and] I stated in evidence along with many other people that I found him arrogant, aloof and very difficult to deal with. And in this report, Judge Lindsay comes out and says that she believes Professor Temperley – having watched him for two weeks or whatever as he was giving evidence – '. . . was not arrogant or aloof or distant'."

Pat Kenny said: "She therefore is dismissing the observations of the families of haemophiliacs who observed very different behaviour?"

Ray interjected: "Who met this man in his domain where he was God and who dealt with him . . . in my case for fourteen years . . . It's dismissing my testimony and other people's testimony." Asked whether he would like to see people on trial for what happened to his son John, Ray said: "I would like to see people having to account for it – what happens after that is immaterial to me . . . I thought we'd see that at the tribunal."

I spoke with Ann, Ray's wife, upstairs in the hospitality room, and I marvelled at her composure. She was angry, but said that she had had no great expectations in the first place. I was just overcome with sorrow for Ray and how he had exposed himself, and for what? He had allowed his son's photograph to be used publicly in a fruitless search for the truth.

On a personal level, I felt Judge Alison Lindsay had let down the sixty-four people who came forward to give personal testimony. In her report, it stated that their evidence was "very important to the work of the tribunal" and was of "considerable assistance". It also acknowledged that these witnesses had to "recall and discuss occasions of great pain and suffering" and as a result the tribunal "owes a debt of gratitude to each of the witnesses who gave personal testimony and acknowledges their courage in coming forward to do so". This was not enough. There was written acknowledgement of the pain and suffering but no account of it. The tribunal's decision to "explore a number of themes that emerged from that testimony" didn't do it for me.

The impression I was left with was that she had listened far more closely to her own colleagues. It felt as if there was a closing of ranks – professionals protecting professionals. The use of such terms as "unreasonable" and "inexplicable" in describing events is of absolutely no benefit to people with haemophilia or the next of kin of those who died. I am still incensed by what has happened to the community. Yet those who were infected, and those whose lives have been shattered, are expected to put up or shut up. Even as a document, the report is impossibly dense. I feel that those involved in the drafting of the report should now hang their heads in shame.

Some people have argued that the Lindsay Tribunal indirectly led to a lot of good measures being put in place for people with haemophilia, such as reforms of the Blood Bank, a new haemophilia treatment centre and a fair financial settlement. However, these are not the reasons the tribunal was established in the first place.

Maybe I am the fool. Maybe I expected too much. I spent four years of my life working on this. I've lost friends because I wasn't around. The absence from my family is something that I can never get back. In times of need or in times of celebration I simply wasn't there. I had thought there would be answers at the end of the tribunal. Answers for Austin and Ray. Answers for the families of Jerome and Dermot. Answers for a tiny community which endured so much pain. Jesus, how foolish can you be? And yet my sacrifice was nothing compared to those who had stepped out of the shadows and into the spotlight to give evidence. What must they be thinking now?

The effect of the media glare was of some benefit. Many members feel they can now speak more openly about their infections and their condition. But I think the truth was delivered in the regular media reports of harrowing testimony. We were always conscious that this was the only method by which the public would have a full understanding of what had happened to the haemophilia community. We felt strongly about this from the outset and it explains why we put so much emphasis on the media. However, I never thought the result of the tribunal would be so bad. The recommendations contained in the report will be of some use, I am sure. But for the pain, the anguish, the effort, the energy and the expectations, Lindsay has been a total and absolute let-down.

Just a few weeks after the Lindsay Report was published, it was followed by the Second Interim Report of the Tribunal of Inquiry into Certain Planning Matters and Payments, known as the Flood Report. It was easy to read, had a summary of conclusions chapter and didn't pull any punches. Events didn't seem to be "inexplicable" or "extraordinary" –

Mr Justice Flood spoke of corrupt payments, concealment and of individuals not acting in the public interest. It was straight talking based on the evidence. On the day it was published I received a call from Ray Kelly. He praised the report for getting to the truth, for meticulous investigation despite the obstacles and for hitting hard when it was necessary. Both of us wondered what language Mr Justice Flood might have applied to the tragedy which befell the haemophilia community. If it could only have been so.

Epilogue

When considering whether or not to write this book, one of the first people I consulted was Austin. We had spent so much time together that our friendship was going to have to feature if a book was to happen at all. He called to my house one afternoon and we sat in the back garden. It was sunny.

At first, we just joked about the idea of me becoming an author. He thought it was a hilarious concept considering I couldn't even type and spelling wasn't exactly my strong point. Would I use my middle initial on the book jacket just to make it look a bit more highbrow? What about posing in a black hat for a bit of mystique?

After a while, we began to meander through some of the eventful times we'd gone through: the conversation in the car on the way to a Wicklow school; the pain of trying to work out when to tell a woman you liked that you were HIV positive; the madness of the Mexican conference surrounded by guard dogs; the joy of his marriage and the happiness it had brought to him.

Austin looked at some of the initial things I was writing. It led us into discussing the number of friends who were no longer alive due to HIV and hepatitis C. As we went through the stories of fun and inevitably pain, it became very emotional.

One thing I lost sight of was the fact that Austin still had to endure his own personal war every day. I had been so busy focusing on the tribunal that I had lost touch. He told me that his major fear was that his immune system would weaken and the cocktail of drugs which stabilised his condition would no longer work. He cried and I cried as we sat in my small suburban Dublin garden with the sun blazing down from on high.

The fact is that while the issue of compensation has been resolved at last and the Irish dimension of what happened has been investigated – the pain continues. Austin was diagnosed with HIV just before his Leaving Cert and here he was, more than fifteen years later, still fighting. What moved me was that Austin never lets himself go, but, for once, he was allowing himself a very brief release.

The afternoon made me reconsider whether or not I could continue doing the job. It had been thirteen long years. The compensation agreement and the tribunal had been significant events, but I didn't believe I had the energy to carry on the next fight. This wasn't a new feeling, but somehow it took on an additional importance. I was running out of steam and needed to take a break if not move on to something altogether different. I applied for a year's leave of absence.

Working in the IHS, however, was never a normal job and walking away, in reality, meant cutting ties and breaking bonds. I didn't realise just what that meant until I made the announcement. There were lots of gatherings, lunches and dinners at which faces I had not seen for years appeared. I also felt, in some way, that I was abandoning them.

It was highly emotional at times. I remember on one occasion meeting a man who had contracted HIV through blood products. We had been close and talked about what might happen to him if the medication ever failed. He came up to me at a quiet time and simply said: "Who is going to look after me when I am dying?" I choked and couldn't find any words to answer him. He wasn't saying it to make me feel bad – it was just the reality of the situation.

The fact was that I had become woven into the fabric of the haemophilia community and will always be a part of it, albeit in a diminished way. There are so many incredible people I have had the privilege of spending time with on different occasions. It's their spirit which is so remarkable and which will ensure that we remain close.

One of the last events I went to before taking time off was a twenty-first birthday celebration. As usual, relatives and friends were there. The only difference between this and similar parties was that the birthday boy had died years earlier due a virus contained in a contaminated blood product. There was grief but, more importantly, there was a desire to celebrate the life that had been and cherish the memories which remained. It's an attitude which is both brave and beautiful. It sums up the haemophilia community.

The tinge of sadness I feel is that the Lindsay Tribunal has failed to bring the closure which so many people with haemophilia had hoped for. For those infected by international pharmaceutical companies, the fight continues for all of the answers. And many questions are still left hanging over the Irish dimension to this tragedy.

This absence of closure leaves people like Martin on edge. I will never forget that car-drive home with him and his wife shortly after the report's publication when he spoke about the death of his son and the feeling of anguish. Martin told me when writing my book to "paint it black". He wanted the full horror of the haemophilia community's story to come out. I hope that I've lived up to his challenge. I also hope that the courage of those infected and their families shines through.

I've now decided to leave the Irish Haemophilia Society. I don't feel I still have the energy needed to do the job. However, the community will be with me always. This book is dedicated to all of them.

Appendix 1

Chronology of Deaths of People With Haemophilia Due to Contaminated Blood Products

YEAR	DEATHS	TOTAL
1984	1	1
1985	0	1
1986	1	2
1987	3	5
1988	4	9
1989	3	12
1990	6	18
1991	6	24
1992	3	27
1993	15	42
1994	10	52
1995	6	58
1996	5	63
1997	1	64
1998	8	72
1999	1	73
2000	2	75
2001	1	76
2002	4	80
2003	1 (To Date)	81

Appendix 2

Chronology Of International Events
Relating to HIV

June 1981: New illness in American homosexual men [i.e. AIDS] first reported in US medical journal *Morbidity and Mortality Weekly Report [MMWR]*

Dec 1981: Similar immune-suppressive disorder identified in homosexual men in France, Netherlands and UK

June 1982: US Centers for Disease Control formulate the first definition of AIDS

AIDS may be sexually transmitted

July 1982: Three haemophiliacs in the US using concentrates reported to have AIDS

Dec 1982: Infant reported to have contracted AIDS after blood transfusion

Four more US haemophiliacs reported to have AIDS

US Food and Drug Administration [FDA] asks blood product manufacturers not to collect donations in high-risk areas

Feb 1983: US scientist Gallo claims that AIDS probably caused by retrovirus

Mar 1983: FDA asks blood and plasma centres to screen out high-risk donors

May 1983: French scientist Montagnier isolates retrovirus that might cause AIDS

First US blood product company recalls concentrates after donor linked to AIDS

Aug 1983: Report of AIDS in UK haemophiliac

Jan 1984: Report of AIDS in the spouse of a US haemophiliac

April 1984: Gallo isolates AIDS virus

May 1984: Gallo publishes results in *Science*

Sept 1984: Levy publishes article showing heat treatment [HT] inactivates retrovirus

Oct 1984: CDC reports fifty-two haemophiliacs in the US have AIDS

Evidence of the efficacy of HT

Dec 1984: Scientific journal *The Lancet* recommends heat treatment [HT] for concentrates

Montagnier and Gallo viruses shown to be related

Feb 1985: *The Lancet* publishes report concluding HT is effective in eliminating HIV in concentrates

Mar 1985: Abbot Laboratories get licence from FDA for HIV test kits

May 1985: HIV antibody testing begins in the US

July 1985: FDA recommends look-back be introduced

Appendix 3

Chronology of Domestic Events Relating to HIV

1968:   Cryoprecipitate becomes available, a major improvement on infusions of whole blood or plasma

1972:   120 registered people with haemophilia in Ireland – ninety-three haemophilia A patients and twenty-seven with haemophilia B

1973:   Concentrates made by Cutter – later Bayer – first used in Ireland

1974:   More concentrates available from manufacturer Travenol – later Baxter

1976:   BTSB-made freeze-dried cryo (i.e. cryo in powdered form) available, but only in small quantities

May 1983: First case of AIDS in Irish patient

           IHS queries AIDS-risk re imported concentrates from Prof Temperley

June 1983: First meeting of BTSB Scientific Committee re AIDS

           National Director of BTSB attends Council of Europe meeting of experts on AIDS – Blood Bank later asks high-risk donors not to donate

           The date which the Lindsay Tribunal found that the medical profession should have been aware of a "significant or substantial risk that AIDS was caused by an infectious agent transmissible by blood and blood products"

Aug 1983: Prof Temperley responds to IHS, advising maintaining the use of concentrates

Oct 1983: BTSB Scientific Meeting re AIDS – Prof Temperley attends

Dec 1983: Prof Temperley writes treatment protocol re AIDS which recommends limiting exposure of Irish haemophiliacs to number of donations

Sept 1984: Prof Temperley writes to National Drugs Advisory Board recommending continued use of non-heat-treated blood products

Nov 1984: Following UK meeting, Prof Temperley reviews advisability of non-heat-treated imported concentrates

Dec 1984: First case of AIDS in an Irish haemophiliac – victim was a child

Prof Temperley writes to the Blood Bank: "Dr P Cotter and I, with the support of Dr Walsh of the Department of Health, have agreed to purchase only heat-treated coagulation Faction VIII and IX concentrates from commercial firms in 1985. We have also agreed to ask you to urgently consider the question of heat treating all BTSB products for the treatment of haemophiliacs."

Beginning of tests on blood samples of Irish haemophiliacs at Middlesex using research test

Dec 1984:   Donor F donates blood. The donation, which was infected with HIV, goes into batch 90753 which is believed to have infected six people with haemophilia who used the Factor IX blood product

Jan 1985:   Commercial heat-treated concentrates available for Factor VIII; however the Blood Bank continues to issue its non-heat-treated Factor IX

BTSB National Director writes to Prof Temperley stating that the heat-treatment of its own Factor IX is "being given urgent attention"

Feb 1985:   BTSB receives commercial heat-treated Factor IX, but continues to issue non-heat-treated product

Mar 1985:   Research test results indicate fifty-four Irish haemophiliacs have HIV antibodies out of 133 blood samples

April 1985: Prof Temperley goes on sabbatical having informed IHS committee of research results, but not the patients themselves

July 1985:   Dr Helena Daly takes over locum position for Professor Temperley. By this time, only eight HIV patients and one negative patient had been informed of their diagnosis

Aug 1985:   Dr Daly meets BTSB over continued manufacture, distribution and use of non-heat-treated Factor IX. Concerns dismissed

The following day a decision is taken by the BTSB to heat-treat Factor IX.

Prof Temperley writes to BTSB after contact visit from Daly in London. Nov 1, 1985 new deadline for only heat-treated Factor IX to be used.

The month the Lindsay Tribunal found that the Blood Bank should have ceased issuing non-heat-treated Factor IX and recalled any still with hospitals, treating doctors and patients. The report stated that had this happened "it is probable that most, though not all, of the seven persons would have avoided infection"

Sept 1985: By the end of the month, Dr Daly has informed thirty-two patients who were HIV positive and fourteen patients who were negative

Oct 1985: HIV antibody test introduced in Ireland. Within two weeks, a donor tests positive for HIV. The Lindsay Tribunal found that this should have prompted the overdue recall of non-heat-treated Factor IX. It didn't happen. The report found that "there was still a prospect that some of the patients may have avoided infection although it seems probable that the majority were already infected"

Nov 1985: Prof Temperley returns

Dr Cotter's Factor IX patient, Andrew, tests HIV positive – the first to do so

Dec 1985:   Confirmation re-test shows he was HIV negative in January. As he only used BTSB non-heat-treated Factor IX, this had to be responsible, but Dr Cotter takes no action. Batch 90633 continues to be used in Cork

Jan 1986:   Beginning of new system making Factor VIII using Irish plasma

The Lindsay Tribunal found that the BTSB was informed that patient Fionn had become HIV positive as a result of its cryo

BTSB letter to Irish hospitals, but does not either seek a return of non-heated Factor IX or explicity state that only heated products should be used. Lindsay Tribunal found "no justification" for this

Feb 1986:   Child patient still using non-heat-treated Factor IX concentrate made by the Blood Bank

Imported blood product made by Armour pharmaceuticals, batch number A28306, infused into young Irish boy who later tests HIV positive and dies

April 1986: Prof Temperley tells the BTSB he is "becoming very concerned" over Factor IX patients testing HIV positive and "urgent attention should be given to the problem". He does not state if Blood Bank material is responsible

June 1986:   Prof Temperley voices concerns at UCD AIDS conference of possibility that Blood Bank-made Factor IX causing HIV infections. While commercial products might be responsible, he stated it was "very worrying"

Withdrawal notice sent to hospitals from BTSB recalling blood products made from donations not tested for HIV

Board of BTSB meets. It's told that the situation with Factor IX is "unsatisfactory" and is being examined "as a matter of urgency". The Lindsay Tribunal found it was "probable" that this reference meant the board was informed of the HIV development with Factor IX patients

A week later, Prof Temperley meets Dr Terry Walsh from the BTSB. According to Dr Walsh's memorandum, there was a "strong possibility" that Blood Bank material was responsible and it "would appear" that non-heat-treated Factor IX was to blame

July 1986:   Board of the BTSB meets, but minutes contain no record of members being informed or discussing the new harder information re BTSB non-heated Factor IX

Aug 1986:   Board of the BTSB meets, but only reference to Factor IX is under finance

Six days later, Prof Temperley writes to Dr Walsh: "As you are aware, I have come to the conclusion that patients with severe haemophilia B may have HIV-antibody seroconverted due to BTSB F IX concentrate."

Sept 1986: Board of the BTSB meets, but no reference to the infectious Factor IX – only production issues

The Lindsay Tribunal concluded it was "unlikely" any further information other than the June update was given to the board of the BTSB regarding the Factor IX infections. The report concluded this was a "serious failure" on the part of the BTSB organisation as a whole and that "Dr Barry and Mr Keyes were principally responsible". The report also found that the board "were not entirely blameless" as they were informed about HIV infections in Factor IX users in June and "should have enquired about them at subsequent meetings"

April 1988: Irish Haemophilia Society seek fund for members infected with HIV

April 1989: Labour Party Private Members Bill passed allowing for £400,000 for fund. Fianna Fáil minority Government refuses to implement Bill. General Election returns Fianna Fáil-Progressive Democrat Coalition which agrees to £1 million for fund

July 1989: Members of the Irish Haemophilia Society infected with HIV initiate legal action against the State

Aug 1990: Donor F gives donation and tests positive for HIV, but the Blood Bank does not institute a look-back procedure to assess where previous donations might have gone. The Lindsay Tribunal found "this should have taken place"

Jan 1991: The Lindsay Tribunal found that "in or around" this date, the Blood Bank made a connection between Donor F, the December 1984 donation and Factor IX batch 90753 which was infected with HIV. This suggests the Blood Bank had absolute proof that its blood products infected people with HIV

Mar 1991: Blood Bank signs affidavit relating to legal action being taken by people with haemophilia infected with HIV. Includes letters between the Blood Bank and Professor Temperley as well as minutes of the board from 1986. Critically, does not include statement of liability re Donor F

May 1991: Government offers £7 million settlement, but it is rejected by IHS

July 1991: Government increases offer to £8 million, but includes legal costs of both sides. This is accepted

April 2001: Government re-opens settlement and allows HIV infected people to make further claims via Compensation Tribunal

Appendix 4

Chronology of International Events
Relating to Hepatitis C

Aug 1974: First identification of virus which is not hepatitis A or B in post-transfusion group of patients by Dr Alfred Prince and others. Given the name Non-A Non-B hepatitis

1975: Professor Mannucci finds initial evidence suggesting that Non-A Non-B hepatitis is relatively mild and non-progressive

Sept 1978: Professor Preston in *The Lancet* publishes evidence that the unidentified virus might be more serious than previously thought

Dec 1983: *British Medical Journal* publishes evidence that very high percentage of people with haemophilia contract Non-A Non-B hepatitis after first use of concentrates

June 1985: *The Lancet* publishes evidence that Non-A Non-B hepatitis is a "potentially serious problem" leading to "cirrhosis"

July 1985: *The Lancet* publishes evidence that Non-A Non-B hepatitis still transmitted in haemophilia blood products which had been heat-treated to eliminate HIV after eleven of thirteen previously untreated patients develop it

April 1987: *New England Journal Of Medicine* publishes evidence that treating concentrates by a process of pasteurisation seems to eliminate Non-A Non-B hepatitis

June 1988: Strong evidence published in *The Lancet* that a viral inactivation system called solvent/detergent eliminates the virus in concentrates

Oct 1988: *The Lancet* publishes evidence that a UK system of heating concentrates to temperatures higher than that used to kill HIV appears to be effective in eliminating Non-A Non-B hepatitis

1989: Hepatitis C is identified

Antibody test developed

The Lindsay Tribunal report states it was only after 1989 that there was international consensus on the scale of the dangers inherent with hepatitis C

Appendix 5

Chronology of Domestic Events
Relating to Hepatitis C

July 1985:   Blood Bank enters into deal with Travenol – later Baxter – in which Irish plasma is converted into concentrates by the company. Travenol use heat treatment method which kills off HIV but not hepatitis C

Jan 1987:   Prof Temperley writes to BTSB about the HIV infection of a young patient – possibly due to cryoprecipitate, concentrates made from Irish donations or products made by Armour Pharmaceuticals. Dr Walsh of the BTSB wrote back to say Armour was probably responsible. Prof Temperley wrote to Armour, but didn't receive a response to his query

April 1987:   Board of BTSB considers Armour as company to make concentrates from Irish plasma, instead of Travenol

June 1987:   BTSB delegation, including Prof Temperley, meet to finalise fractionation deal with Armour under which the concentrates would be using a method of viral inaction known not to protect against Non-A Non-B hepatitis

              The Lindsay Tribunal found the BTSB should "have been seeking protection" against Non-A

Non-B hepatitis by this date. If this wasn't possible for all products, it should have "obtained and provided a special product for previously untreated patients"

June 1988: BTSB decides to continue with Armour arrangement for 1989 and supplies the company with an indemnity from "liability in respect of HIV, hepatitis and other viral infection". Prof Temperley stated in a letter to the board that Armour's viral inactivation method "seems inadequate to destroy" the Non-A Non-B hepatitis. However, he argued Armour should be given the contract as "virtually all" treated haemophiliacs had the virus already and previously untreated patients could get a safer product

The Lindsay Tribunal found that the BTSB "ought it have been distinctly unhappy and uncomfortable at the prospect of continuing to supply a product with a system of viral inactivation believed to be inadequate to destroy Non A Non-B hepatitis

June 1989: BTSB committee decides to change from Armour to Octapharma because its solvent detergent method was able to kill off what's now known as hepatitis C

Lindsay Tribunal finds that three children, two of them brothers, were "probably infected" with hepatitis C by BTSB Factor IX batch 9885 some time after this date. It found that they wouldn't have received this product "had a policy of providing special product for previously untreated patients been in place"

Aug 1989:   Board approves decision on Octapharma

                Last batch of plasma sent to Armour for fractionation

Jan 1990:   BTSB begins to supply Octapharma Factor VIII and Factor IX treated with the solvent detergent method of killing off HIV and hepatitis C

Sept 1990:   Luke receives two treatments of solvent detergent Factor IX for dental extraction

Oct 1990:   Luke receives the old BTSB Factor IX. It turns out to be batch 9885 which is deemed to be the "probable source" of his hepatitis C infection by the Lindsay Tribunal. It found that he "clearly should not h a v e been treated" with this product – on the basis t h a t he only ever had two previous infusions and these were Octapharma. The tribunal said it was "probably inappropriate" for it to have been used on any patient by this date

Dec 1990:   Test results show that three of Felicity's children were positive for hepatitis C antibodies

Dec 1991:   Latest date deemed by Lindsay Tribunal, allowing for confirmatory testing, that Felicity should have been told of infections

1993:   Two people with haemophilia die as a result of hepatitis C infection

1994:   Test results show more than 150 members of haemophilia community infected with hepatitis C

Oct 1995:   Felicity is informed of diagnosis – and then by accident rather than design

                First case by IHS successfully taken to Hepatitis C Compensation Tribunal

Appendix 6

Dictionary Of Terms

AIDS:

>Acquired Immune Deficiency Syndrome. A breakdown in the immune system resulting from infection with the human immunodeficiency virus – known as HIV. The breakdown leads to a series of specific infections which are not normally seen in a person with a normal functioning immune system.

Antibody:

>Protein substances produced by the immune system which circulate in the blood in response to a foreign organism being detected.

Blood:

>A complex mixture of specialised cells [white cells, red cells and platelets], proteins and other molecules. Among its functions is the transport of oxygen and nutrients to body tissues; the removal of carbon dioxides and other wastes; transfer of hormonal messages between organs; the prevention of bleeding; and the transport of antibodies and infection-fighting cells.

Coagulation:

>The process of clotting blood. The plasma protein prothrombin (Factor II) is converted to thrombin. This in turn causes the soluble plasma fibrinogin (Factor I) to insoluble fibrin creating a clot.

Coagulation Factors:

Naturally occurring proteins in plasma [like Factor VIII and Factor IX] that aid coagulation of the blood

Concentrates:

A product employed to treat bleeding either from a Factor VIII or Factor IX deficiency. It's a freeze-dried powder made from large pools of donated human plasma. It's subjected to purification and viral-inactivation methods to kill off viruses and eliminate foreign substances. It's stored in sterile bottles.

Cryoprecipitate:

Known as simply cryo, it's the solid substance left when fresh-frozen plasma is thawed between two and four degrees Celsius. The product is rich in clotting factors needed to treat people with haemophilia.

Custom Fractionation:

Process whereby Irish plasma is converted into concentrates on behalf of the Blood Bank by commercial company.

Factors I to XII:

Refers to the classification of the multiple factors involved in coagulation. For example, Factor VIII is the deficiency in people with haemophilia A whereas Factor IX is the deficiency in people with haemophilia B.

Fibrinogin:

Factor I. A plasma protein synthesised in the liver, which is involved in coagulation as a precursor of fibrin.

Fresh Frozen Plasma:

The fluid portion of the blood which is frozen after the blood cells are removed. FFP was at one time the only treatment for haemophilia.

Freeze Dried Cryoprecipitate:
> A powder form of cryo.

Haemophilia:
> A rare bleeding disorder, usually hereditary, caused by a deficiency to synthesise one of the coagulation proteins like Factor VIII or Factor IX.

Haemophilia A:
> A blood disorder where there is a deficiency in synthesising Factor VIII. Also known as classical haemophilia.

Haemophilia B:
> A less common blood disorder where there is a deficiency in synthesising Factor IX. Also known as 'Christmas Disease' after the scientist who first identified it.

Heat Treatment:
> A method employed to either inactivate or destroy a virus by heating. The factor is heated in a dry state to a certain temperature for a certain length of time to kill the virus but without damaging the factor molecule.

Hepatitis:
> Inflammation or infection of the liver. It can cause lifelong damage to the liver. It can be fatal.

Non-A Non-B Hepatitis:
> The name given to hepatitis C, before it had been identified.

Hepatitis C:
> A viral liver disease which can be acute, chronic or even life-threatening.

HIV:
> Human immunodeficiency virus. This is the virus which

causes AIDS. There are three different types – HIV-1, HIV-2 and HIV type O. HIV-1 is by far the most common.

Immune System:

The body's mechanisms for fighting infections and eradicating dysfunctional cells.

Interferon:

A type of antiviral protein which stimulates the immune system.

Jaundice:

A yellowing of the skin and the whites of the eyes associated with liver or gall bladder problems.

Kaposi's Sarcoma:

Lesions on the skin and/or internal organs caused by abnormal growth of blood vessels. Associated with AIDS.

Look-back:

A procedure whereby once a donor tests positive for HIV, the Blood Bank checks back to see if any of their previous donations were also infectious and were transfused into other patients.

Opportunistic Infection:

A disease or infection caused by a micro-organism that does not ordinarily cause disease but, under certain conditions [impaired immune responses e.g. HIV], becomes pathologic e.g. pneumonia.

PCR

Polymerese Chain Reaction. A method of amplifying fragments of genetic material so they can be detected. Used as a definitive test for hepatitis C.

Plasma:
> The liquid portion of the blood. It contains nutrients, electrolytes [dissolved salts], gasses, albumin, clotting factors, wastes and hormones. Accounts for 10 per cent of the blood.

Retrovirus:
> Family of viruses to which HIV belongs that are distinguished by their use of our genetic material RNA [ribonucleic acid].

Seroconvert:
> A person changes their status from being deemed negative for a virus following a test to positive.

Shingles:
> Condition caused by a herpes viral infection, involving painful blisters on the skin. Sometimes associated with AIDS.

Virus:
> A subcellular microscopic organism comprised of genetic material and protein. It's only able to reproduce within the living cell of the organism it infects. When viruses infect a cell they can cause disease, often ultimately killing the host. Though they vary greatly, all viruses have genetic material surrounded by at least one protein shell. Viruses may subvert the host cell's normal functions, causing the cell to behave in a manner determined by the virus.

Appendix 7

Biography Of Key People

IRISH HAEMOPHILIA SOCIETY:

Rosemary Daly:
> Administrator up to October 2002. Joined in 1989 as AIDS coordinator.

Brian O'Mahony:
> Former chairman 1987 to 2003. Previous vice-chairman Joined executive in 1982. Three-term president of World Federation of Haemophilia.

Margaret Dunne:
> Administrator since October 2002. Joined in 1990 as secretary.

Margaret King:
> Former haemophilia nurse at Saint James's Hospital, she was a counsellor, volunteer and executive member of the IHS.

BLOOD BANK:

Dr Jack O'Riordan:
> National director until his retirement in December 1985. Combined roles of chief medical consultant and chief executive officer.

Dr Vincent Barry:
> Chief medical consultant from the beginning of 1986 until the end of 1987.

Dr Terry Walsh:
> Consultant haematologist. Chief medical consultant from 1988 until 1995.

Dr Emer Lawlor:
> Consultant haematologist. Current deputy medical director of the Blood Bank.

Edward Ryan:
> Accountant and personnel officer from 1974 until retirement in 1988.

TREATING DOCTORS:

Prof Ian Temperley:
> Medical director of the National Haemophilia Treatment Centre based at Saint James's Hospital from its creation in 1971 to 1995. Board member of the BTSB from 1987 to 1999. Professor of Haematology. Dean of the Faculty of Health Services in Trinity College 1987 to 1993.

Dr Paule Cotter:
> Consultant haematologist and head of the Munster Regional Haemophilia Treatment Centre.

Prof Ernest Egan:
> Consultant haematologist and head of the Galway Regional Haemophilia Treatment Centre.

Dr Helena Daly:
> Stood in for Prof Temperley at Saint James's Hospital for a number of months in 1985 when he went on sabbatical.